DISPENSING TRUTH

Divine Prescriptions
to Restore and Maintain Good Health

My son, give attention to My words, incline your ear to My sayings. Do not let them depart from your sight; keep them in the midst of your heart. For they are life to those who find them, and health to all their whole body.
Proverbs 4: 20-22

DR. RON GIRARDIN

ISBN 978-1-64299-532-9 (paperback)
ISBN 978-1-64299-533-6 (digital)

Second printing 2022

Christian Faith Publishing
832 Park Avenue
Meadville, PA 16335
www.christianfaithpublishing.com

Printed in the United States of America

FOREWORD

Several years ago, I was the guest speaker at a youth softball banquet given by Prairie Avenue Foursquare Church in Torrance, California. The youth leaders shared the gospel that night with those in attendance from the perspective of Charlie Brown and Lucy, two characters created by the late Charles Schultz for his famous cartoon strip *Peanuts*. They shared the good news with such a fervor that there was no doubt in my mind that these two had a special relationship with the "Author and Finisher" of our faith, the Lord Jesus Christ. That night, I not only got to speak to the youth about my years in professional baseball, but I also had the pleasure of meeting Ron and Lu Girardin, a.k.a. Charlie Brown and Lucy.

God's Word tells us that He will direct our path (Proverbs 3:5, 6). Ron's path led him to the University of Southern California where he received his degree in pharmacy. Later his path led him to prepare for Christian ministry at L.I.F.E. Bible College and then Talbot Theological Seminary. Now, years later, after trials, testing, and the experience of seeing the healing power of God revealed through faith in Jesus Christ and His Word, he presents to us prescriptions for life.

Ron had just finished his studies at U.S.C. when God called me out of baseball and into full-time ministry. Since then, I have discovered few books that have served me as other books might serve a seminary student. These are the books I periodically turn to for a refreshing of my faith. Books such as *Ever Increasing Faith* by Smith Wigglesworth and *A Shepherd Looks at the 23rd Psalm* by Philip Keller. You will discover *Dispensing Truth* to be a refreshing and insightful book that ties the will of God (Psalms 103:2, 3) to the person of Jesus Christ (Matthew 4:23) and the anointed ministry of His disciples (Matthew 10:1-8, Luke 9:1, 2), to the continuing ministry of the church (Mark 16:15-18, Acts 14:7-9), and the assurance that Jesus is still freeing people today from the power of sin and sickness (Hebrews 13:8) and releasing them into an abundant life (John 10:10).

Please allow these pages to bring the healing that Christ desires for you and then allow them to provide healing for others through you.

May I give you my friend and modern-day knight who shows us how to use the sword of God's word to defeat the wiles of the devil, Dr. Ron Girardin.

May God bless you as you take to heart these prescriptions for health and abundant life.

Sincerely,

Albie Pearson

Albie Pearson played major league baseball for 9 years and was honored by being selected Rookie of the Year, as well as, being the starting centerfielder for the American League All Star team. Soon after his playing days were over the Lord directed him to begin a youth foundation. That faithful beginning has resulted in churches being planted in all of North America and spreading into Europe, Asia and Africa, where a Bible college now exists. The results of his ministry have reached into South America where an orphanage has been established in Ecuador. He is the founder and president emeritus of United Ministries International.

INTRODUCTION

In the beginning God created the heavens and the earth.
Genesis 1:1

The very first verse in the Bible tells us the origin of all things. It also reminds me of a cute story. The story goes something like this. One Sunday afternoon, a family of three was heading home from church. The father asked his son, who was seated in the rear of the car, "What did you learn in Sunday school today?" The boy thought a moment and then replied, "We learned about creation." And then he quickly added, "Oh yeah, Dad, I learned that God is a baseball fan!" That response caused the father who was driving, and his mother, who was also in the front seat to turn and look at each other in mild puzzlement. Then the boy's mother asked her son, "Really! Where did you learn that?" Their son proudly announced, "Mom, it's in the very first verse of the Bible." That's when the lad's father and mother again turned and looked at each other. Only this time, they shared a knowing smile. Then the boy's father asked his son, "What does it say, son?" Their son, without hesitation, answered, "In the big inning God created the heavens and the earth."

DISPENSING TRUTH also traces its beginning back to God. Allow me to explain. I started this book soon after three remarkable events took place. The first event involved our pet dachshund, Ebony. One morning I awoke to discover she was unable to walk on her hind legs. Our veterinary looked at her and said we had two choices: do nothing and let her live the balance of her natural life in her present condition, or we could put her to sleep. Ebony appeared in good health in all other respects, and she wasn't advanced in years. We decided to think about our choices. A few days passed. Then one day, while I was reading the last chapter of Mark's gospel, a section jumped out at me: "And these signs shall accompany those who have believed: in My name . . . they will lay hands on the sick, and they will recover"

(Mark 16:17, 18). I thought for a moment and then realized I could do that for Ebony. Her belief didn't matter. All that mattered was my belief. So I laid my hands on her and prayed in Jesus' name. The very next morning, Ebony was walking on all four legs. Yes, you could say there was joy in the Girardin household that day.

Several months passed before the second incident occurred. One evening, a young lady in her late teens came into the Thrifty drug store in Cathedral City where I was employed as a pharmacist. She was accompanied by a gentleman on her right and another lady on her left side. She was wearing a bandana on her head, and her two companions were helping her to walk. She handed me several prescriptions written by an emergency room doctor at Desert Hospital in Palm Springs. One of the prescriptions called for 100 tablets of a sleeping medication. That quantity is very unusual for an emergency room doctor to prescribe, so I called the doctor to confirm the quantity. He thanked me for my caution, and then he explained that the young lady had brain surgery twice for a cancerous tumor that could not be removed. He said she was terminal, and this quantity was appropriate. I was shocked. This young lady was only nineteen years old. She took a partial amount of the sleeping medication and said the balance would be picked up later. A couple of days passed and then the gentleman returned for the balance. I asked him if he would take a note back to Patricia, which was the young lady's name. He consented, and I wrote something like the following.

Patricia,

You're probably going to think I'm crazy, but God loves you, and He doesn't want you to have a brain tumor. If you would like to hear more, call me later tonight.

Ron, your pharmacist

I hoped she would call, but frankly, I didn't expect it to happen. Surprise! Later that same evening, she called me at home. Two hours later, a Christian friend of mine, Ron Reed, and myself were sharing the good news about Jesus with her. She said she had accepted Jesus as her Savior some years back. We asked if she would like God to remove the brain tumor. She answered *Yes*, but with obvious doubt. So I told her she didn't have to believe He would. All she had to do was ask Him. Her expression immediately changed. Then we read the verses from Mark's gospel. We explained it was Ron Reed and I who had to believe. This seemed to make it much easier for her, and she asked God to heal her. Then we placed our hands on her and commanded the cancer to leave. Two months or more passed, and then she called Ron from Santa Barbara. She had just received the results from her latest brain scan, and there was no evidence of a tumor. Our joy had just reached a new level. Five years later, we learned she was married and raising a family.

The third and single most important event occurred several months later. One evening, I had a dream. In this dream, Jesus appeared above the foot of our bed. He expanded my understanding of three biblical truths, and then He told me I was to write a book on divine healing. When I awoke, the dream remained crystal clear in my mind. It was then that I knew the dream was very real. You see, I don't remember my dreams. I considered all the great men and women of God I have had the privilege to know or know about, and I wondered, *Why me?* The Lord knows I hate failure, and the thought of failing Him was nearly unbearable. Nonetheless, I had a tremendous desire to start writing.

It was sometime later that I realized the first two incidents had a lot in common. Both centered upon hopeless conditions. Both needs were met through the same promise of God. And as breathtaking as it is to me, both occurred because I believed God's promise. As I considered these facts, they eventually brought forth their own purpose. It was then that I believed God revealed to me the answer to my original question, *Why me?* One day, I was reading the parable of the talents (Matthew 25:14-29). I could see myself in that parable, but I wasn't sure who I was. You see, I not only hate failure, I also fear it. I was considering the parable when I believe the person of the Holy Spirit encouraged me. It was like He was exhorting me and saying, *You were faithful with a single promise when you applied it to Ebony. Later, you were given an opportunity to share the same promise with Patricia, and you were faithful again. Now you are being given three biblical truths to share. Be faithful and experience the joy it will bring you.*

So, I read a portion of that parable again: "His master said to him, 'Well done good and faithful slave; you were faithful with a few things, I will put you in charge of many things; enter into the joy of your master'" (Matthew 25:23). Fear and everything that goes along with it began to leave me. I was confident the Lord, who had provided the first three truths, would continue to provide the truths and the motivation to continue. "For I am confident of this very thing, that He who began a good work in you will perfect it until the day of Christ Jesus" (Philippians 1:6). I had a tremendous amount of assurance that the Lord would continue to supply my need, and I knew that need would be met from His word.

I needed to choose a Bible translation for a reference. There are so many good sources available. Finally, I selected the New American Standard translation. Other translations will also be quoted and appropriately noted.

Now that these pages are finally being published, I would like to be sure my intentions are perfectly clear.

Watchman Nee in his book titled *The Normal Christian Life*, points out that it is the *life* inside of a seed that is responsible for the growth that results after it has been sown.

When Jesus explained to His disciples the parable of the sower and the seed (Matthew 13:18-23), the seed always germinated regardless of the condition of the ground it fell on. Jesus referred to the seed as the word of God's kingdom. If there was a problem after the germination of God's word, which never failed, then it was a result of the condition of the ground, not the seed.

DISPENSING TRUTH could be considered nothing more than a package of health and restoration seed and the reader as nothing more than the ground that seed falls upon.

Inside this package there is more than enough seed to produce the desired results.

Consequently, my motivation is more than merely sowing seed. It is also to help prepare the ground to receive the seed so it not only will germinate, which God guarantees, but that it will grow to its fullest potential and produce the desired fruit.

In concluding this introduction, I want to say, I consider myself to have been blessed beyond measure. I have been particularly blessed by those whom I have had an opportunity to know and whom I either assisted in ministry or they have ministered to me. If I attempted to remember all of them I would surely fail, and you know how I feel about failure. My mind can't recall them all, which is a fact I regret. Every one of them has contributed to my maturity and my ministry. However, I would like to take a brief moment to thank the Lord for some of those He has used to help shape me.

In the very beginning, Lord, I want to thank You for those whom I have absolutely no knowledge, those who mentioned my name in prayer. At this moment, only You know how essential their faithful prayer was to my life and ministry. Specifically, I would like to thank You for the Reverend Paul Garrison, who helped bring me to You. I also want to thank You for the Reverends George and Nancy Johnson, who, for over thirty-five years, demonstrated to me the meaning of commitment. George has been like the big brother I never had or the dad whom I lost before I became a teenager. Thank You so much for the Reverend Paul Hackett, who You used to bring to life Your precious Old Testament truths and made them so exciting.

In addition, I want to thank You for the Reverend Jack Hayford. I first met Reverend Hayford while I was a student at LIFE Bible College in Los Angeles. I got to know him even better as my wife and I served for a brief season at The Church on the Way, in Van Nuys. Since then, I have watched him be extremely faithful with the many gifts provided to him by You, Lord. Amidst the enormous success the Lord has brought his way, I still see a servant who has remained human in the very best sense of the word. Lord, You know how instrumental the writings of T. L. Osburn and Frank and Ida Mae

Hammond have been to my ministry. Although I never observed their ministries, their writings have brought their ministries to me.

And, dear Jesus, I want to give You special thanks for the powerful and loving ministry of Albie Pearson. His ministry has had a life-changing impact on my own ministry. Over the past forty-five years, he has always been available whenever my family has required his ministry. Also, I want to thank You for the Reverend Ralph Moore. Our family's association and service with brother Ralph during his first five years at Hope Chapel in Manhattan Beach, was an eye-opening experience. His vision to develop leaders and birth new fellowships beautifully aligns itself with Your great commission.

I would like to give a special thanks to a dear friend and brother in Jesus, Ted Weber for his countless hours spent in proof reading.

Now, dear Father, there is a special thank you I've saved for last. I thank You so very much for the wife You gave me, Luetta-Rae. She has tolerated me since 1969 and has spent countless and selfless hours inputting my notes into our personal computer. Actually, the final thanks goes to You, dear Father. May I always be thankful to You and Your Son and the person of the Holy Spirit, who have made all of this possible.

Since the initial publication I've decided to to take some of the most salient information from parts II an III and include it in this revised version. My principal concern was that the most important material be available.

So get comfortable and together let's become better informed about divine prescriptions that can restore and maintain good health.

May our Lord, Savior, and yes, Healer, bless His word and increase your faith as you go from sections *Diagnosis* through *Restoration*.

Sincerely,

Ron Girardin

Ron Girardin

SECTION ONE

 DIAGNOSIS

When it comes to healing, diagnosis is the key to therapy and eventual recovery. A wrong diagnosis can delay or even prevent proper treatment. That is why this section appears first in our file of prescriptions. When we understand the cause of our condition, then a course of therapy can be prescribed which will best treat our problem.

PRESCRIPTIONS 1-14

Prescription File No. 1

(Table of Contents)

Rx 1

YOU HAD BETTER BELIEVE IT!

"Which one of you convicts Me of sin? If I speak truth, why don't you believe Me?"
John 8:46

I don't remember where I was or what I was doing, but I'll never forget that sound. A thundering *va-voom* echoed in my ears, and everything seemed to stop for a split second. I thought I felt the ground moving beneath my feet, and I could feel my fight-or-flight response kicking in. What happened? Was there an explosion, an earthquake, or what?

It was just a few days earlier that we had rehearsed an air raid drill in school. An alarm had sounded its distinct warning and our teacher had told us to "drop". We dropped to the floor and curled up under our desks, resting on our knees, with our faces to the ground and our hands clasped protectively around the backs of our heads. Could this be what was happening? Were we having an air raid?

The year was 1948, and I was just a seven-year-old, but I remember turning my attention to the sky. It wasn't long before my eyes focused on a dark trail of smoke streaking through the blue haze. I just stood there, staring at this strange sight. I had seen sky writers before, but this wasn't like any sky writer I had ever seen. Then I noticed the small silver shaft at the front of the trail. Together, they looked like a needle pulling a thread across the heavens. However, the needle-and-thread explanation seemed a little far-fetched even to a seven-year old. Was this a flying saucer, which was something I had overheard my mother and father once discussing? About then things returned to normal speed, and I heard someone nearby ask, "What do you think of that?" Frankly, I wasn't sure what to think. Then the person told me that a jet aircraft had just broken the sound barrier. I thought, wow. I had just experienced my first sonic boom. Only, then I didn't know it was called a sonic boom.

Some years later, a former pilot told me how important it is for a *jet jockey* to trust his instrument panel. He said, "A pilot needs to trust that panel even more that he trusts his own senses." He said, "If your instruments tell you one thing and your senses tell you something else, then you better believe that panel. Yes sir, YOU HAD BETTER BELIEVE IT! Your life depends on it."

We have all discovered there are some things we can trust through observation. For instance we may trust someone because we have seen over a period of time that they are trustworthy. This is one type of trust. On the other hand, there are times we trust something before we discover it is "trustworthy". Consider the seatbelt in a car. We have been told a seat belt will protect us, so we trust it and use it. However, we have never seen it work. This is another form of trust. The first type of trust can be described as *seeing is believing*. The second form of trust can be referred to as *believing is seeing*. This form of trust accepts as fact something it has never seen. The Bible refers to this type of trust as faith.

A BIBLICAL DEFINITION OF FAITH

Only faith can guarantee the blessings that we hope for, or prove the existence of the realities that at present remain unseen.
Hebrews 11:1 (Jerusalem Bible)

I can think of two examples of this type of faith. Most of us might find either example practical whenever we go on a long trip in a car. In the first example, we are traveling through the desert, and we see a gas station less than a quarter mile up the road. The next thing we do is to check our gas gauge. Let's say it reads almost empty. Then we look up and see a road sign that reads "Next gas 85 miles." So what do we do? We stop at the station, and we fill our tank. We believe the next gas station is eighty-five miles away. The last station is staring us in the face. In the second example, we are farther down the highway, and we come to a fork in the road. We aren't sure which way to go. So what do we do? Well, we happen to have a map, so we look at the map. It shows we should take the road to the right. Do we believe it, or do we take our chances going another way? Well, if we believe the map, then we go to the right and discover it is correct. Any other decision would indicate that we have no faith in what the map is informing us. Who would ignore either help? However, do we realize we have a panel, a road sign, a map available to us that can direct us to a better life? This panel provides the readings that can keep us healthy or enable us to return to sound health. Unfortunately, most of us are so busy with the struggle to provide a halfway decent standard of living for our families and ourselves that the few brief moments of free time we have are spent with TV, talk shows, tabloids, and texting. Consequently, some of us are unaware of this magnificent and infallible panel. True, a few of us realize it exists, but we rarely find the time to check its readings. Unfortunately, some of us who manage to refer to it disregard what it says and decide to follow our own senses.

"What panel is that?" "What panel are you referring to?" The word of God, the Bible, containing the Old and New Testaments. The Bible has been around for centuries, and except for a few notable periods of history, it has been collecting dust. Our problem is, we tend to judge the Bible by those who are its proponents. Instead, we should allow it to speak for itself. The Bible claims to be the word of God.[1] It claims to be God's message to all mankind. Now, forgetting for a moment the personal lives of those who make this claim for the Bible, we must realize that if the Bible itself claims to be the word of God,

---

[1]   Harold Lindsell, *Battle for the Bible*, (Grand Rapids: Zondervan Publishing House, 1976), p. 34.

then that claim is either true or false.[2] Therefore, it is a claim each of us would do well to investigate. Should we accept what we have heard about the Bible when we can read it ourselves? Let me illustrate the importance of this last question. Have you heard someone say that the fall of mankind was the result of Adam and Eve eating the forbidden apple? Would it be a surprise to learn the Bible doesn't say they ate an apple.[3] Maybe it is your understanding that three wise men came to see baby Jesus at the manger scene. Just think of all those manger scenes we see at Christmas time. Well, guess what! The Bible never says there were three wise men,[4] and they certainly didn't find Jesus in a manger but rather in a house.[5] Have I made my point?

The Bible is filled with claims that impact everyone's daily lives. Shouldn't we read it for ourselves and investigate those claims before we discard it, or should we be numbered with those who allow it to continue to collect dust? Just read a few of the claims the Bible makes for itself.

A FOOL GIVES GOD NO EAR

*"**The fool says** in his heart, **there is no God.**"*
Psalm 53:1

Okay, we certainly want to be fair to ourselves and the Bible as well. So what can we do that will help us make an informed and rational decision? Isn't that a fair question? I have found that the God of the Bible welcomes any individual who makes the time to reason.

---

[2] John Murray, *"The Attestation of Scripture"* in *The Infallible Word,* N.B. Storehouse and P. Woolley, eds., (Nutley: Presbyterian and Reformed, 1946), pp. 4, 5.

[3] George Ricker Berry, *Interlinear Hebrew-English Old Testament,* (Grand Rapids: Kregel, 1974), pp. 8, 9.

[4] Alfred Marshall, *The Interlinear Greek-English New Testament,* (London: Samuel Bagster and Sons, 1967), pp. 4, 5.

[5] David Brown, *A Commentary: Critical, Experimental and Practical, Vol. III-The Gospel According Matthew,* (Grand Rapids: Eerdman's Publishing Company, 1976), p. 6.

GOD WANTS TO REASON WITH US

"Come now, and let us reason together," says the Lord, *"Though your sins are as scarlet, they will be white as snow; though they are red like crimson, they will be like wool."*
Isaiah 1:18

Here, the Bible informs us of God's willingness to reason with us regarding sin and how that problem is to be resolved. If God is willing to reason with us concerning sin, then He might be willing to reason with us regarding sickness and healing also.

The Bible is a big book, so where do we begin? Actually, we have already begun. Please allow me to explain. There was a time when I thought that many of the biblical accounts were just stories. You know, David and Goliath, Samson and Delilah, and Daniel in the lions' den. I thought they were just stories used to make a point, something like a fable. When I realized that the Bible was either the word of God or just another religious book, I started to read it with an open mind. That turned out to be one of the two best decisions I ever made. For whatever reasons, I had always thought of Jesus as an extraordinary person, so I began to read about Him in the gospels of Matthew, Mark, Luke, and John. Then I read the remainder of the New Testament, and that's when I discovered something I could sink my teeth into, something I could test for myself.

GOD'S WORD WILL CREATE FAITH

So faith comes from hearing, and hearing by *the word of Christ.*
Romans 10:17

If the Bible or any part of it is God's word, then the more familiar I am with Christ's words, the more I will believe it to be true. This is something that would either occur or not occur. This is something I could find to be true or untrue. Plus, this is something I had already begun to do. I must admit, I was a little excited. This wasn't going to be so difficult after all. To make a long story short, I discovered the more I read the Bible, the more I accepted it as true. The Old Testament stories became fact to me, and eventually the entire Bible. Faith was created in me to believe the Bible is what it claims to be: the word of God.

Sometime after I had accepted the Bible as the word of God, I noticed that the Jews in Jesus' day believed God spoke to Moses.

MOSES KNEW GOD'S WORD

> *"We know that God has spoken to Moses; but as for this man (Jesus), we do not know where He is from."*
> John 9:29

They considered the Old Testament the word of God, but how did Jesus view the Old Testament?

MOSES, THE PROPHETS AND THE PSALMS ARE GOD'S WORD

> Now He (Jesus) said to them. *"These are My words which I spoke to you while I was still with you, that **all things which are written about Me in the Law of Moses and the Prophets and the Psalms must be fulfilled."***
> Luke 24:44

Jesus could have said, "You accept the Old Testament as God's word, and you should. Well, it talks about Me." Jesus said nothing to discredit one's belief in the Old Testament. Then in Christ's famous Sermon on the Mount, He refers to the Proverbs at least ten times. In essence, Jesus endorses the entire Old Testament as the word of God, but how did His contemporaries view Him?

JESUS: A TEACHER

*Now there was a man of the Pharisees, named Nicodemus, a ruler of the Jews; this man came to Him (Jesus) by night, and said to Him, **"Rabbi, we know you have come from God as a teacher;** for no one can do these signs that you do unless God is with him."*
John 3:1, 2

JESUS: A MAN FROM GOD

*"If this man were not **from God,** He (Jesus) could do nothing."*
John 9:33

JESUS: A PROPHET

*And the multitudes were saying, **"This is the prophet, Jesus, from Nazareth in Galilee."***
Matthew 21:11

JESUS: THE PROPHESIED CHRIST

*And He (Jesus) continued by questioning them, "But who do you say that I am?" **Peter answered and said to Him, "Thou art the Christ."***
Mark 8:29

JESUS: THE KING OF ISRAEL AND SON OF GOD

*Nathanael answered Him (Jesus), **"Rabbi, you are the Son of God; You are the King of Israel".***
John 1:49

JESUS: GOD'S WORD IN THE FLESH

In the beginning was the Word, and the Word was with **God and the Word was God** (v. 1). **And the Word became flesh** *(Jesus),* **and dwelt among us,** *and we beheld His glory, glory as of the only begotten from the Father, full of grace and truth* (v. 14).
John 1:1, 14

Jesus was recognized by His contemporaries as a teacher, a prophet, the rightful king of Israel, the prophesied Messiah or Christ, one sent from God, the Son of God, the Word of God and even God living in flesh. This recognition came from the multitudes; it came from those whose lives He touched. It came from His disciples and it even came from a ruler of the Pharisees, a teacher of the Jews. This recognition came from a broad spectrum of the populace. Did Jesus agree with their conclusions? The answer is absolutely, yes!

JESUS AGREED: HE IS A TEACHER

"You call Me **Teacher** *and Lord; and you are right,* **For so I am.***"*
John 13:13

JESUS AGREED: HE WAS SENT FROM GOD

Jesus said to them, "If God were your Father, you would love Me, for **I proceeded forth and have come from God,** *for I have not even come on My own initiative, but* **He sent Me.***"*
John 8:42

JESUS AGREED: HE WAS A PROPHET

And He (Jesus) said to them, "No doubt you will quote this proverb to Me, 'Physician heal yourself!'" Whatever we

*heard was done at Capernaum, do here in your hometown as well. And He said, "**Truly I say to you, no prophet is welcome in his hometown.**"*
Luke 4:23, 24

JESUS AGREED: HE IS THE MESSIAH, THE CHRIST

*The woman said to Him, "**I know that the Messiah is coming** (He who is called the Christ); when that One comes, He will declare all things to us." **Jesus said to her, "I who speak to you am He."***
John 4:25, 26

JESUS AGREED: HE IS THE KING OF THE JEWS (ISRAEL)

*And Pilate asked Him (Jesus), saying, "**Are you the King of the Jews?**" And He (Jesus) answered him and said, "**It is as you say.**"*
Luke 23:3

JESUS AGREED: HE IS THE SON OF GOD

*"If he called them gods, to whom the word of God came (and the Scripture cannot be broken), do you say of Him, whom the Father sanctified and sent into the world, 'You are blaspheming,' because **I** (Jesus) **said, 'I am the Son of God?'**"*
John 10:35, 36

JESUS AGREED: HE IS GOD IN THE FLESH

*"**I** (Jesus) **and the Father** (God) **are one.**" The Jews took up stones again to stone Him. Jesus answered them, "I showed you many good works from the Father, for which of them are you stoning Me?" The Jews answered Him, "For*

a good work we do not stone you, but for blasphemy; and because **you, being a man, make yourself out to be God.** "
John 10:31-33

I realize that Jesus never denied any of these before mentioned things that were said about Him. Instead, He only reaffirmed them. I'm sure that if God had not created faith within me by His word, then I would be faced with a decision, a decision that all who have heard the good news of God's kingdom and Jesus Christ must make. Jesus was either what He claimed to be, or what others recognized Him to be, or Jesus was a fraud, a real con man, or possibly a religious fanatic who was self-deceived and suffering from delusions of grandeur. Jesus was either a fraud, a fanatic or for real. Because I believe Jesus is for real, the primary ingredient in this prescription is the following:

JESUS IS LORD

"You call me Teacher and Lord; and you are right, for so I am."
John 13:13

The extreme importance of this statement will be fully explained in Rx 5. But for right now, let me just say, YOU HAD BETTER BELIEVE IT. Divine therapy and healing begin right here.

THIS PRESCRIPTION PROVIDES
THE FOLLOWING BENEFITS

1. Confidence that the Bible is the Word of God
2. Confidence that Jesus is who He and others claimed Him to be
3. Confidence that Jesus should be called Lord

$Rx2$

WHEN WE ASSUME

There is a simple memory device to help one remember how to spell the word *assume*. It briefly states that when we assume we make an *ass* out of *u* and *me*.

Now, an "ass" according to *Webster's New Universal Unabridged Dictionary* is first "a long-eared, slow, patient, surefooted, domesticated mammal, Equas asinus, related to the horse, used chiefly as a beast of burden." However, this is not the definition implied in the memory device. That definition is found further down in *Webster's* list of definitions, and it states that *ass* is also a term used to describe someone who acts like a blockhead or a fool.

In Rx 1 we read that a fool is someone who says in his heart there is no God.

Webster further states that a synonym for the word *assumption* is "guess".[1] Now when it comes to one's eternal destiny, who wants to assume or guess? If there was a source of information available, one that could take all the guesswork out, would you take advantage of it?

Let me illustrate the dangers inherent in assumptions.

---

[1] *Webster's New Universal Unabridged Dictionary*, (New York: Barnes & Noble, 1994), p. 89.

BELIEVE IT OR NOT

It was on Christmas Day 1893 that Santa Rosa, California witnessed the birth of Robert LeRoy Ripley. It was Robert Ripley who became a famous newspaper cartoonist. He would present the most unbelievable yet factual happenings in his cartoons. One day Mr. Ripley went too far. He definitely stepped over the line of public opinion and belief. What was it he said that was so unbelievable? He claimed that Charles Lindbergh was not the first man to make a non-stop flight across the Atlantic Ocean. Outrageous! Everyone knew Lindbergh had received $25,000 for making that first nonstop flight from New York City, New York to Paris, France.[2] Everyone knew he had received decorations and honors from various European nations for his achievements. Such a statement was bordering on insanity. However Ripley did not stop there. He also claimed sixty-six other people had also performed a non-stop flight across the Atlantic. Had Ripley lost his mind or had he simply done his homework and discovered the truth? Ripley's research revealed that earlier two men in a single aircraft had accomplished a non-stop transatlantic flight. It also revealed the fact that sixty-four other men in two dirigibles had also accomplished the feat.[3] Ripley was correct, not insane, and his cartoons were entitled "Believe It or Not."

Ripley wasn't the first one to step over the line of public opinion and make a statement that at first appeared to be an unbelievable claim. Jesus made a claim even His closest friends and confidants assumed was in error.

I WILL RETURN FROM THE GRAVE

*And while they were gathered together in Galilee, Jesus said to them, "The Son of Man is going to be delivered into the hands of men; and they will kill Him, and **He will be raised on the third day.**" And they were deeply grieved. Matthew 17:22, 23*

---

[2] "Robert Ripley," *Encyclopedia Americana XXII*, (1964), p. 536.
[3] "Charles Lindbergh," *Encyclopedia Americana XVII*, (1964), p. 540.

His disciples didn't doubt the probability He would be killed because they grieved, but if they believed He was going to come back from the grave, then where is their rejoicing? It's absent. If anyone had believed Him, then there would have been ample rejoicing. This portion of Jesus' announcement was His guarantee of their own resurrection, as well as, the resurrection of believers in every age.

HIS GUARANTEE: BELIEVERS WILL BE RESURRECTED

I am the resurrection and the life; **he who believes in Me shall live even if he dies**.
John 11:25
Do not marvel at this, for an hour is coming in which all who are in the tombs shall hear His voice, and shall come forth; **those who did the good to a resurrection of life**, *those who committed the evil to a resurrection of judgment.*
John 5:28, 29

If Jesus was wrong, and He did remain in the tomb, then our concern is lessened. However, if He did return from the grave, then we better do our *homework* instead of allowing our eternal future to be determined by the assumption and guess work of others. In addition, if Jesus did return from the grave, then we better understand what Jesus meant when He said, "the good" and "the evil".

The Bible claims Jesus was raised from the dead on the Sunday following His crucifixion. Why should we believe this claim to be accurate? The answer to this question could be rather lengthy, so I will endeavor to keep it as brief and concise as possible. However, I hope many readers will be encouraged to do even more homework.

Let's have some fun and imagine we have been selected to be part of a first-century jury. We must decide if those who claim Jesus of Nazareth has risen from the grave are correct, or the other side, who claims these storytellers actually have stolen His body are correct. It would be very easy to render a verdict on assumption alone, but we have learned earlier that this is not a good practice. So we will listen to the arguments, claims and evidence favoring each side before making a decision.

THIS PRESCRIPTION PROVIDES
THE FOLLOWING BENEFITS

1. Confidence that it is a bad practice to make assumptions regarding important issues
2. Confidence that examining the facts before making a crucial decision is the best procedure

Rx3

JUST THE FACTS

The 1950s featured a popular television series known as *Dragnet*. It was a police-theme-based show featuring the Los Angeles Police Department and re-enacting accounts of actual crimes. It gained such popularity that they made a movie based on the series, which was also titled *Dragnet*. The lead character was a police sergeant named Joe Friday. Whenever he questioned a witness, he would cut right through the fluff and get to the heart of the investigation. He would repeatedly use the same matter-of-fact statement to obtain that goal. Whenever he felt a witness was getting carried away with their account, he would simply say, "All we want are the facts ma'am." He knew that the truth could only be obtained from the facts.

Remember that you are a member of a jury who must decide if the account of Jesus' resurrection is fact or fantasy. Maybe it's a hoax or a conspiracy. At any rate, you have been called to order, and the evidence is about to be presented.

Would those who are presenting the case against the resurrection of Jesus of Nazareth please proceed.

THE ARGUMENT OPPOSING JESUS' RESURRECTION

DIRECT EXAMINATION (by disbelievers of the resurrection):

For whatever reason, just or unjust, Jesus was arrested and taken first to Annas who was the father-in-law of Caiaphas, the high priest, (John 18:13), and then He was taken to Caiaphas, himself (Matthew 26:57). Eventually, He was tried and sentenced by the Roman governor of Judea, a man named Pontius Pilate. What was Pilate's decision?

RESPONSE (from the testimony of the Bible):

> He delivered Him to them **to be crucified.**
> John 19:16

CROSS-EXAMINATION (by believers of the resurrection):

Are you aware Jesus predicted this would occur?

RESPONSE (from the Bible):

> And it came about that when Jesus had finished all these words, He said to His disciples, "You know that after two days the Passover is coming, and the **Son of Man is to be delivered up for crucifixion."**
> Matthew 26:2

DIRECT EXAMINATION (by disbelievers):

Was the sentence carried out?

RESPONSE (from the Bible):

> They took Jesus therefore, and He went out, bearing His own cross, to the place called the Place of a Skull, which is

called in Hebrew, Golgotha. **There they crucified Him,** *and with two other men, one on either side, and Jesus between.*
John 19:17, 18

CROSS-EXAMINATION (by believers):

The question, "Didn't He predict this would happen?" has been asked and answered, but didn't the Hebrew Scriptures also mention He would die among criminals?

RESPONSE (from the Bible):

> *Therefore, I will allot Him a portion with the great, and He will divide the booty with the strong;* **because He poured out Himself to death, and was numbered with the transgressors;** *yet He Himself bore the sin of many, and interceded for the transgressors.*
> *Isaiah 53:12*

OBJECTION (by disbelievers):

Irrelevant!

CROSS-EXAMINATION (by believers):

No further questions.

DIRECT EXAMINATION (by disbelievers):

Did Jesus die?

RESPONSE (from the Bible):

> *The soldiers therefore came, and broke the legs of the first man, and of the other man who was crucified with Him; but*

*coming to Jesus, **when they saw that He was already dead,** they did not break His legs; but one of the soldiers pierced His side with a spear, and immediately there came out blood and water.*
John 19:32-34

CROSS-EXAMINATION (by believers):

With the court's permission, I would like to refer to the Hebrew scriptures one more time and ask, "Doesn't the Old Testament state the Messiah would not suffer any broken bones, but that He would be pierced?"

RESPONSE (from the Bible):

> ***He keeps all His bones; not one of them is broken.***
> *Psalms 34:20*

> *And I will pour out on the house of David and on the inhabitants of Jerusalem, the Spirit of grace and of supplication, so that **they will look on Me whom they have pierced;** and they will mourn for Him, as one mourns for an only son, and they will weep bitterly over Him, like the bitter weeping over a first born.*
> *Zechariah 12:10*

OBJECTION (by disbelievers):

This line of questioning is not relevant to the deciding if this man Jesus has actually risen from the dead.

DIRECT EXAMINATION (by disbelievers):

What happened next?

RESPONSE (from the Bible):

> *And after these things Joseph of Arimathea, being a disciple of Jesus, but a secret one, for fear of the Jews, asked Pilate that he might take away the body of Jesus; and Pilate granted permission. He came therefore, and took away the body. And Nicodemus came also; who had first come to Him by night,* **bringing a mixture of myrrh and aloes, about a hundred pounds weight.** *And so they took the body of Jesus, and bound it in linen wrappings with spices, as is the burial custom of the Jews.*
> *John 19:38-42*

CROSS-EXAMINATION (by believers):

That means the final wrapped body weighed approximately an additional one hundred pounds.[1]

DIRECT EXAMINATION (by disbelievers):

Was Jesus then buried?

RESPONSE (from the Bible):

> *And* **Joseph took the body,** *and wrapped it in clean linen cloth, and* **laid it in his own new tomb,** *which he had hewn out in the rock; and* **he rolled a large stone against the entrance of the tomb** *and went away.*
> *Matthew 27:59, 60*

CROSS-EXAMINATION (by believers):

How large was the stone? Isn't it true one individual has estimated the stone could have weighed between 1,500 and 2,000

---

[1] Josh McDowell, *Evidence That Demands A Verdict,* Vol. 1, (San Bernardino: Campus Crusade for Christ International 1972), p. 214.

pounds?[2] And another has suggested it would take as many as 20 men or more to remove it?[3]

OBJECTION (by disbelievers):

That is mere speculation and hearsay.

DIRECT EXAMINATION (by disbelievers):

Did the Jewish leadership take any precautions to secure the tomb from theft?

RESPONSE (from the Bible):

> *Now on the next day, which is the one after the preparation, the Chief Priests and the Pharisees gathered together with Pilate, and said, "Sir, we remember that when He was still alive that deceiver said, 'After three days I am to rise again.' Therefore give orders for the grave to be made secure until the third day, lest the disciples come and steal Him away and say to the people, 'He has risen from the dead,' and the last deception will be worse than the first." Pilate said to them, "**You have a guard; go, make it as secure as you know how.**"*
> *And they went and made the grave secure, **and along with the guard they set a seal on the stone.***
> *Matthew 27:62-66*

CROSS-EXAMINATION (by believers):

[2] Herbert Lockyer, *All The Miracles of the Bible*, (Grand Rapids: Zondervan, Publishing House, 1978), p. 246.
[3] Josh McDowell, *Evidence That Demands A Verdict, Vol. 1*, (San Bernardino: Campus Crusade for Christ International, 1972), p. 216.

How many soldiers guarded the tomb? Could it have been as little as four,[4] or maybe as many as 30?[5] Was there a centurion in charge?[6] No matter. What does matter is that Christ's enemies were confident there was no way His disciples would be able to steal the body.[7] Isn't that right? No further questions.

DIRECT EXAMINATION (by disbelievers):

None the less, sometime early Sunday morning, the third day after His death, His disciples did take the body?

OBJECTION (by believers):

Excuse me, but isn't that what we are here to determine?

DIRECT EXAMINATION (by disbelievers):

At any rate, the guards were unable to secure the body in the tomb. So what did the guard do next?

RESPONSE (from the Bible):

> *Some of the guard came into the city and reported to the Chief Priests all that had happened. And when they assembled the elders and counseled together . . . they said, "You are to say,* **'His disciples came by night and stole Him away while we were asleep.'"**
> *Matthew 28:11-13 (with selected portions omitted)*

---

[4]   Ibid., pp. 222, 223.
[5]   Albert Roper, *Did Jesus Rise From the Dead?*, (Grand Rapids:Zondervan Publishing House, 1965), p. 23
[6]   Josh McDowell, Evidence That Demands A Verdict, Vol. 1, (San Bernardino: Campus Crusade for Christ International 1972), p. 219.
[7]   Ibid., p. 224.

CROSS-EXAMINATION (by believers):

Excuse me, but if the guards were asleep how did they know anyone took the body, let alone who took the body? Don't bother to answer. The answer seems obvious.

Isn't it true that any guard found asleep on duty could be put to death?[8] However this guard was willing to say they were all asleep? Not even one guard was arrested! Why is that?

RESPONSE (from the Bible):

> *They (the Chief Priests) gave a large sum of money to the soldiers, (v. 12). and said, . . . "And if this should come to the governor's ears, we will win him over and keep you out of trouble (v. 14)."*
> *Matthew 28:12, 14*

OBJECTION (by disbelievers):

May those remarks be stricken from the record?

CROSS-EXAMINATION (by believers):

So what did the guard do next?

RESPONSE (from the Bible):

> *And they took the money and did as they had been instructed; and this story was widely spread among the Jews.*
> *Matthew 28:15*

This concludes the case for those favoring Jesus did not rise from the dead.

---

8   Ibid., p. 221.

We will take a brief recess, and then we will hear the case from those stating He has risen from the dead.

THIS PRESCRIPTION PROVIDES THE
FOLLOWING BENEFITS:

1. Confidence that Jesus died on a cross
2. Confidence that Jesus was buried in a secured tomb

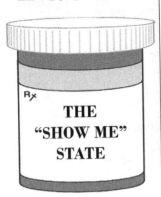

Rx4

Jesus said to him, "Because you have seen Me, have you believed? Blessed are they who did not see and yet believe." John 20:29

THE "SHOW ME" STATE

Missouri is one of fifty states in the United States of America. It is known as the "show me" state.[1] The people of Missouri take great pride in saying, "I won't believe it unless you show me."

There is nothing wrong with expecting proof from one who makes a claim, especially if that claim seems unbelievable or too good to be true. So now let's hear from those who claim Jesus rose from the dead.

THE ARGUMENT FAVORING JESUS' RESURRECTION

OPENING REMARKS

This case reminds me of the story about the boy who was walking home from school one day only to see a classmate of his playing in a game of baseball. He stopped for a moment and asked his classmate about the score. His friend told him the score was 15 to 0, in favor of the other team. The boy blurted out, "You're getting killed!" Then his classmate replied, "Yeah, I know, but we ain't got up yet."

Now it's our turn to be up.

---

[1]   Mark Jonas Viles, *Encyclopedia Americana, Vol. IXX,* (1964), p. 261.

DIRECT EXAMINATION (by believers of the resurrection):

What did the disciples do when Jesus was arrested?

RESPONSE (from the testimony of the Bible):

> So the Roman cohort and the commander, and the offi-
> cers of the Jews arrested Jesus and bound Him.
> John 18:12

> And **they** (His disciples) **all left Him and fled. And
> a certain young man** was following Him, wearing nothing
> but a linen sheet over his naked body; and they seized him.
> **But he** left the linen sheet behind and **escaped naked**.
> Mark 14:50-52

CROSS-EXAMINATION (by disbelievers of the resurrection):

Did all the disciples run away?

RESPONSE (from the Bible):

> **And Peter had followed Him at a distance**, right
> into the courtyard of the high priest; and he was sitting with
> the officers and warming himself at the fire.
> Mark 14:54

CROSS-EXAMINATION CONTINUED (by disbelievers):

Does this sound like the action of someone who is afraid?

REDIRECT EXAMINATION (by believers):

May I continue? I would like all of us to be perfectly clear on
this point. How many disciples followed Jesus into the courtyard

after His arrest? One? Did this disciple show any visible support for Jesus?

RESPONSE (from the Bible):

> And as Peter was below in the courtyard, one of the servant-girls of the high priest came, and seeing Peter warming himself, she looked at him, and said, **"You too, were with Jesus the Nazarene." But he denied it** saying, "I neither know nor understand what you are talking about." And he went out onto the porch. And the maid saw him, and began once more to say to the bystanders, "This is one of them!" **But again he was denying it**. And after a little while the bystanders were again saying to Peter. "Surely you are one of them, for you are a Galilean too." But he (Peter) began to curse and swear, **"I do not know this man you are talking about!"**
> Mark 14:66-71

DIRECT EXAMINATION (by believers):

Do we know any special course of action by any other of His disciples?

RESPONSE (from the Bible):

> Then when Judas, who had betrayed Him, saw that He had been condemned, he felt remorse and returned the thirty pieces of silver to the chief priests and elders saying, "I have sinned by betraying innocent blood." But they said, "What is that to us? See to that yourself!" And he threw the pieces of silver into the sanctuary and departed; and **he went away and hanged himself**.
> Matthew 27:3-5

DIRECT EXAMINATION CONTINUED (by believers):

So, what has been said so far is that His disciples fled rather than be taken prisoner. One of His disciples repeatedly denied Him and another committed suicide. Would you say that these are the types of individuals who could form the nucleus of a band of men capable of stealing a corpse away from an expectant Roman guard or any guard for that matter.

OBJECTION (by disbelievers)

Counsel is leading the witness and asking for a conclusion.

DIRECT EXAMINATION (by believers):

Let's move forward to the morning of the third day following His crucifixion. What happened that morning?

RESPONSE (from the Bible):

Now on the first day of the week Mary Magdalene came early to the tomb, while it was still dark.
John 20:1

DIRECT EXAMINATION CONTINUED (by believers):

Did anyone else besides Mary Magdalene go to the tomb?

RESPONSE (from the Bible):

And when the Sabbath was over, Mary Magdalene, and Mary the mother of James, and Salome, brought spices that they might come and anoint Him.
Mark 16:1

DIRECT EXAMINATION (by believers):

Were they concerned about the stone in front of the tomb, and if so why?

RESPONSE (from the Bible):

> And they were saying to one another, "Who will roll away the stone for us from the entrance of the tomb?" And looking up, they saw **the stone had been rolled away, although it was extremely large.**
> Mark 16:3, 4

DIRECT EXAMINATION CONTINUED (by believers):

So women, not men, were the first followers of Jesus to the tomb? And even with a sizable guard on duty they were concerned how such a large stone would be moved? What did they find?

RESPONSE (from the Bible):

> **They found the stone rolled away** from the tomb, but when they entered, **they did not find the body of the Lord Jesus.**
> Luke 24:2, 3

DIRECT EXAMINATION (by believers):

We are going to attempt to be as fair as we can to the other side, so please avoid, as much as possible any references to supernatural beings, such as angels, in answering the following questions. Thank you. So, what did the women do next?

RESPONSE (from the Bible):

> **And they departed quickly** *from the tomb with fear and great joy and ran* **to report it to His disciples.**
> *Matthew 28:8*

DIRECT EXAMINATION (by believers):

And what was the reaction of the disciples?

RESPONSE (from the Bible):

> *And so she (Mary Magdalene) ran and came to Simon Peter, and to the other disciple (John) whom Jesus loved, and said to them,* **"They have taken away the Lord out of the tomb,** *and we do not know where they have laid Him."*
> *John 20:2*

> *And these words appeared to them as nonsense, and* **they would not believe them.**
> *Luke 24:11*

CROSS-EXAMINATION (by disbelievers):

Would you say the disciples didn't believe Mary because they knew they had taken the body?

OBJECTION (by believers):

The witness is asked to draw a conclusion.

DIRECT EXAMINATION (by believers):

The disciples did not believe these women, but did any of them show any curiosity?

RESPONSE (from the Bible):

> *Peter therefore went forth, and the other disciple (John)* *and* **they were going to the tomb. And the two were running together;** *and the other disciple ran ahead faster than Peter, and came to the tomb first; and stooping and looking in, he saw the linen wrappings lying there but he did not go in. Simon Peter therefore also came, following him, and entered the tomb; and he beheld the linen wrappings lying there, and the face-cloth, which had been on His head, not lying with the linen wrappings, but rolled up in a place by itself. So the other disciple who had first come to the tomb entered then also, and he saw and believed (vv. 2-8). So the disciples went away to their own homes (v. 10).*
> *John 20:2-8, 10*

DIRECT EXAMINATION (by believers):

Who claimed to have first seen the risen savior?

RESPONSE (from the Bible):

> *But Mary (Magdalene) was standing outside the tomb weeping; and so, as she wept, she stooped and looked into the tomb; and she beheld two angels in white.*
> *John 20:11, 12*

OBJECTION (by disbelievers):

I thought we were going to avoid this type of testimony?

RESPONSE CONTINUED (from the Bible):

> *And she beheld two angels in white sitting, one at the head, and one at the feet, where the body of Jesus had been*

*lying. And they said to her, "Woman, why are you weeping?"
She said to them, "Because they have taken away my Lord,
and I do not know where they have laid Him."*

*When she had said this, **she turned around and beheld
Jesus standing there**, and did not know that it was Jesus. Jesus
said to her, "Woman, why are you weeping? Whom are you seeking?" Supposing Him to be the gardener, she said to Him, "Sir, if
you have carried Him away, tell me where you have laid Him,
and I will take Him away." Jesus said to her, "Mary!" She turned
and said to Him in Hebrew, "Rabboni!" (Which means, Teacher.)*
John 20:11-16

CROSS-EXAMINATION (by disbelievers):

Do we understand you correctly? Did you say Mary saw two
angels, but Peter and John didn't? Did you say Mary saw a gardener,
but it was actually the risen Jesus? Now please think before you
answer this next question. Did she see the tooth fairy also? No further questions.

DIRECT EXAMINATION (by believers):

Would you say Mary even for a brief moment, thought the disciples had taken the body of Jesus? Did Mary even consider God had
raised Him from the dead? Did Mary believe someone had taken His
body? I believe the answers to these questions are self evident. More
importantly, what did Mary do next?

RESPONSE (from the Bible):

*She went and reported to those who had been with Him,
while they were mourning and weeping. And when they heard
that He was alive, and had been seen by her, **they refused to
believe it.***
Mark 16:10, 11

CROSS-EXAMINATION (by disbelievers):

Let's see, Mary Magdalene was the first one to see the empty tomb, and no one believed her. So now she was the first one to see the *risen* Jesus, and still no one believed her. It seems this Mary had a first-century *attention deficit disorder*, if you will pardon the pun. It would appear Mary enjoyed being the center of *attention*.

OBJECTION (by believers):

The cross-examiner is attempting to testify.

DIRECT EXAMINATION (by believers):

Did any of His male followers ever claim to have seen the risen Jesus?

RESPONSE (from the Bible):

> *And after that, **He appeared in a different form to two of them**, while they were walking along on their way to the country, and they went away and reported it to the others, but they did not believe them either.*
> *Mark 16:12, 13*

CROSS-EXAMINATION (by disbelievers):

If I had stolen a corpse, I would find it difficult to believe it was now alive. Wouldn't you?

OBJECTION (by believers):

The cross-examiner is again attempting to testify.

DIRECT EXAMINATION (by believers):

Did any of the remaining disciples ever claim to have seen the risen Jesus?

RESPONSE (from the Bible):

> *When therefore it was evening, on that day, the first day of the week, and when the door was shut where the disciples were, for fear of the Jews,* **Jesus came and stood in their midst,** *and said to them, "Peace be with you." And when He said this, He showed them both His hands and His side.* **The disciples therefore rejoiced when they saw the Lord.**
> *John 20:19, 20*

DIRECT EXAMINATION (by believers):

The disciples didn't rejoice at Jesus' announcement concerning His future resurrection, but now they rejoiced? Were all eleven remaining disciples present?

RESPONSE (from the Bible):

> **Thomas, one of the twelve, called Didymus, was not with them when Jesus came.** *The other disciples therefore were saying to him, "We have seen the Lord!" But he said to them, "Unless I shall see in His hands the imprint of the nails, and put my finger into the place of the nails, and put my hand into His side,* **I will not believe."**
> *John 30:24, 25*

DIRECT EXAMINATION (by believers):

Did Thomas ever change his mind?

RESPONSE (from the Bible):

> *And after eight days again His disciples were inside and Thomas with them. Jesus came, the door having been shut, and stood in their midst, and said, "Peace be with you." Then He said to Thomas, "Reach here your finger, and see My hands; and reach here your hand, and put it into My side; and be not unbelieving, but believing."* **Thomas answered and said to Him, "My Lord and my God!"**
> *John 20:26-28*

CROSS-EXAMINATION (by disbelievers):

It appears you want us to believe that Jesus not only was raised from the dead, but He could enter a room without walking through the doorway. Is that correct?

OBJECTION (by believers):

That has already been answered.

DIRECT EXAMINATION (by believers):

Were there any other witnesses of the risen Jesus?

RESPONSE (from the Bible):

> *After that He appeared to more than* **five hundred brethren** *at one time.*
> *1 Corinthians 15:6*

DIRECT EXAMINATION (by believers):

We have seen that the disciples voiced considerable doubt. When did this doubt begin to fade?

RESPONSE (from the Bible):

> To these **He presented Himself alive**, *after His suffering*, **by many convincing proofs**, **appearing to them over a period of forty days**, *and speaking of the things concerning the kingdom of God. And gathering them together He commanded them not to leave Jerusalem but wait for what the Father had promised, "Which", He said, "you heard from Me".*
> Acts 1:3, 4

DIRECT EXAMINATION (by believers):

Did they do anything at this time to indicate they believed He was alive and how impressed they were with His resurrection?

RESPONSE (from the Bible):

> (Remember that Judas one of the twelve, had taken his life.) *And at this time Peter stood up in the midst of the brethren (v. 15), and said, . . . "It is therefore necessary that of the men who have accompanied us all the time that the Lord Jesus went in and out among us – beginning with the baptism of John,* **until the day that He was taken up from us . . . one of these should become a witness with us of His resurrection** *(vv. 21, 22).*
> Acts 1:15, 21-22

DIRECT EXAMINATION CONTINUED (by believers):

If the disciples had taken His body, there wouldn't have been a resurrection, let alone an ascension. Wouldn't they have known this would make it impossible to find someone who witnessed the resurrection? Considering that proposition this next question may seem unnecessary, but how successful were they at finding someone to fill Judas's position?

RESPONSE (from the Bible):

> *And they put forward **two men**, Joseph called Barsabbas . . ., and Matthias (v. 23). And they drew lots for them, and the lot fell to Matthias; and he was numbered with the eleven apostles (v. 26).*
> *Acts 1:23, 26*

DIRECT EXAMINATION CONTINUED (by believers):

If Jesus had not been resurrected, then this task would have been impossible, correct? So with an impossible task before them, they not only found one candidate that qualified, but two? Pardon me for finding this amusing, but I guess it wasn't impossible after all.

OBJECTION (by disbelievers):

Now who is trying to testify?

DIRECT EXAMINATION CONTINUED (by believers):

Let's move on. When did His followers begin to speak openly?

RESPONSE (from the Bible):

> *And when the day of Pentecost had come, they were all together in one place. And suddenly there came from heaven a noise like a violent, rushing wind, and it filled the whole house where they were sitting (vv.1, 2). Now there were Jews living in Jerusalem, devout men, from every nation under heaven. And when this sound occurred, the multitude came together, and were bewildered (vv. 5, 6) . . . But Peter, tak-*

ing his stand with the eleven, raised his voice and declared to them (v. 14) . . . "Men of Israel, listen to these words: Jesus the Nazarene, a man attested to you by God with miracles and wonders and signs which God performed through Him in your midst, just as you yourselves know — this Man, delivered up by the predetermined plan and foreknowledge of God, you nailed to a cross by the hands of godless men and put Him to death (vv. 22, 23) . . . **This Jesus God raised up again, to which we are all witnesses** *(v. 32)." . . . And Peter said to them, "Repent, and let each of you be baptized in the name of Jesus Christ for the forgiveness of your sins (v. 38)."*
Acts2:1, 2, 5, 6, 14, 22, 23, 32, 38

DIRECT EXAMINATION (by believers):

Had their fears been reasonable? Was there really anything to fear?

RESPONSE (from the Bible):

(Not long after this, Peter and John had restored a lame man's legs in Jesus' name) . . . *and as they were speaking to the people,* **the priests and the captain of the temple guard, and the Saducess, came upon them, being greatly disturbed because they were teaching the people and proclaiming in Jesus the resurrection from the dead.** *And they laid hands on them, and put them in jail until the next day, for it was already evening.*
Acts 4:1-3

DIRECT EXAMINATION CONTINUED (by believers):

So they were arrested for proclaiming Jesus had been resurrected from the dead and in Him there is resurrection for all. So what happened the next day?

RESPONSE (from the Bible):

> *And it came about on the next day, that **their rulers and elders and scribes were gathered together in Jerusalem;** and **Annas** the high priest was there, **and Caiaphas** and John and Alexander, and all who were of high-priestly descent. And when they had placed them (Peter and John) in the center, they began to inquire, "By what power, or in what name, have you done this (miracle)?"*
> Acts 4:5-7

DIRECT EXAMINATION (by believers):

And what was their reply?

RESPONSE (from the Bible):

> *Then Peter, filled with the Holy Spirit, said to them, "Rulers and elders of the people (v. 8), . . . let it be known to all of you, and to all the people of Israel, that by the name of **Jesus Christ the Nazarene, whom God raised from the dead – by this name this man stands here before you in good health** (v. 10)."*
> Acts 4:8, 10

DIRECT EXAMINATION CONTINUED (by believers):

Wow! That took some kind of boldness and courage to say. Did the high priest, the elders, and the rulers realize these were two of the men whom they had accused of stealing Jesus' body?

RESPONSE (from the Bible):

> *Now as they observed the confidence of Peter and John, and understood that they were uneducated and untrained*

*men, **they** were marveling, and **began to recognize them as having been with Jesus.***
Acts 4:13

DIRECT EXAMINATION CONTINUED (by believers):

Boy, I bet that made them happy. Now they had in custody two of the very men responsible for violating a Roman seal, grave robbing, and starting this incredible hoax. With a little effort, they probably could get them to tell where they hid the corpse. Just one more question. What did the leaders do next?

RESPONSE (from the Bible):

> *But when they had ordered them (Peter and John) to go aside out of the Council, they began to confer with one another, saying, "What shall we do with these men? For the fact that a noteworthy miracle has taken place through them is apparent to all who live in Jerusalem, and we cannot deny it. But in order that it may not spread any further among the people, let us warn them to speak no more to any man in this name (vv. 15-18)." **And when they had threatened them further, they let them go** (finding no basis on which they might punish them) (v. 21).*
> Acts 4:15-18, 21

DIRECT EXAMINATION CONTINUED (by believers):

Excuse me, am I missing something here? Annas and Caiaphas are the same priests who had heard the testimony of the guard from the tomb, correct? And it was decided that the disciples of Jesus had taken the body, correct? They knew Peter and John would have been part of that band of followers, correct? What's wrong with this picture? If they truly believed His followers had taken His body from the grave, then all they would have to do to dispel this *hoax* would be to have Peter and John take them to where they had hidden His body. Doesn't it appear they knew that was impossible because Jesus had risen from the dead? No further questions.

OBJECTION (by disbelievers)

Here we go again. Now who is attempting to testify?

THIS PRESCRIPTION PROVIDES THE
FOLLOWING BENEFITS:

1. Confidence that no real effort was put forth to apprehend those who *stole* the body of Jesus
2. Confidence that Jesus was seen alive after His body allegedly was stolen
3. Confidence that even stubborn disbelievers acknowledged that Jesus had risen from the grave

Rx5

"Everyone therefore who shall confess Me before men, I will also confess him before My Father who is in heaven."
Matthew 10:32

YOUR VERDICT, PLEASE

Would everyone please come to order? It is now time for each side to present their closing argument. Would the side opposing the resurrection of Jesus please present your argument?

THE CLOSING ARGUMENT SUPPORTING JESUS' BODY WAS STOLEN

There are only two positions being voiced.[1] Both sides agree Jesus was crucified. Both sides agree Jesus died. Finally, both sides agree He was buried. The dispute is what happened to the body after its entombment. Did His disciples steal the body, or did God raise Jesus from the dead? But why is there a dispute? How difficult a decision can this be? Does anyone really believe the absence of Jesus' body from the tomb is enough evidence to prove He had risen from the dead? Remember the guards who were professional soldiers testified it was the disciples who took the body. Surely, you are all logical people. Certainly, you are not going to allow the other side's obsession with details distract you from the fact that Jewish carpenter was as dead as a doornail.[2] You're not going to allow a bunch of religious

---

[1]   Lee Strobel, *The Case for Christ*, (Grand Rapids: Zodervan, Publishing House, 1998), p. 212.

[2]   Paul E. Little, *Know Why You Believe*, (Colorado Springs: Cook Communications, 1999), pp. 45, 46.

57

fanatics steal your focus away from this unchangeable fact and cause you to doubt the testimony of a centurion and his men. Who are you going to believe: the guardians of the peace or a small basically insignificant cross section of mediocrity? The decision you must make is very easy! Give me a break! There is only one logical decision. Jesus did not rise from the dead!

Thank you very much. Now would the side claiming God did raise Jesus from the dead please present your closing argument at this time.

THE CLOSING ARGUMENT SUPPORTING JESUS' RESURRECTION

The other side would like you to ignore your intellectual capacity to honestly examine the record. They would rather you choose to believe that a small group of fearful doubters plotted to go to a tomb that bore a Roman seal, a tomb that was guarded by a sufficient number of soldiers to ease the concerns of the Jewish leaders and their attempt to steal the body of Jesus. You are supposed to believe that at the tomb, this forewarned guard of soldiers was totally neglecting its duty, and all were asleep. This would have been an offense that could have cost each guard his life.[3] The other side would also like you to believe that these fearful doubters were able to move the extremely large stone without arousing the guard. Then they took the time to unwrap the heavy grave clothes from the corpse and then rewrap or fold them. Then and only then did they leave with the body. However, one or more soldiers must have awakened. And although it was dark they were close enough to the thieves to recognize them as disciples of Jesus, but not close enough to capture even a single perpetrator. Not even the one carrying the body.[4] Are you following this? Shortly thereafter, certain women reported to those *thieves* that Jesus body

---

[3] Josh McDowell, *Evidence That Demands A Verdict, Vol. I*, (San Bernardino: Campus Crusade for Christ International, 1972), p. 221.

[4] John Peter Lange, *Lange Commentary on the Holy Scriptures, Matthew-Luke, Vol. VIII*, (Grand Rapids Zondervan, Publishing House, 1978), p. 552.

had been taken. Guess what happened? Two of these *guilty* disciples returned to the scene of the crime, only this time, in broad daylight. They didn't even consider they might be putting themselves in harm's way. It seems like this was the only scenario that could have taken place if the testimony of the guard was truthful. Does it seem reasonable to you? Now, consider that there were no disciples arrested for this crime although they were recognized. And there were no guards disciplined either. Then there is the interesting problem of what did happen to the body. It seems that the simple act of recovery would have put an end to this hoax, if it was a hoax.

Again, the other side would have you believe that by being responsible and thoughtfully considering the testimony of each side, you will be distracted from the fact that Jesus was declared dead. In reality, an examination of the record will focus your attention on a collective body of evidence that makes your decision something far removed from a mere assumption. To assume Jesus is still dead would be easy. To assume He had been resurrected from the dead would be next to impossible. But how else can you explain the actions of His disciples? Soon after the resurrection they were no longer doubters or fearful. Instead, they placed their own physical well-being secondary to telling others about Jesus' life, His sacrificial death, His resurrection, and the benefits of accepting Him for who He is. Benefits like forgiveness of sin (Acts 5:31), a personal relationship with God (Acts 4:24-31), and healing for one's temporal body (Acts 4:10).

Now, those were the actions of His disciples, but what is truly a mystery are the actions of those opposing the resurrection, the Jewish leaders. When they were provided with the perfect conditions in which to disprove the resurrection, when they had Peter and John in their custody, they chose to take no action. Hello! Doesn't this imply that it was easier for them to claim that Jesus' body was stolen than to prove there wasn't a resurrection of His body? If they truly believed they could prove there wasn't a resurrection, and if they could show Jesus was still dead, then they could have put an end to this hoax. All they needed to do would have Peter and John take them to the body of Jesus. If they had done that when they had the opportunity, then we wouldn't be conducting this proceeding now. So why didn't they do it? Did they fear, believe, or know God had raised Him from the dead? Isn't the answer obvious?

Those who lived in the first-century Jerusalem were far more privileged than we are when it came to making a decision regarding this matter. They were living in those historical moments themselves. We, on the other hand, are nearly two thousand years removed, and still counting. However, keep that imagination working. It can be very helpful. For instance, what if a first-century jury was not only deliberating the above testimony, but they also had to deliberate another question: *can mere mortals place a man on the moon?* Which do you think they would have found more believable? They had heard about Jesus calling a four-day-old corpse, Lazarus, from the grave. Hard to believe? Yeah! Up until about thirty days before His own death. But not any longer. Some of the people in Jerusalem certainly knew Lazarus personally. What was there to doubt?

But now, about that other question. Can man place another man on the moon? What do you think the first-century assumption and decision would have been to that question? Do you think they would have thought it was nonsense or even laughable? If so, they would have been very mistaken. So don't allow two thousand years of history and opinions prejudice your thinking. We have not experienced the full meaning or consequences of men walking on the moon, but we have been informed of the consequences of God raising Jesus from the dead and the decision to ignore that fact.

THE MEANING AND CONSEQUENCES OF JESUS' RESURRECTION

I am the resurrection and the life; **he who believes in Me shall live even if he dies.**
John 11:25

Do not marvel at this, for an hour is coming in which all that are in the tombs shall hear His voice, and shall come

> *forth;* ***those who did the good to a resurrection of life,*** *those who committed the evil to a resurrection of judgment.*
> *John 5:28, 29*

Resurrection may or may not be a question for some of us, but it's not even a consideration to God. It's a definite for everyone. The only thing in question is, will it be a resurrection to life or to judgement? God says it will be a resurrection of life for those who did the good. Now that brings us back to the meaning of *the good. The good* is to believe and confess two key things about Jesus. First, He is Lord, as mentioned in Rx 1, and second, God raised Him from the dead, as discussed in Rx 2-5.

THE GOOD

> ***If you will confess*** *with your mouth* ***Jesus as Lord,*** ***and believe*** *in your heart* ***that God raised Him from the*** ***dead,*** *you shall be saved; for with the heart man believes, resulting in righteousness, and with the mouth he confesses, resulting in salvation.*
> *Romans 10:9, 10*

My wife will, on occasion, reveal to others that she accepted Jesus as a little girl. She will also confess her motive was to have Jesus as fire insurance against the flames of hell. There's nothing wrong with that. However, the last portion of the twentieth-century has provided an additional motivation and that motivation is to insure against the all-consuming flames of medical costs.

Health insurance is a must for anyone whose employer does not provide it. And even those who are insured frequently feel the need for supplemental insurance. We all understand health insurance only insures that out-of-pocket expenses will be kept to a minimum. It certainly doesn't ensure recovery from illness or maintaining good health.

Maybe you remember in Rx 1, I said I started to read the Bible with an open mind; I mean as if it was the first time I had encountered any of the information inside. I also said that was the second-best decision I had ever made. You probably are wondering what I consider the best decision I ever made. The absolute best decision I ever made was to do *the good* thing and to confess Jesus is Lord and that God has raised Him from the dead. The moment I did that, I knew heaven's gates were open wide, and I had just entered the kingdom of God and the salvation of our Lord Jesus Christ. In addition, I had just become a member of God's supplemental health plan. Now just listen to some of the features of His plan: no enrollment fee, no monthly premiums, no deductibles, no co-payments, no exclusions, no appointments necessary, all visits are preapproved, and there is no limit, even for well visits. It even allows for house calls. In addition, it has the most preventive, as well as, advanced therapeutic treatment available, and both are provided by the finest equipped, most qualified team of caring providers in the universe. If I had refused such an offer, it would have been like doing *the evil.* Now, that's a pretty scary thought. I mean a resurrection unto judgement. To be perfectly honest, I don't believe it would be unkind of me to say, "Such a decision really doesn't have much going for it. If you get my drift."

I trust your verdict is in favor of Jesus' resurrection, which is a reasonable and well-thought-out decision.

Now that you have made that decision, may I let you in on a little secret? When the disciples initially gave their testimony, the decisions of the first two juries were overwhelming. The verdict of the first jury found about three thousand individuals believing Jesus was resurrected (Acts 2:41), and the second jury's verdict was even greater, about five thousand men alone believed God had raised Jesus from the dead (Acts 4:4). Oh, I'm sorry! Some of you may not have made a decision yet. Please don't let my little slip influence your final decision. Take your time. At any rate, for those who have made *the good* decision, welcome aboard! Let's begin to examine His plan together, and maybe when we have finished, you'll all agree with me. It has marvelous benefits, and it has given me a very positive attitude and outlook about my present and future physical well-being.

A word of caution to those who haven't made a decision, remember, Jesus said,

THE GOOD AND THE EVIL

I am the resurrection and the life; he who believes in Me shall live even if he dies.
John 11:2

Do not marvel at this, for an hour is coming in which all who are in the tombs shall hear His voice, and shall come forth; **those who did the good to a resurrection of life,** *those who committed the evil to a resurrection of judgment.*
John 5:28, 29

Resurrection isn't the question in Christ's thinking. His concern is whether you will make the *good decision* about Him or the *evil decision*. Hopefully, no one will make or maintain the latter position. Why? Prescription number 1 provides the authority for healing: Jesus is Lord. How does that apply to healing?

JESUS HAS AUTHORITY OVER DISEASES

*And when He had entered Capernaum, a centurion came to Him, entreating Him, and saying, "**Lord**, my servant is lying paralyzed at home suffering great pain." And He said to him, "I will come and heal him." But the centurion answered and said, "**Lord**, I am not worthy for You to come under my roof, but **just say the word, and my servant will be healed. For I, too, am a man under authority**, with soldiers under me; and I say to this one 'Go!' and he goes, and to another 'Come!' and he comes, and to my slave, 'Do this!' and he does it." Now when Jesus heard this He marveled and said to those who were following, "**Truly I say to you, I have not found such great faith with anyone in Israel.**"*
Matthew 8:5-10

Prescription numbers 2 through 5 provide the miraculous power that enforces our Lord's authority. God raised Jesus from the dead. This power is set in motion by the joint response of your heart and your mouth. It is set in motion by your confession. So, let's hear YOUR VERDICT PLEASE.

THE VERDICT

If you confess with your mouth Jesus as Lord, and believe in your heart that God raised Him from the dead, you shall be saved.
Romans 10:9

The meaning of the word *saved* is more than forgiveness of sin and eternal life. Healing is also contained in its meaning,[5] and this will be explained in prescriptions WHERE'S THE BEEF? and SEEK AND YOU SHALL FIND.

But for right now, let's turn our attention to the origin of our sicknesses.

THIS PRESCRIPTION PROVIDES THE FOLLOWING BENEFIT

1. Confidence in your decision that God raised Jesus from the dead

---

[5] T.L.Osborn, *Healing The Sick,* (Tulsa: Harrison House, Inc., 1986), pp. 84, 85.

Rx6

Rx

CAN WE LEAVE THIS PART OUT?

How many of us look forward to going to our dentist, or maybe the D.M.V.? There was a time when I didn't look forward to eating spinach or liver, and I'm sure you can think of something right now that you would rather avoid. For instance, if we were asked if we would like to avoid death, all of us who are strong and healthy in body and mind would no doubt say, "Of course." Maybe you have heard the old saying that goes something like this, "Everybody wants to go to heaven, but no one wants to die." This rather accurately describes the feelings of most.

Why do we grow old and die? Here is another old adage: "Some questions are best left unasked." And even though I would like to LEAVE THIS PART OUT of our talk, it is essential we understand the origin of our situation.

The opening chapter of the Bible informs us that it was God who brought forth the heavens, the earth and all living things including man. God looked at His completed work and found it was very good.

GOD WAS PLEASED

> *And God saw all that He had made, and behold, **it was very good**.*
> *Genesis 1:31*

What went wrong? How did sickness and all the woes of the world enter a situation that began as *very good*? The familiar abbreviation, KISS, or keep it simple stupid, is something I don't believe God would ever say, but "keep it simple son" would surely fit into His vernacular. He follows this same principle Himself. For instance, God initially had only one simple prohibition.

A ONE-RULE WORLD

> *And the Lord God commanded the man, saying, "From any tree of the garden you may eat freely; **but from the tree of the knowledge of good and evil you shall not eat, for in the day you eat from it you shall surely die.***"*
> *Genesis 2:16, 17*

Take note, God did not say, "You shall surely become sick and die." Let's focus on the one rule. Rather simple, wasn't it?

In addition, Adam, the man God had created, was placed in charge of planet earth.

MAN RULED OVER EVERY LIVING CREATURE

> *And God created man in His own image, in the image of God He created him; male and female He created them. And God blessed them; and God said to them, "Be fruitful and multiply, and fill the earth, and subdue it, and **rule** over the fish of the sea, and over the birds of the sky, and **over every living thing** that moves **on the earth.***"*
> *Genesis 1:27, 28*

Man had no need to know there was another highly intelligent being who existed on this planet. All man needed to know was as long as he obeyed God, he would not die. However, Satan, the other highly intelligent being desired this planet for himself. He wanted to be in charge instead of being ruled over.

SATAN IS VERY INTELLIGENT

> **Now** the serpent (Satan) **was more crafty than any beast of the field** which the Lord God had made.
> Genesis 3:1

Satan knew if he could get Adam to believe him instead of God, then he, Satan, would actually be in charge of planet Earth. So here is what he did.

SATAN SETS HIS TRAP

> And he (the serpent, Satan) said to the woman, "Indeed **has God said**, 'You shall not eat from any tree of the garden?'"
> Genesis 3:1

Could animals speak before man's fall in the garden? Possibly! We know one could, for sure. At any rate, the fact that a serpent spoke to Eve did not seem to alarm or alert her in any way. After all, Adam and Eve were ruling over every living creature. It might serve us well to recognize that the things we hear with our ears do not always come from man's spirit. It could be a mixture of man's spirit, God's spirit, or even a spirit from Satan. All things should be measured against God's word.

We know Satan is very crafty. He knows that it is not good strategy to directly attack the object of someone's admiration without expecting a counterattack. A far more successful approach is to plant a seed of doubt regarding the one who is admired. Satan knows if we doubt someone, soon our trust in them will begin to wane. Our confidence will waver. Gradually, we will not be sure if we should believe that person. If something doesn't change, eventually we will not have any faith in that individual or what that person says.

So Satan hurls the fiery dart of doubt toward the mind of Eve. Remember that it was the apostle Paul who informed us how to defend ourselves against such attacks.

DEFENSE AGAINST DOUBT

> *In addition to all,* **taking up the shield of faith with**
> **which you will be able to extinguish all the flaming mis-**
> **siles of the evil one.**
> *Ephesians 6:16*

Eve's protection and our protection against being wounded by doubt is the shield of faith, but where do we find this shield? This shield comes directly from God's word.

GOD'S WORD IS OUR SHIELD

> **So faith comes** *from hearing, and hearing* **by the word**
> **of Christ**.
> *Romans 10:17*

But what was Eve's response? Did she use the shield of faith? If so, did she use it correctly?

EVE MISUSED THE SHIELD

> *And the woman said to the serpent, "From the fruit of*
> *the trees of the garden we may eat; but from the fruit of the*
> *tree which is in the middle of the garden, God has said, 'You*
> *shall not eat from it* **or touch it**, *lest you die'."*
> *Genesis 3:2, 3*

Did Eve misunderstand God's word? Did she misinterpret God's word? Did she forget God's word? Did she doubt God's word? I don't know. Who does? But what is for sure is that she misquoted God's word and that is misuse of God's shield, and it simply is not effective against such a crafty opponent.

Eve's defense should have been to correctly remind Satan of what God had said. She had the opportunity to do so. Satan was confident that when she failed to do so, he could take her by the figurative hand and lead her down the path of deception. The next fiery dart that he launched displays his confidence. Satan directly attacked God, the object of her love.

SATAN CALLS GOD A LIAR

> *And the serpent said to the woman, "**You surely shall not die!** For God knows that in the day you eat from it your eyes will be opened, and you will be like God, knowing good and evil."*
> *Genesis 3:4, 5*

One more time, Eve had an opportunity to raise the shield of faith. Read how our Lord, Jesus of Nazareth, responded.

JESUS USED THE SHIELD OF FAITH

> *And the devil said to Him (Jesus), "If you are the Son of God, tell this stone to become bread." **And Jesus answered him, "It is written, 'Man shall not live on bread alone'."***
> *Luke 4:3, 4*

Unfortunately, Eve didn't use the shield of faith. Consequently, the fiery darts of doubt found the shield of faith down, and they hit their mark. When we miss the mark, we can count on Satan hitting the mark.

WE HAVE ALL MISSED THE MARK

> *For all have sinned and fall short (missed the mark) of the glory of God.*
> *Romans 3:23*

The seeds of doubt sprung up fast as Eve considered the tree and the fruit.

CONSIDER THE POSSIBILITIES

> *When the woman saw that **the tree was good for food**, and that **it was a delight to the eyes**, and that **the tree was desirable to make one wise**, she took from its fruit and ate; and she gave also to her husband with her, and he ate.*
> *Genesis 3:6*

Eve considered all the possibilities but one. Maybe God wasn't a liar. Maybe God was telling the truth.

GOD DOES NOT LIE

> *"**God is not a man, that He should lie**, nor a son of a man, that He should repent; has He said and will He not do it?"*
> *Numbers 23:19*

Maybe Eve should have considered the possibility that it was the serpent who was lying.

SATAN NATURALLY LIES

> *"He (the devil) was a murderer from the beginning, and does not stand in the truth, because **there is no truth in him**. Whenever he speaks a lie, he speaks from his own nature; for **he is a liar**, and the father of lies."*
> *John 8:44*

Well, Eve didn't consider this possibility, and she and Adam did eat of the fruit. The rest is history. Satan won the day and established his kingdom on planet earth.

NEW LEADERSHIP FOR PLANET EARTH

> *We know that we are of God, and **the whole world lies in the power of the evil one.***
> *1 John 5:19*

Things suddenly became ugly on planet earth. The immediate results of Adam and Eve's actions were and are as follows:

MANKIND HAD A NEW AWARENESS

> ***Then the eyes of both of them were opened,*** *and they knew they were naked; and they sewed fig leaves together and made themselves loin coverings.*
> *Genesis 3:7*

Not only did man have a new awareness of himself, but that awareness caused him to fear God.

MAN BECAME AFRAID OF GOD

> *Then the Lord God called to the man, and said to him, "Where are you?" And he (the man) said, "I heard the sound of Thee in the garden, and **I was afraid** because I was naked, so I hid myself."*
> *Genesis 3:9, 10*

Man's fear may have been very justified. Didn't God say man would die the day he ate from the Tree of the Knowledge of Good and Evil? Now man knew right from wrong. Adam and Eve knew they blew it, and they could have been afraid that God was out to get them. So what's new? Isn't this how man thinks today?

Man may have been worried about death, physically, but he had already died spiritually.[1] When man fell, he pulled the plug on his spiritual life source and plugged in to a completely different source.

MAN PLUGGED INTO SIN AND DEATH

> **And you were dead in your trespasses and sins,**
> *in which you formerly walked according to the course of the world, according to the prince of the power of the air, of the spirit that is now working in the sons of disobedience.*
> *Ephesians 2:1, 2*

We are all born spiritually dead, but very alive to the plan embraced by the leader of this planet,[2] Satan. It is his spirit and power that begins to work in us at birth.

Adam and Eve did not fall over dead when they ate the forbidden fruit, but they immediately had a new life source working within them, a source that fears God Almighty. However, we are well aware that all men will die physically.

PHYSICAL DEATH COMES TO ALL

> *And in as much as* **it is appointed for men to die once** *and after this comes judgment.*
> *Hebrews 9:27*

God is out to get us, but not for the reason we naturally fear. God wants to restore us. He wants to restore us to right relationship with Himself, and to be full heirs to His kingdom, and He wants to restore our health. However, there is one part of us that God will one day replace rather than return to its former state. That part of us is

---

[1]   W. Robertson Nicoll, ed., *The Expositor's Greek Testament, Vol. III*, (Grand Rapids: Eerdmans, 1974), p. 283.
[2]   Ibid., p. 284.

our bodies. Since the fall, our bodies have had a serious defect. They hate God's will.[3]

OUR BODY, OUR ENEMY

> *But I say, walk by the Spirit, and you will not carry out the desire of the flesh.* **For the flesh sets its desire against the Spirit,** *and the Spirit against the flesh;* **for these are in opposition to one another,** *so you may not do the things that you please.*
> *Galatians 5:16, 17*

There is plenty of hope for the spirit of man, but his body will eventually die. It is not a pleasant fact, but it would be horrible to live forever with a body that was fighting God all the way. Instead of pleasing God naturally, our spirit and God's Spirit are and would be continually at task to keep our body in check. Do you want to live forever with this problem? Or would you rather have a body that rejoices along with your soul, your spirit, and God's will? No contest! Right? Of course, and God agrees with you. So, that is why He did not allow that to happen.

PHYSICAL DEATH AND FULL FREEDOM

> *Then the Lord God said, "Behold, the man has become like one of Us, (the Father, the Son and the Holy Spirit), knowing good and evil; and now lest he stretch out his hand,* **and take also from the tree of life, and eat, and live forever** *(v. 22)." So He drove the man out; and at the east of the garden He stationed the cherubim, and the flaming sword which turned every direction, to guard the way to the tree of life (v. 24).*
> *Genesis 3:22, 24*

---

[3]   Albert Barnes, Barnes' Notes on the New Testament, Galatians, (Grand Rapids: Kregel Publications, 1974), p. 955.

But before God drove man from the garden, He confronted Adam. God desires humility, honesty, and confession from His children.

GOD DESIRES HONESTY

> *And He said, "Who told you that you were naked?* **Have you eaten from the tree which I commanded you not to eat?"**
> *Genesis 3:11*

God also desires confession, but before Adam made his honest confession, he became the father of all excuses.

ADAM'S CONFESSION AND EXCUSE

> *And the man said, "The woman whom Thou gavest to be with me, she gave me from the tree, and* **I ate.***"*
> *Genesis 3:13*

Adam eventually did confess, "I ate." But, in the process was he trying **to con**vince **God** that he had been an innocent victim? Was Adam trying **to con**vince **God** that he had no idea where the fruit came from? Maybe, maybe not, but it certainly sounds like a **con** job, and a lot like something we all have said at one time or another.

However, the only **con** job any of us can pull off on God is a true **con**fession. God desires confession from all His children. So, He inquires of Eve.

WOMAN, ARE YOU GUILTY?

> *Then the Lord God said to the woman,* **"What is this you have done?"**
> *Genesis 3:13*

Now, it's Eve's turn to confess, and yes, before her confession is finished she becomes the mother of all excuses.

EVE'S CONFESSION AND EXCUSE

> And the woman said, "The serpent deceived me, and **I ate**."
> Genesis 3:13

It could go unnoticed, but God does not desire or expect a confession from Satan. We already know he is a liar, thus, expecting an honest confession would be pointless. In addition, Satan is without hope of forgiveness. Indeed he is the very reason God created a place of eternal fire and punishment. Fallen man certainly was not the reason.

A FIERY PUNISHMENT FOR SATAN

> "Then He will also say to those on His left, 'Depart from Me, accursed ones, into **eternal fire which has been prepared for the devil and his angels**';"
> Matthew 25:41

Satan can't escape the fiery eternity, which is his destiny, and since Adam fell, all mankind must face physical death. On the other hand, Christ has made it possible for all mankind to escape spiritual death and the fiery eternity that awaits Satan, his demons and all who reject God's gift of eternal life in Christ Jesus.

How many of us at one time or another have wished we could do something over? You know, thoughts like, *I wish I hadn't said that*, or *If I could do it over, I would have done it differently*. Do you think Adam ever had those kinds of thoughts? Without a doubt! I mean, Eve was deceived, but Adam knew exactly what he was doing.

ADAM KNOWINGLY SINNED

> *And it was not Adam who was deceived,* but the woman being quite deceived, fell into transgression.
> 1 Timothy 2:14

Adam probably was haunted by thoughts like these all the days of his life, but he couldn't do it over. That job was left for Jesus of Nazareth, and thank God, Jesus did it right. He did what Adam wished he could do over. Jesus became the last Adam.

Are you in Christ? Then you shall be made alive.

We have already stated, the devil cannot escape his fiery eternity, but God has made it possible for fallen man to escape.

JESUS: THE LAST ADAM

> But God demonstrates His own love towards us, in that while we were yet sinners, *Christ died for us.*
> Romans 5:8

> For as in Adam all die, so also *in Christ all shall be made alive.*
> 1 Corinthians 15:22

> For as through the one man's disobedience many were made sinners, *even so through the obedience of the One (Jesus) the many will be made righteous.*
> Romans 5:19

> *So also it is written, "The first man, Adam, became a living soul. The last Adam (Jesus) became a life-giving Spirit."*
> 1 Corinthians 15:45

THIS PRESCRIPTION PROVIDES
THE FOLLOWING BENEFIT

1. Confidence that sin, not God, ushered in sickness and disease

Rx7

INSTRUCTIONS

Be of sober spirit, be on the alert, the devil prowls about like a roaring lion, seeking someone to devour.
1 Peter 5:8

Did you ever hear the old joke that went something like this: Do you know why none of Mr. and Mrs. Cannibal's neighbors will accept an invitation to come over for dinner? They discovered that to accept such an invitation meant that they were not only going for dinner, but they were dinner! I understand that today's concept of humor considers this form of humor as being rather corny, but here in our neighborhood that we call planet earth, we have a very similar but not-so-corny situation. We have invited the Cannibals over for dinner, and as you can imagine, we are still the main course.

Maybe you can envision a husband calling his wife one day from work and asking her this question: "GUESS WHO'S COMING TO DINNER?" She inquires, "Who?" Then her husband informs her that he has invited a European nobleman, Count Dracula, over for dinner. His wife hesitates for a moment and then she replies, "Darling, wouldn't breakfast be better?"

Okay, so much for humor. The last chapter gave us a glimpse of our situation. It's a situation millions ignore and refuse to accept. It's a situation with life-long, as well as, eternal consequences. Moreover, it is a situation that must be accepted before any lasting relief can be obtained. It is an ugly situation, without question. Nevertheless, it is a situation that is not hopeless. On the contrary, it is a situation filled with hope, promise, and positive certainty. So let's move on and examine the long-term results of this situation, and in so doing let's discover the true source of mental and physical maladies.

Adam and Eve had just confessed. They admitted that they had eaten from the Tree of Knowledge of Good and Evil. Up to this point, God had placed Adam and Eve on a need-to-know basis. That is to say, all they needed to know was the one simple rule (Genesis 2:17). They didn't need to know about the serpent, and they didn't need to know any of the additional consequences that would result from disobedience. All they needed to know was to believe and to follow God's word. Would not the avoidance of dying be sufficient reason to obey God's word? It would if you believed it, but Satan deceived Eve into believing something else. Satan deceived Eve into doubting God. Satan deceived Eve into believing she needed to know more. Now God was going to let all of them know the additional consequences of disobedience and breaking the one rule.

We saw that Adam confessed first (Genesis 3:12) and pointed his finger at Eve, who confessed and pointed her finger at the serpent (Genesis 3:13), who is the devil, Satan himself.

THE SERPENT, THE DEVIL, SATAN

> And the great dragon was thrown down, **the serpent, of old who is called the devil and Satan**, who deceives the whole world; he was thrown down to the earth, and his angels were thrown down with him.
> Revelations 12:9

God did not begin to detail the long-term consequences of the fall to Adam. First, He had a surprise in store for Satan.

SATAN CURSED

> And the Lord God said to the serpent. "Because you have done this, **cursed are you** more than all cattle, and more than every beast of the field; on your belly shall you go, and

*dust shall you eat all the days of your life; And **I will put enmity between you and the woman**, and between your seed and her seed; **He shall bruise you on the head**, and you shall bruise Him on the heel."*
Genesis 3:14, 15

Satan may have earlier won the day and the planet, but all of a sudden things were just a little less rosy. Satan was cursed and informed that *dust* would be his principle diet. These were immediate consequences. Next, he was informed that a state of hostility, dare I say, a state of war, would exist between the woman and himself, indeed between his offspring and her's.[1]

Eventually, her seed, Jesus, would deal a permanent *deathblow* to Satan, although Jesus would suffer a temporary injury.[2] God is foretelling Satan of the events of the crucifixion[3] and the resurrection of Jesus, and He is promising all mankind that a time is coming when the results of the fall can be reversed and man's authority will be restored.

Next, God spoke to Eve and enlarged upon the consequence of being deceived.

BEING DECEIVED CAN BE PAINFUL

*To the woman He said, "**I will greatly multiply your pain in childbirth**, in pain you shall bring forth children; yet your desire shall be to your husband, and he shall rule over you."*
Genesis 3:16

In the spring of 1973, Lu and I were anticipating the birth of our first child. Lu had decided she wanted to experience natural child-

---

[1]   H. C. Luepold, *Barnes' Notes on the Old & New Testaments, Genesis, Vol. I,* (Grand Rapids, Baker Book House, 1975), p. 166.

[2]   Ibid.

[3]   Ibid., p. 170.

birth. So we enrolled in a natural childbirth class offered through Torrance Memorial Hospital. The instructor offered encouragement to all the expectant mothers in many ways, but the one thing she said I remember most is that Chinese women have been known to work in the rice fields up to the moment of delivery. Then she went on to say it wasn't unheard of for some Chinese women to return to work the same day that they gave birth. That seemed so unbelievable to my Western mind. However, it did remind me that God designed the woman's body.

Obviously, God's word informs us that the process of childbirth would be more uncomfortable than He originally intended. The instructor also stated, that the woman's body has a built-in anesthetic process that serves to lessen the degree of pain she experiences during childbirth. Our loving God could have easily removed this benefit completely, but apparently, He only decreased its original capability. God does not delight in His children having to experience pain. Please note there is no direct mention of sickness or disease in God's words to Eve.

God has finished updating both Satan and Eve regarding their current situation. Now it's Adam's turn.

ADAM, YOU ARE DUST

*Then to Adam He said, "Because you have listened to the voice of your wife, and have eaten from the tree about which I commanded you saying, 'You shall not eat from it;' cursed is the ground because of you; in toil you shall eat of it all the days of your life. Both thorns and thistles it shall grow for you; and you shall eat the plants of the fields; by the sweat of your face you shall eat bread, till you return to the ground, because from it you were taken; for **you are dust**, and to dust you shall return."*
Genesis 3:17-19

God spoke to both Adam and Eve, and yet He did not directly mention sickness and disease as a consequence of the fall. We all recognize that wars, murders, suicides, and accidents are all means of ending physical life but with their exceptions, are we to assume that it is God's will to use sickness and disease as His means of destroying our bodies until we return to the dust from whence we came? And if we consciously or unconsciously make such an assumption, then are we not categorizing God in very much the same way as the inventor in the following story?

THE MAD SCIENTIST

Contemplate this fictional story. You have a friend who is a brilliant scientist and inventor. One day, he phones you and invites you to drop by and see his latest invention. So, you do. Your friend takes you to his backyard and points to a figure standing near a tree, and he says, "Well, there he is. That's Adam." There you see this incredible lifelike humanoid with only a battery pack on its back to suggest it is anything less than human. Your friend, with great contentment, tells you Adam can do anything a human can do, even talk. Next, he demonstrates its capabilities. It trims the tree, picks weeds, and waters the plant beds. It's astounding. Your friend asks you if you would like to go into the house and have something to drink. You answer, "Sure."

Then he turns to Adam and instructs him to mow the lawn, but to be sure he avoids the flower beds. You get your refreshments and return to the yard only to discover that Adam not only mowed the lawn but the flower beds as well. Your friend is greatly disturbed, and he asks Adam if he mowed the flowers. Adam confesses, "Yes." The next thing you know, your friend has picked up a nearby baseball bat and is demolishing Adam despite Adam's pleas to stop. You stand there completely stunned. You don't know what to think. Your friend was so pleased with his invention. What went wrong? Did he have to react so violently? Couldn't he have simply removed the battery?

My dear brothers and sisters in Christ, God doesn't have to destroy our bodies with cancer or some other lesser-known but equally terminal condition. He only needs to *remove its life source,* and that is His only intention. If God can bring our physical lives to such a painless close, then why doesn't it happen that way all the time? Do you remember when God reminded Adam, *"You are dust"*? Do you remember God told Satan, *"And dust shall you eat* all the days of your life"? The human race is a gigantic smorgasbord, a bountiful buffet, for Satan's insatiable hunger. Nevertheless, he still can't just barge in and help himself. Satan needs an invitation.

SATAN'S APPETITE IS LIKE A LION'S

> Be of sober spirit, be on the alert. **Your adversary, the devil, prowls about like a roaring lion, seeking someone to devour.**
> *1 Peter 5:8*

Just how does Satan satisfy his ungodly hunger?

SATAN'S HUNGER SATISFIED

> **"The thief comes only to steal, and kill and destroy;**
> *I (Jesus) came that they might have life, and might have it abundantly."*
> *John 10:10*

Satan is satisfied by being able to destroy our lives or take our life any way he can. His means are manyfold, but sickness and disease are two of his favorite selections.

We know Satan is in our neighborhood, and we know our neighborhood looks like restaurant row. So what can we do to prevent him from stopping by for dinner? The following chapters will deal with this question as well as others, but for right now, just be sure your establishment is:

CLOSED

> *But He gives a greater grace. Therefore it says, "God is opposed to the proud, but gives grace to the humble." Submit therefore to God.* **Resist the devil and He will flee from you.**
> *James 4:6, 7*

THIS PRESCRIPTION PROVIDES
THE FOLLOWING BENEFIT

1. Confidence that Satan, not God, is the one who afflicts the human race with sickness and disease

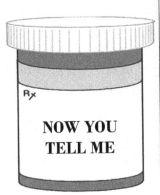

Rx8

INSTRUCTIONS

**My son give attention to my wisdom, incline your ear to my understanding; Lest you give your vigor to others, and your years to the cruel one; and groan at your later end, when your flesh and your body are consumed.
Proverbs 5:1, 9, 11**

My father died before I entered my teen years, so my mother raised me. And I can remember Mom saying to me, "You're going to have to learn the hard way." Mom would try to share with me her accumulated wisdom and experience. She wanted my life to be easier than hers had been, whenever possible. I understood that, and I loved her for it. But let's face it, I was a teenager and all moms and dads live in the dark ages or so I thought. So when Mom's ideas and my own differed, I usually believed my opinions were based on more contemporary information and consequently superior. It's not so difficult to admit today, but it was then. I, more often than not, discovered Mom's advice wasn't so bad, after all. You could easily say that between my fifteenth and my thirtieth birthday, Mom's intelligence and wisdom grew by leaps and bounds. By the time I was thirty years old, I finally realized Mom was a pretty sharp gal. Does any of this sound familiar? Can any of you relate to what I have just said? If you are thirty years of age or older, the answer is probably yes.

Mom was trying to warn me that some of my decisions and actions were going to cost me. Frequently I didn't listen to her advice, and I paid the price. Does our heavenly Father offer us any such sound advice? Does He give us any warning so that we can avoid any of the physical and emotional conditions that so frequently occur in life, emotional conditions such depression and dreadful physical conditions, such as heart disease that rob us of our quality of life even life itself?

Below is a list of warnings, promises if you will, examples and implications that God gives us in advance to tell us how our physical and emotional well-being can be affected by certain attitudes and actions. No! You can't skip this section.

HEREDITARY CONDITIONS: RELATED TO SIN

"You shalt not make for yourself an idol, or any likeness of what is in heaven above, or on the earth beneath or in the waters under the earth. You shalt not worship them or serve them; for I, the Lord your God, am a jealous God, visiting the iniquity of the fathers on the children, on the third and the fourth generations of those who hate Me. But showing lovingkindness to thousands, to those who love Me and keep My commandments."
Exodus 20:4-6

CHRONIC AND TERMINAL ILLNESS RELATED TO SIN

But it shall come about, if you will not obey the Lord your God, to observe to do all His commandments and His statutes, which I charge you today, that all these curses shall come upon you and overtake you (v. 15). If you are not careful to observe all the words written in this book, to fear this honored and awesome name, the Lord your God, then the Lord will bring extraordinary plagues on you and your descendants, even severe and lasting plagues, and miserable and chronic sickness. And He will bring back on you all the diseases of Egypt of which you were afraid, and they shall cling to you. Also every sickness and every plague which, not written in the Book of the Law, the Lord will bring on you until you are destroyed (vv. 58-61).
Deuteronomy 28:15, 58-61

EMOTIONAL PROBLEMS RELATED TO SIN

> *"But Samuel said to Saul, 'I will not return with you;*
> *for* **you have rejected the word of the Lord,** *and the Lord*
> *has rejected you from being king over Israel.'"*
> 1 Samuel 15:26

> *Now the Spirit of the Lord departed from Saul, and* **an**
> **evil spirit from the Lord terrorized him.**[1]
> 1 Samuel 16:14

It is interesting to note that medical science acknowledges that emotions could be responsible for nearly all sickness.[2]

The Ten Commandments that God gave to Moses and the subsequent statutes and ordinances of God do not promise eternal life. The New Testament makes it perfectly clear that the Law was powerless to justify anyone.

THE LAW: POWERLESS TO JUSTIFY

> **Nevertheless knowing that a man is not justified by**
> **the works of the Law but through faith in Christ Jesus,**
> *even we (the Jewish Christians) have believed in Christ Jesus,*
> *that we may be justified by faith in Christ, and not by the*
> *works of the Law;* **since by the works of the Law shall no**
> **flesh be justified.**
> Galatians 2:16

The Law was not given by God to provide eternal life; rather it was given to make it clear there was no way any of us are deserving

---

1   Robert Jamieson, *A Commentary: Critical, Experimental and Practical, Vol. I,*
    Part Two, 1 Samuel (Grand Rapids: Eerdmans, 1976), pp. 175, 176.
2   S.I. McMillen, *None of These Diseases,* (Old Tappan: Fleming H. Revell
    Company, 1968), preface.

of eternal life. It was provided so we would realize our only hope for our eternal future is Jesus Christ.

THE LAW: OUR TEACHER

> **Therefore the Law has become our tutor to lead us to Christ**, *that we may be justified by faith.*
> *Galatians 3:24*

Although the Law could not promise a future eternal life with God, it did make some promises about this life that reveal very pertinent spiritual information. This information informs us that our attitudes and actions play an important role in our physical and emotional well being. Christ did nothing to dispute this revelation at His first coming.

JESUS CONFIRMS OLD TESTAMENT TRUTH

> *Jesus said to him, "Arise, take up your pallet and walk* (v. 8)." *Afterward Jesus found him in the temple and said to him,* **"Behold, you have become well; do not sin anymore, so that nothing worse may befall you** (v. 14)."
> *John 5:8, 14*

We find a thread of this truth running throughout the balance of the New Testament. It should not be necessary to state, but I will, that Jesus didn't change previously revealed spiritual truth. He merely clarified that truth.[3]

PHYSICAL HANDICAPS: RELATED TO SIN

> *And behold, they were bringing to Him a paralytic, lying on a bed; and Jesus seeing their faith said to the paralytic,* **"Take courage, my son, your sins are forgiven** (v.

---

[3]   W. Robertson Nicoll, ed., *The Expositor's Greek Testament, Vol. I,* (Grand Rapids: Eerdmans, 1974), p. 104.

2). *But in order that you may know that the Son of Man has authority on earth to forgive sins" - then He said to the paralytic - "Rise, take up your bed and go home (v. 6)."*
Matthew 9:2, 6

Do believers have this same authority today? (1 Timothy 4:10).

DEATH: A CONSEQUENCE OF (SPECIFIC) SIN

It is actually reported that there is immorality among you, *and immorality of such a kind as does not exist even among the Gentiles,* ***that someone has his father's wife*** *(v. 1).* ***I have decided to deliver such a one to Satan for the destruction of his flesh,*** *that his spirit may be saved in the day of the Lord Jesus (v. 5).*
1 Corinthians 5:1, 5

GENERATIONAL CONDITIONS: RELATED TO SIN

"And to the angel of the church in Thyatira write: the Son of God, who has eyes like a flame of fire, and His feet are like burnished bronze, says this: 'I know your deeds, of late are greater than at first. But I have this against you, that you tolerate the woman Jezebel, who calls herself a prophetess, and she teaches and leads my bond-servants astray, so that they commit acts of immorality and eat things sacrificed to idols. And I gave her time to repent, and she does not want to repent of her immorality. ***Behold I will cast her upon a bed of sickness,*** *and those who commit adultery with her into great tribulation, unless they repent of her deeds.* ***And I will kill her children with pestilence;*** *and all the churches will know that I am He who searches the minds and hearts; and I will give to each one of you according to your deeds.'"*
Revelation 2:18-23

These can be disturbing words to read, and yet they are the words and advice (warnings and promises, if you will) of our heavenly Father. These scriptures are not the well-meaning opinions and views of our earthly parents, but rather the certain words of the all-knowing God. These words were spoken to Old Testament saints who lived under the legal system of the Ten Commandments and the statutes and ordinances of God. And these are also the words spoken to the New Testament saints who live in a time of grace, a time after Jesus incurred the penalty for man's sinful nature. However, they are words that caution us about the reality of consequences in the now rather than where we might spend eternity, consequences resulting from sins of the flesh. These are words we should genuinely consider and heed. Our physical and emotional well-being are at stake, as well as the physical and emotional well-being of our children and grandchildren.

As you can see from the above verses, sin and sickness are like sunup and sundown, one follows the other.

It was Smith Wigglesorth, who was an early twentieth-century evangelist who's ministry was endorsed by the person of the Holy Spirit with healing after healing and even resurrections, who said, "Sickness is the direct result of sin". [4]

He was simply pointing out what the Bible clearly states in both the Old and New Testaments.

THE OLD TESTAMENT

> But He was pierced through for our transgressions, He was crushed for our iniquities (sin); the chastening for our well being fell upon Him, and **by His scourging we are healed**. Isaiah 53:5

THE NEW TESTAMENT

[4]   Smith Wigglesworth, Healing, (New Kensington. PA., Whitaker House, 1999), p. 183.

*And He Himself bore our sins in His body on the cross,
so that we might die to sin and live to righteousness; **for by
His wounds you were healed**.*
1 Peter 2:24

Great! I've been a Christian for all this time, and NOW YOU TELL ME!

Cheer up. You're probably not the only one. However, look at those last two verses closer. They both point out an equally important truth.

If the *sin problem* is solved, and of course it is, then so is the *sickness problem*. These two verses tell us that Jesus solved our *sin problem*, on the cross and our *sickness problem* by His lashing. In other words, He took our sicknesses upon Himself.

Maybe this illustration will make that truth easier to understand. If you were wearing a coat and your brother took it off you and put it on himself, then who would be wearing the coat? You or him? Now, what if your coat was made of sin and sicknesses, then who would have your sins and sicknesses?

Jesus not only allowed Himself to be crucified for our sins, but He also allowed Himself to be unmercifully beaten so He could take our sicknesses in His body. We no longer need to have them in our bodies.

If you have been forgiven, redeemed, and saved, then you have been delivered, set free, and healed.

Who said, "Hallelujah!?"

THIS PRESCRIPTION PROVIDES
THE FOLLOWING BENEFIT

1. Confidence that Satan uses bad decisions or personal sin to bring on sickness and disease

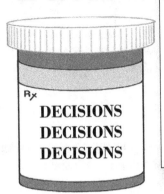

Rx9

There is a way which seems right to man, but its end is the way of death.
Proverbs 14:12

Rx
DECISIONS
DECISIONS
DECISIONS

I admit I really enjoy this next illustration, and I hope some of you have not heard it. It certainly makes the point. Have you heard of the fellow who had the same dream over and over one night? In his dream, a large number 5 appeared before his face, and a voice repeatedly said, "Five, five, five". When he awoke it was five o'clock in the morning. He got up and picked up his newspaper and discovered it was the fifth day of the fifth month of the year. Next, he turned to the sports section, section 5. He automatically turned to page 5 and saw the racing entries for the day. He looked at the fifth race and discovered the fifth choice was a horse named Five by Five at odds of 5 to 1. He noticed that the horse had post-position number 5. This couldn't be coincidence, could it? He was speechless. So he got dressed, went to the bank, and then to the track. There he bet five hundred dollars on number 5 in the fifth race to win. Some of you, no doubt, have guessed what happened next. Number 5 ran fifth, and this poor chap threw his hands in the air and said, "It seemed like a good idea at the time."

Man's way of living, his decisions, frequently leave something to be desired. I know when I'm given two choices, somehow my decision never reflects the odds are fifty-fifty. The fellow in our story isn't so different from most of us. All of us are born with a basic knowledge of good and evil; we know right from wrong.

MAN KNOWS RIGHT FROM WRONG

> *"For God knows that in the day you eat from it your eyes will be opened, and **you will be like God, knowing good and evil.**"*
> Genesis 3:5

Satan is a liar, but he hit the nail on the head in the above verse. The fellow in our story certainly should have recognized his actions were foolish. Please say amen.

God loves man so much that even though He equipped him with a conscience to discern right from wrong, He goes not one, but two steps further. First, God informs us what will happen if we choose to ignore His word, His warnings.

ADVANCED WARNING SYSTEM

> *"But from the tree of the knowledge of good and evil you shall not eat, for in **the day that you eat from it you shall surely die.**"*
> Genesis 2:17

And second, if we decide to ignore His word, then He has both a desire to and a way to restore us.

GOD'S WAY

> *"And I will put enmity between you (Satan) and the woman, and between your seed and her seed; **He** (Jesus) **shall bruise you** (Satan) **on the head**, and you shall bruise Him on the heel."*
> Genesis 3:15

God could have looked at Adam and Eve in the aftermath of the fall and said, "It seemed like a good idea at the time." God could have said, "Oh well," and walked away, leaving us alone in a world with a creature who was going to make life and death as miserable as possible. But He didn't. Instead of leaving us, He stuck around and provided a way or a plan for us to be reunited with our Creator and, in the process, to be healed and restored as well.

God didn't have to warn us, but He did, and He certainly didn't have to go to such great expense to Himself to bail us out, but He did. How fair can He be?

God didn't hesitate. He decided immediately to show Adam and Eve the right way.

MAN'S WAY

> *Then the eyes of both of them were opened and they knew they were naked; and* **they sewed fig leaves together and made themselves loin covering.**
> *Genesis 3:7*

GOD'S WAY

> **And the Lord God made garments of skin** *for Adam and his wife, and clothed them.*
> *Genesis 3:21*

We see man's way doesn't work and that God's way is best. Here God introduced the fact that innocent blood is part of His requirement to make things right.[1] Later in Genesis, He again illustrates man's way versus His way. In Rx 20, He gives us more details. Abraham feared that the king of Gerar would desire his wife and take her and kill him. So Abraham did things his way, man's way, the wrong way. Abraham lied to the king in an attempt to protect himself and allowed the king to take his wife. Man's way falls considerably short of God's way. God informed the king by a dream that adultery carries a death

---

[1] Robert Jameison, *A Commentary-Critical, Experimental and Practical, Vol. I, Genesis*, (Grand Rapids: Eerdmans, 1976), p. 61.

penalty (even though the Ten Commandments had not been given yet) and that Abraham had lied. In addition, all the women in the king's household were unable to conceive children. So the king confronted Abraham, and this time Abraham did things God's way.

GOD'S WAY WORKS

> And Abraham prayed to God; and **God healed Abimelech and his wife and his maids,** so that they bore children. For the Lord had closed fast all the wombs of the household of Abimelech because of Sarah, Abraham's wife. Genesis 20:17, 18

God's way always works. Finally, Abraham was honest about his situation, and in humility, he confessed his actions were wrong, and he no longer held to his former attitude. He repented, and God showed forgiveness through the king, and through Abraham's prayer, God healed and restored the women in Abimelech's kingdom, and yes, unbelievably, Abraham was blessed.

You would think by now that a godly person would begin to understand that it pays to do things God's way. Right? Nevertheless, God continues to reveal the fact that He designed our bodies to be healthy, but when we make wrong decisions, when we sin, God's will is to heal and restore our lives

Let's look at the exodus of the Jews from Egypt.

GOD IS OUR HEALER

> And He said, "**If you will give earnest heed to the voice of the Lord your God,** and do what is right in His sight, and give ear to His commandments, and keep all His statutes, I will put none of the diseases on you which I have put on the Egyptians; for **I, the Lord, am your Healer.**" Exodus 15:26

Here, the Lord makes three things extremely clear: First, deciding on obedience ensures health.[2] Second, deciding on disobedience ushers in sickness.[3] Third, God is our Healer.[4] But, what commandments and statutes are to be kept? The Ten Commandments were not given until Exodus 20. What decisions did the children of Israel make in obedient faith that allowed the Lord to heal them? It is very likely that over two million Jews, including women and children, left Egypt, and all were sound in body.[5]

HUNDREDS OF THOUSANDS LEAVE

*Now the sons of Israel journeyed from Rameses to Succoth, **about six hundred thousand men on foot aside from children.***
Exodus 12:37

ALL HEALTHY

*Then He brought them out with silver and gold; **and among His tribes there was not one who stumbled.***
Psalms 105:37

The children of Israel were given simple instructions to follow, and this time, they choose to heed (believe) the voice of the Lord.

PLAIN AND SIMPLE

*Then Moses called for all the elders of Israel, and said to them, "Go and take for yourselves lambs according to your families, and slay the Passover lamb. **And you shall take a***

---

2   Finis Dake, *Dake's Annotated Refference Bible, Old Testament*, (Atlanta, Dake Bible Sales, Inc., 1963), p. 80.

3   Ibid.

4   Ibid.

5   T.L. Osborn, *Healing The Sick*, (Tulsa: Harrison House, Inc., 1986), p. 257.

bunch of hyssop and dip it in the blood which is in the basin, and apply some of the blood that is in the basin to the lintel and the two doorposts; and none of you shall go outside the door of his house until morning. For the Lord will pass through to smite the Egyptians; and when He sees the blood on the lintel and on the two doorposts, the Lord will pass over the door and will not allow the destroyer to come into your house to smite you."
Exodus 12:21-23

Very simple. Put the blood of the lamb on the designated areas and stay inside till morning. Those who believed the Lord and followed His way of doing things lived, and those who needed physical healing were restored for their journey.

Our journey begins with birth, and as we grow older, we discover we are faced with a multitude of desires and decisions. Unfortunately, our fallen nature doesn't leave us with a fifty-fifty chance of making the right decision. However if we heed the word of the Lord and follow God's plan we can make the right decision every time.

A PLAN TO FOLLOW

But I say, walk by the Spirit, and you will not carry out the desire of the flesh. For the flesh sets its desire against the Spirit, and the Spirit against the flesh; for these are in opposition to one another, so that you may not do the things that you please.
Galatians 5:16, 17

THIS PRESCRIPTION PROVIDES
THE FOLLOWING BENEFIT

1. Confidence that bad decisions can be avoided and good decisions can be made

Rx10

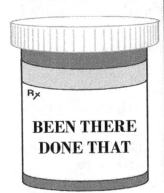

Rx

**BEEN THERE
DONE THAT**

If I regard wickedness in my heart, the Lord will not hear . . .
Psalms 66:18

Can you imagine what it would be like if Jesus was physically walking the face of the earth today?

Maybe you are one who is suffering from an incurable condition. Maybe you incur periodic but unbearable headaches. Maybe you suffer from depression to the point that it is destroying your life. Maybe you experience violent outbursts of anger. Maybe you have an addiction you cannot seem to overcome. Or maybe you've even considered ending your life.

Can you imagine how you would feel if you heard Jesus was going to be the guest speaker at your fellowship this week? Can you imagine the hope that would spring up inside you? Can you imagine trying to beat the crowds in order to have a good seat? Can you imagine having an opportunity to actually speak to Jesus? This is what you were hoping would occur. Can you imagine asking Him to heal you of your condition? Now, can you imagine Jesus seemingly ignoring your request? He's not responding. Nothing is happening! It is just like He doesn't hear a word you're saying. There is no change! Is this unthinkable to you? Imagine Jesus now turning His attention to another. Can you imagine your hopes sinking into the pit of your stomach as you stand there in total bewilderment? Now, imagine the person next to you saying, "I know why that happened." Can you imagine focusing your complete attention on this individual and asking, "Why?"

Today there are countless thousands of believers who can relate to this type of situation.

THEY HAVE BEEN THERE, AND THEY HAVE DONE THAT

They have prayed or they have asked for prayer, and nothing seems to have happened. Not being healed seems to be the rule instead of the exception today. However, didn't Jesus personally guarantee positive results?

JESUS' GUARANTEE

> "Until now you have asked for nothing in My Name;
> **ask and you will receive**, that your joy may be full."
> John 16:24

He certainly did! So why does this unthinkable and unacceptable conflict exist? How can I ask God for something He wants to give to me, and yet He doesn't seem to hear a word I say?

Below is a list of biblical reasons God gives to explain the existence of this seeming contradiction. You can't skip this either.

BY REBELLING[1]

> "For in the wilderness of Zin, during the strife of the congregation, **you** (Moses) **rebelled against My command** to treat Me as holy before their eyes at the water."
> Numbers 27:14

---

[1] J.M. Fuller, *Barnes' Notes on the Old & New Testaments, Deuteronomy* (Grand Rapids, Baker Book House, 1975), p. 27.

BY MAKING GOD ANGRY[2]

> *'Let me, I pray, cross over and see the fair land that is beyond the Jordan, that good hill country and Lebanon.'* "But the Lord was angry with me *on your account, and* would not listen to me, *'Enough! Speak to me no more of this matter'."*
> Deuteronomy 3:25, 26

BY NOT BEING HUMBLE, SEEKING GOD'S FACE OR TURNING FROM WICKEDNESS[3]

> "(If) My people who are called by My name **humble themselves and pray, and seek My face and turn from their wicked ways,** *then I will hear from heaven, will forgive their sin, and will heal their land."*
> 2 Chronicles 7:14

BY FORSAKING GOD[4]

> Now the Spirit of God came upon Azariah the son of Oded, and he went out to meet Asa and said to him, "Listen to me Asa, and all Judah and Benjamin: The Lord is with you when you are with Him. And if you seek Him, He will let you find Him; but **if you forsake Him, He will forsake you.**"
> 2 Chronicles 15:1, 2

BY REGARDING WICKEDNESS[5]

---

2   Finis Dake, *Dake's Annotated Reference Bible, Old Testament,* (Atlanta, Dake Bible Sales Inc., 1963), p. 663.
3   Ibid.
4   Ibid.
5   Ibid.

*If I regard **wickedness** in my heart, the Lord will not hear.*
Psalms 66:18

BY IGNORING THE POOR[6]

He who shuts his ear to the cry of the poor *(he) will also cry himself and not be answered.*
Proverbs 21:13

BY IGNORING GOD'S WORD[7]

He who turns away his ear from listening to the law, *even his prayer is an abomination.*
Proverbs 28:9

BY BEING UNJUST, UNKIND, UNCOMPASSIONATE, OPPRESSIVE AND EVIL[8]

*Then the word of the Lord came to Zechariah saying, "Thus has the Lord of Hosts said, '**Dispense true justice, and practice kindness and compassion each to his brother; and do not oppress the widow or the orphan, the stranger or the poor; and do not devise evil in your hearts against one another.**' But they refused to pay attention, and turned a stubborn shoulder and stopped their ears from hearing. And they made their hearts like flint so that they could not hear the law and the words which the Lord of hosts had sent by His Spirit through the former prophets; therefore great wrath came from the Lord of hosts. **And it came about that just as He called and they would not listen, so they called and I would not listen, says the Lord of hosts.**"*
Zechariah 7:8-13

---

6   Ibid.
7   Ibid.
8   Ibid.

BY SEEKING THE ATTENTION AND RESPECT OF OTHERS[9]

> *"And when you pray, you are not to be as the hypocrites; for they love to stand and pray in the synagogues and on the street corners, **in order to be seen by men.** Truly I say to you, they have their reward in full."*
> *Matthew 6:5*

BY TRYING TO IMPRESS GOD[10]

> *"And when your are praying, do not use meaningless repetitions, as the Gentiles do, **for they suppose they will be heard for their many words.**"*
> *Matthew 6:7*

BY NOT BEING ABLE TO FORGIVE OTHERS[11]

> *"**For if you forgive men for their transgressions, your heavenly Father will also forgive you.** But if you do not forgive men, then your Father will not forgive your transgression (when you ask for forgiveness, implied)."*
> *Matthew 6:14, 15*

BY UNBELIEF[12]

> *And Jesus answered and said to them, "Truly I say to you, **if you have faith, and do not doubt,** you shall not only do what was done to the fig tree, but even if you say to this mountain, 'Be taken up and cast into the sea,' it shall*

---

[9]   Ibid.
[10]   Ibid.
[11]   Ibid.
[12]   Ibid.

*happen. And **all things you ask in prayer, believing, you shall receive.***"
Matthew 21:21, 22

BY BEING DISCOURAGED AND LOSING HEART[13]

*Now He was telling them a parable to show that **at all times they ought to pray and not to lose heart** (v. 1). "Now shall not God bring about justice for His elect, who cry to Him day and night, and will He delay long over them (v. 7)?"*
Luke 18:1, 7

BY BEING SELF-RIGHTEOUS[14]

And He also told this parable to certain ones who trusted in themselves and that they were righteous, and view others with contempt: *"Two men went up into the temple to pray, one a Pharisee, and the other a tax-gatherer. The Pharisee stood and was praying thus to himself, 'God I thank Thee that I am not like other people: swindlers, unjust, adulterers, or even like this tax-gather. I fast twice a week, I pay tithes of all that I get.' But the tax-gatherer, standing some distance away, was even unwilling to lift up his eyes to heaven, but was beating his breast, saying, 'God, be merciful to me, the sinner!' I tell you, this man went down to his house justified rather that the other; for everyone who exalts himself shall be humbled, but he who humbles himself shall be exalted."*
Luke 18:9-14

BY ASKING WITH THE WRONG MOTIVE[15]

---

[13]   Ibid.
[14]   Ibid.
[15]   Ibid.

You ask and do not receive, because you ask with wrong motives, so that you may spend it on pleasures. You adulteresses, do you not know that friendship with the world is hostility toward God? Therefore whoever wishes to be a friend of the world makes himself an enemy of God.
James 4:3, 4

BY MAINTAINING A NON-BIBLICAL MARRIAGE RELATIONSHIP[16]

In the same way, you wives, be submissive to your husbands so that even if any of them are disobedient to the word, they may be won without a word by the behavior of their wives (v. 1). Thus Sarah obeyed Abraham, calling him Lord, and you have become her children if you do what is right without being frightened by any fear. You husbands likewise, live with your wives in an understanding way, as with a weaker vessel, since she is a woman; and grant her honor as a fellow heir of the grace of life, **so that your prayers may not be hindered** *(vv. 5-7).*
1Peter 3:1, 5-7

It is easy for us to deceive ourselves into thinking that as Christians we don't behave in such a manner.

DO NOT DECEIVE YOURSELF

If we say that we have no sin we are deceiving ourselves, *and the truth is not in us.*
1John 1:8

However, when we look at the above list of reasons we notice that the very first reason involved Moses (Numbers 27:12-14) and

---

16   Ibid.

that Abraham got caught up in the last reason (Genesis 20:2, 10, 11). Are not Abraham and Moses believers?

ABRAHAM AND MOSES: BELIEVERS

> *"But regarding the fact that the dead rise again, have you not read **in the book of Moses**, in the passage about the burning bush, how God spoke to him, saying, **'I am the God of Abraham, and the God of Isaac, and the God of Jacob?' He is not the God of the dead, but of the living; you are greatly mistaken**."*
> Mark 12:26, 27

We could also entertain another thought that might deceive us into believing this list of reasons is very subjective. Who can be sure any of these reasons apply to any of us personally? Let us turn our attention to the very last reason on the list: maintaining a nonbiblical marriage relationship. This is a reason that can be measured objectively as well as subjectively evaluated. Statistics will sadly inform us of the continuing increase in the divorce rate among professing Christians. In fact, Christian couples are more likely to divorce than atheists.[17] Unfortunately, this list contains reasons that have applied to all of us at one time or another, so it doesn't hurt us to be informed of these possible hindrances to our prayers.

HARDNESS OF HEART AND DIVORCE

> *And some Pharisees came up to Him, testing Him whether it was lawful for a man to divorce a wife. And He answered and said to them, "What did Moses command you?" And they said, "Moses permitted a man to write a certificate of divorce and send her away." But Jesus said to them, **"Because of your hardness of heart he wrote you this command-***

---

[17]   Kerby Anderson, *Kerby Anderson's Commentaries, Divorce Statistics*, (January 12, 2000), (www. prob.org), p. 1.

ment. But from the beginning of creation, God made them male and female. For this cause a man shall leave his father and mother, and the two shall become one flesh; consequently they are no longer two, but one flesh. **What therefore God has joined together, let no man separate.***"*
Mark 10:2-9

In this particular example, we can see how maintaining a non-biblical relationship led to another reason, the hardening of one's heart, and finally to divorce. The fact that two of the reasons on this list can be clearly demonstrated as existing in the lives of believers today should convince us that any of these reasons can arise or exist in our lives.

Jesus used parables that are truths the people clearly understood from everyday life and placed them alongside spiritual truths.[18] Jesus did this to help us comprehend the workings of the kingdom of God. With that in mind, let's look at a couple of illustrations from the twentieth-century that are designed to help us understand how we can believe God specifically for His promises and provisions regarding healing and how we can approach Him and pray, believing He will hear our prayers and answer, and yet nothing seems to happen.

Have you ever been near a jackhammer when it was in use? A jackhammer is used to break up concrete and asphalt. It is extremely loud. If you were standing next to someone who was operating a jackhammer it would be pointless for the operator to say anything to you and expect you to hear what was said. Maybe you have known someone who enjoyed listening to music with the volume turned to nearly maximum? If so, then you know how difficult it is to carry on a conversation under such conditions. In fact, there are things we can do that make it impossible for others to hear us, and God is saying that we can decide to do certain things that keep Him from hearing us. Spiritually, our actions can speak louder than our words.

---

[18] W.E. Vine, *Expository Dictionary of New Testament Words, Vol. III*, (Old Tappan: Fleming H. Revell Company, 1966), p. 158.

Let's concede the possibility that at least one reason on the list might pertain to us. What should we do? Well, we know God wants us healthy in both body and soul (3 John 2),[19] and we also know that if we ask anything according to His will, we have what we ask. However, if we are doing something that spiritually prevents God from hearing us, then we need to stop doing that very thing or those very things. This answer appears profoundly simple. Of course, what is easy to say is not always easy to do. Nonetheless, we first need to identify any reason or reasons that could be responsible for hindering our prayers.

We begin to do this by reviewing the above reasons.

1.	By rebelling and provoking God	Numbers 27:13, 14; Deuteronomy 3:25, 26
2.	By refusing to be humble	2 Chronicles 7:14
3.	By not turning from sin	Isaiah 59:1, 2
4.	By not seeking God's face	2 Chronicles 7:14
5.	By forsaking God	2 Chronicles 15:1, 2
6.	By regarding wickedness in one's heart	Psalms 66:18
7.	By ignoring the cry of the poor	Proverbs 21:13
8.	By ignoring what the Law says	Proverbs 28:9
9.	By being unjust, unkind, uncompassionate	Zechariah 7:9, 13
10.	By oppressing widows, orphans, strangers and the poor	Zechariah 7:10, 13
11.	By devising evil against one another	Zechariah 7:10, 13
12.	By hardening one's heart against what God has said	Zechariah 7:11-13
13.	By being hypocritical	Matthew 6:5

---

[19] Finis Dake, *Dake's Annotated Reference Bible, New Testament,* (Atlanta, Dake Bible Sales, Inc., 1963), p. 282.

14. By trying to impress God   Matthew 6:7
15. By not forgiving others   Matthew 6:14, 15
16. By not believing God's word   Matthew 21:21, 22
17. By being discouraged   Luke 18:1, 7
    and losing heart
18. By being self-righteous   Luke 18:9-14
19. By asking with the wrong   James 4:3, 4
    motive and loving the world
20. By maintaining a nonbibli-   1 Peter 3:1, 5-7
    cal marriage relationship

We can see that in both the Old and the New Testaments, God mentions specific reasons that keep Him from hearing or answering our prayers. However, we would be doing ourselves a disservice if we thought that this list is complete and all-inclusive. We must keep in mind that anything we do that is against God's revealed will can produce the same amount of *spiritual noise*. Obviously, the longer we allow certain attitudes and actions to continue then the longer it will take before God is *able* to hear and answer our prayers.

SIN ACTS LIKE A SILENCER

> *Behold, the Lord's hand is not so short that it cannot save; neither is His ear so dull that it cannot hear.* **But your iniquities have made a separation between you and your God, and your sins have hidden His face from you, so that He does not hear.**
> *Isaiah 59:1, 2*

WHEN YOU'RE RIGHT, YOU RECEIVE

*Beloved, if our heart does not condemn us, we have con-
fidence before God;* **and whatever we ask we receive from
Him, because we keep His commandments and do the
things that are pleasing to His sight.**
1 John 3:21, 22

If we sincerely examine our hearts and lives, our attitudes and actions, then the Holy Spirit can put His finger on the thing or things that we need to change. When the changes are made, we know God will hear and answer our prayers. If we seem unable to change certain attitudes and actions, it may indicate we have a need that requires spiritual ministry and assistance from other members of the body of Christ, His blood-bought church. This is a subject that will be discussed more fully in a later prescription, DIAL 911.

In the prescription, READ MY LIPS, we will become aware of the importance of knowing God's will, meaning our intellect being aware of God's will for our bodies and souls. Then in the prescription WHERE THERE'S A WILL, THERE'S A WAY, we will discover that our will plays a significant role in our ability to approach God. In this chapter we have learned, that our attitudes and actions can actually keep God from hearing our prayers and doing the things He promises to do.

Our spiritual condition was healed the instant we placed our faith in Jesus of Nazareth as our Savior. That is the gospel we all heard, and that is the gospel we all received. However, many of us did not hear the gospel that declared that God's love, for us as demonstrated by the life and sacrifice of His Son, also includes physical and emotional healing along with spiritual healing. Consequently, emotional and physical healing can be postponed indefinitely. In the meantime, we all go through various learning processes and experiences that can make it more difficult to accept these portions of the gospel when we do become exposed to them or when our need for them arises. On a more positive note, if we believe God's Word, overcome our emotional roadblocks and giants, and decide to believe and act according to His Word, then healing for our bodies and souls will occur. It is His promise. It is His guarantee.

GOD'S WORD CONTAINS HEALTH

> *My son, give attention to my words, incline your ear to my sayings* (v. 20). *For **they are life to those who find them, and health to all their body*** (v. 22).
> *Proverbs 4:20, 22*

THIS PRESCRIPTION PROVIDES
THE FOLLOWING BENEFIT

1. Confidence that the things that keep God from hearing our prayers can be eliminated

Rx11

My covenant will I not violate nor will I alter the utterance of my lips.
Psalms 89:34

READ MY LIPS

The 1988 campaign for the presidency of the United States made famous an old expression READ MY LIPS. This expression was used by one of the candidates to emphasize his promise that there would be no new taxes. So much for the promises of men. On the other hand, when God makes a promise, you can count on it (Numbers 23:19).

GOD KEEPS HIS WORD

> *What then? If some did not believe, their unbelief will not nullify the faithfulness of God, will it? May it never be! Rather,* **let God be found true, though every man be found a liar,** *as it is written. "That Thou mightest be justified in Thy words, and mightest prevail when Thou art judged."* *Romans 3:3, 4*

In previous prescriptions, we learned what role Satan plays in the drama of our lives. To Satan, our bodies are the best-looking item on his menu, and he will eat us alive whenever possible.

Sooner or later, we must realize that the quality and, very likely, the duration of our existence in these temporal bodies depends on whether we listen to God, believe what He says, and follow His instructions.[1] Keeping that in mind, what does God reveal to us about His will for our bodies? Does God want any of us to suffer sickness and disease? It may surprise some of us, but our Creator begins to reveal His answer to these questions with our very bodies, themselves. Let's look at the apostle Paul's letter to the believers who lived in Rome.

GOD'S WILL IS NOT HIDDEN

> For since the creation of the world His (God's) invisible attributes, **His eternal power and divine nature have been clearly seen, being understood through what has been made** (like our bodies), **so that they are without excuse.**
> Romans 1:20

Does that mean if we examine our bodies we can better understand God's nature and will? Of course! And what do we learn? First, if we cut ourselves, it bleeds, a scab forms, and healing takes place. Second, if we have the flu or catch a cold, we get a runny nose and maybe a fever, aches, pains, and a cough. But after a few days, our immune system fights off the infection, and we recover. Third, if we accidentally break a bone, we set it, immobilize it, and given proper time, it repairs itself. What have we discovered? God created our body with the remarkable capacity to heal and restore itself. Why is that? Because it's God's will we be healthy and free from sickness and disease. We might hastily conclude that God intended natural death to result from a heart attack. Occasionally, we will hear others say words similar to this: "What a blessing to be taken so quickly (by a heart attack)."

Some of us probably have said "amen" to such a remark, but what would our response have been if we had realized our Lord designed our bodies so that during a heart attack, the body initially

---

[1]   E. W. Kenyon, *Jesus the Healer*, (USA: Kenyon Gospel Publishing Society, 1968), pp. 62-64.

comes to the rescue of the heart?[2] If we follow the above criteria, then it seems obvious that heart attacks are not God's will for His children.

We can see that God, in His infinite love, designed our bodies with an incredible ability to restore health. He knew sickness and other such things would come our way, and regardless of our beliefs and feelings about Him personally, He equipped each of us with a built-in self-preservation system. God did not show partiality.

GOD'S LOVE IS FREE TO ALL

"But I say to you, love your enemies, and pray for those who persecute you. In order that you may be sons of your Father who is in Heaven: **For He causes His sun to rise on the evil and the good, and sends rain on the righteous and the unrighteous.***"*
Matthew 5:44, 45

God knew that eventually, each of our bodies would be the object of Satan's desire, so He equipped each of us with a measure of self-preservation. This is His basic health plan. In addition, He created His universe with built-in principles that, when followed, supplement our bodies' own system of self-preservation.

For example, few of us would willingly stick our hand into a fire, walk on broken glass or drink poison. Anyone who treated his or her body in such a manner would probably be considered very strange and possibly to have a self-destructive nature. God certainly isn't in that category. Is He? If God, Himself, put sickness upon His children, how would He be any different?[3] If you wouldn't treat your body that way, why would God treat His body that way?

OUR BODIES BELONG TO GOD

---

2   Sandra L. Chase, *"New Frontiers in the Treatment Strategy of Heart Failure." Pharmacy Times,* (July 2001), p. 58.

3   H. C. Luepold, *Barnes' Notes on the Old & New Testaments, Genesis, Vol. I,* (Grand Rapids: Baker Book House, 1975), p. 165.

> *Or do you not know that **your body is a temple of the Holy Spirit who is in you,** whom you have from God, and that **you are not your own?** For you have been bought with a price; therefore glorify God in your body.*
> *1 Corinthians 6:19, 20*

It is Jesus who states that God does not operate in such a manner.

GOD'S NATURE: RESTORING NOT DESTROYING

> *Then there was brought to Him (Jesus) a demon-possessed man who was blind and dumb. And He healed him, so that the dumb man spoke and saw (v. 22). But when the Pharisees heard it, they said, "This man casts out demons only by Beelzebub the ruler of the demons." And knowing their thoughts He (Jesus) said to them, "**Any kingdom divided against itself is laid to waste;** and any city or house divided against itself shall not stand. And if Satan casts out Satan he is divided against himself; How then shall his kingdom stand (vv. 24-26)?"*
> *Matthew 12:22, 24-26*

Jesus makes a very clear statement here. If God makes us sick, only to heal us later, then His kingdom could hardly be eternal. It could not last forever.

GOD'S KINGDOM IS FOREVER

> *And He showed me a river of water of life, clear as crystal, coming from the throne of God and the Lamb (v. 1). And there shall no longer be any curse; and the throne of God and of the Lamb shall be in it, and His bond-servants shall serve Him (v. 3); and there shall no longer be any night; and they shall not have need of the light of a lamp nor the light of the*

sun, because the Lord God shall illumine them; **and they shall reign forever and ever** *(v. 5).*
Revelations 22:1, 3, 5

God's restoring nature should be very easy to understand and to accept. Have you ever had a problem with pests where you live? Have you ever had friends over to visit only to have them see some of those undesirable creatures scurrying across your floor, crawling over your countertop, or buzzing around their faces? You know, ants, flies, roaches, mice, etc. Embarrassing, isn't it? Without question! If you discover ants in your kitchen you take immediate action to eliminate them. So why should God be any different? God doesn't want any pests residing within one of His temples that is, your body or my body. How would that glorify Him? Frankly, it's embarrassing. Jesus came in the flesh to reveal the nature of God.

WHAT IS GOD LIKE

God, after He spoke long ago to the fathers in the prophets in many portions and in many ways, in these last days has spoken to us in His son, whom He appointed heir to all things, through whom also He made the world. **And He** *(Jesus)* **is the radiance of His** *(God's)* **glory and the exact representation of His nature.**
Hebrew 1:1-3

No guesswork involved on our part here. Jesus shows us exactly who God is and what He is like.

JESUS REVEALED GOD'S WILL

Jesus therefore answered and was saying to them, **"Truly, truly, I say to you the Son can do nothing of Himself,** *unless it is something He sees the Father doing,* **for whatever**

the Father does, these things the Son also does in like manner."
John 5:19

And just what is the will of our Heavenly Father?

JESUS HEALED ALL WHO WERE OPPRESSED

*"You know **Jesus of Nazareth** how God anointed Him with the Holy Spirit and with power, and how **He went about doing good, and healing all who were oppressed by the devil; for God was with Him."***
Acts 10:38

Again, no guesswork involved here. Jesus came to restore our bodies as well as make our spirits one with His. He came to eliminate every pest and every demonic destroying scheme from our lives. So whenever a plea goes out to Jesus asking for healing (pest control), Jesus always answers the call.

If the call is for:

Leprosy (Matthew 8:3)	Jesus answers the call
Paralysis (Matthew 8:5-13)	Jesus answers the call
Fevers or infection (Matthew 8:14, 15)	Jesus answers the call
Diseases and demons (Matthew 8:16, 17)	Jesus answers the call
Hemorrhaging (Matthew 9:20-22)	Jesus answers the call
Untimely death (Matthew 9:18-25)	Jesus answers the call
Blindness (Matthew 9:26-30)	Jesus answers the call
Dumbness (Matthew 9:32, 33)	Jesus answers the call
Restoring body parts (Matthew 15:30)	Jesus answers the call
Convulsions or epilepsy (Mark 1:23-26)	Jesus answers the call
Withered limbs or nerve damage (Mark 3:1-5)	Jesus answers the call

Mental disorders (Mark 5:1-13)	Jesus answers the call
Deafness (Mark 7:32-35)	Jesus answers the call
Terminal illness (Luke 7:2-10)	Jesus answers the call
Osteoporosis (Luke 13:11)	Jesus answers the call
Inherited or genetic conditions (John 9:1-7)	Jesus answers the call

Is there any problem Jesus can't eliminate? Well, if the Bible were the yellow pages, then God's ad would read, "No problem too big."

JESUS ELIMINATES EVERY PROBLEM

> *"Bless the Lord, O my soul, and forget none of His benefits; Who pardons all your iniquities; **who heals all your diseases.**"*
> *Psalms 103:2, 3*

I'll say it one more time: there is "no guesswork involved". Every time Jesus healed anyone, God was saying, "READ MY LIPS! This is my will for you!" It is God's will that we be healthy: spiritually, mentally, and physically.

ASK GOD TO RESTORE YOUR HEALTH

> *And this is the confidence which we have before Him, that, **if we ask anything according to His will, He hears us. And** if we know that He hears us in whatever we ask, we know that **we have the requests which we have asked from Him.***
> *1 John 5:14, 15*

THIS PRESCRIPTION PROVIDES
THE FOLLOWING BENEFIT

1. Confidence that God doesn't want anyone to suffer sickness and disease

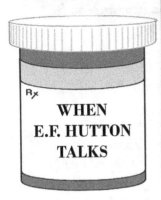

Rx12

**WHEN
E.F. HUTTON
TALKS**

If you have something you want to sell, then you put a considerable amount of thought to what might be the best way to promote your product or yourself. Several years ago a well-known investment firm decided to promote itself with the slogan "WHEN E. F. HUTTON TALKS, PEOPLE LISTEN." Their TV ads were very striking. A room of people would be abuzz with conversation, but as soon as someone would say, "E.F. Hutton says," a dramatic hush would come over the entire room, and everyone would strain to hear exactly what E.F. Hutton says.

How much more should we Christians be concerned with what God says? God reminds us in every major section of the Bible that it is His will for us to be physically sound. It is also His will for us to experience an abundant life, and He has a way for both to come about. Read what God says:

THE LAW (Genesis through Deuteronomy)

> *Then it shall come about, because you listen to these judgments and keep and do them, that the Lord your God will keep with you His covenant and His loving kindness which He swore to your forefathers* (v. 12). ***And the Lord will remove from you all sickness; and He will not put on you any of***

123

the harmful diseases of Egypt which you have known, but
He will lay them on all who hate you (v. 15).
Deuteronomy 7:12, 15

THE HISTORICAL BOOKS (Joshua through Job)

*If I shut up the heavens so that there is no rain, or if I command the locust to devour the land, or if I send pestilence among My people. **And if My people who are called by My name shall humble themselves and pray, and seek My face and turn from their wicked ways, Then I will hear from heaven, will forgive their sin, and will heal their land.***
2 Chronicles 7:13, 14

THE POETIC BOOKS (Psalms through Song of Solomon)

*Bless the Lord, O my soul, and forget none of His benefits; **Who pardons all your iniquities; Who heals all your diseases;***
Psalm 103:2, 3

THE PROPHETS (Isaiah through Malachi)

Surely He has borne our sicknesses *and carried our sorrows; yet we regarded Him as a stricken one, smitten of God, and afflicted. But He was pierced for our transgressions; He was bruised for our iniquities; the punishment which procured our peace fell upon Him, **and with His stripes we are healed.***
Isaiah 53: 4, 5 (Berkeley)

THE GOSPELS (Matthew through John)

And Jesus was going about *all the cities and villages, teaching in their synagogues, and **proclaiming the gospel***

of the kingdom, and healing every kind of disease and every kind of sickness.
Matthew 9:35

THE BOOK OF ACTS

"And now Lord, take note of their threats, and **grant that Thy bond-servants may speak Thy word with all confidence while Thou dost extend Thy hand to heal, and signs and wonders take place** *through the name of Thy holy servant Jesus (vv. 29, 30)."* **And with great power the apostles were giving witness to the resurrection of the Lord Jesus,** *and abundant grace was upon them all (v. 33).*
Acts 4:29, 30, 33

THE EPISTLES (Romans through Jude)

Is anyone among you sick? Let him call for the elders of the church, and let them pray over him, anointing him with oil in the name of the Lord. **And the prayer offered in faith will restore the one who is sick, and the Lord will raise him up,** *and if he has committed sins they will be forgiven him.*
James 5:14, 15

THE BOOK OF REVELATION

And to the angel of the church in Thyatira write (v. 18): But I have this against you, that you tolerate the woman Jezebel, who calls herself a prophetess, and she teaches and leads My bond-servants astray, so that they commit acts of immorality and eat things sacrificed to idols. **And I gave her time to repent of her immorality. Behold, I will cast her upon a bed of sickness, and those who commit adultery with her into great tribulation, unless they repent of her deeds** *(vv. 20-22).*
Revelation 2:18, 20-22

We have seen from cover to cover, from Genesis to Revelations, that God has taken great effort to inform His children that it is His will for all of us to be free from pain and sickness. If people were advised to pay close attention to what a certain investment firm had to say, how much more should God's children listen to His Word? How many times does God have to say something for it to be so? We have also seen that God has a specific way to avoid sickness as well as a specific way to be healed and restored from its ill effects.

In addition to the above, God promises that a day is coming when Satan, the destroyer, will be removed from our presence forever.

AND AWAY GOES TROUBLE

> ***And the devil who deceived them was thrown into the lake of fire and brimstone,*** *where the beast and the false prophet are also; and they will be tormented day and night forever and ever.*
> *Revelations 20:10*

Nice future you have there, Satan! Now, you snake, listen to our future.

OUR FUTURE

> *And I saw a new heaven and a new earth; for the first heaven and the first earth passed away (v. 1), And I heard a loud voice from the throne, saying, "Behold, the tabernacle of God is among men, and He shall dwell among them, and they shall be His people, and **God Himself shall be among them**, and He shall wipe away every tear from their eyes; and **there shall no longer be any death; there shall no longer be any mourning, or crying, or pain;** the first things have passed away (vv. 3, 4)."*
> *Revelation 21:1, 3, 4*

If I weren't already a Christian, I'd be interested in knowing how to become a child of God. Satan may not be completely out of the picture yet, but his power is now challenged. Those who have entered the kingdom of God have been given power and spiritual authority over Satan and his kingdom. God has begun to reclaim planet earth for His own.

SATAN'S POWER OF DEATH GONE

Since the children share in flesh and blood, He Himself (Jesus) likewise also partook of the same, that through death **He might render powerless him who had the power of death, that is, the devil;** *and might deliver those who through fear of death were subject to slavery all their lives. Hebrews 2:14, 15*

Satan's use of fear allowed him to control our lives and keep us in all forms of bondage, including a deteriorating physical being.

The death, burial, and resurrection of Jesus changed all that forever.

JESUS HOLDS THE KEYS OF DEATH

"Do not be afraid; I am the first and the last, and the living one; and I was dead, and behold, I am alive forever-more, and **I have the keys of death and of Hades."** *Revelations 1:17, 18*

Old age is no longer something we need to dread. Did you know, even before Christ, that is under the law, godly men aged differently? How much more under grace should we look forward to our advanced years?

THE GODLY AND THE GOLDEN YEARS

*Although Moses was one hundred and twenty years old
when he died, **his eye was not dim, nor his vigor abated.***
Deuteronomy 43:7

Oh, you say, "But that was Moses." Well, Moses has no advantage over any of us at living a godly life. On the contrary, I can imagine Satan attacking Moses more aggressively than he does most of us. Yet, Moses died in sound health, and he is our example for our later years. However, we have additional encouragement.

A FULL HEALTHY LIFE

You will come to the grave in full vigor, *like the
stacking of grain in its season.*
Job 5:26

God wants us to have a full, healthy, and abundant life, a life free from the worry of sickness and death.

JESUS FREED OUR MINDS AND OUR BODIES

The sting of death is sin, and the power of sin is the law.
***But thanks be to God, who gives us the victory through
our Lord Jesus Christ.***
1 Corinthians 15:56, 57

Did you just read what I read? Look again. "The sting of death is sin." Notice, it doesn't say, "The sting of sin is death." It is sin that makes death painful.[1] We are all going to die, but we all do not have to be stung with the pain of Satanic diseases and causes when we die. Jesus *gives us*, right now, victory over sin. The presence of God's

---

[1]   R.C.H. Lenski, *The Interpretation of I and II Corinthians*, (Minneapolis: Augsburg Publishing House, 1963), pp. 748, 749.

Spirit makes it possible to heed the voice of God and keep all His commandments

GOD'S SPIRIT IS WITH US

> *"And I will ask the Father, and **He will give you another Helper**, that He may be with you forever."*
> *John 14:16*

Okay, God's Spirit is with us, but how can we keep every commandment and statute of God? Remember KISS? Keep It Simple Son.

LOVE FULFILLS THE LAW

> ***For the whole law is fulfilled in one word**, in the* statement, *"You shall **love** your neighbor as yourself."*
> *Galatians 5:14*

If we accept God's helper, the Holy Spirit, and allow His Spirit to help us love others as we love ourselves we will fulfill the whole Law. Then we won't have to be concerned about old age and sickness.

THIS PRESCRIPTION PROVIDES
THE FOLLOWING BENEFIT

1. Confidence that God reveals in every major division of the Bible that it is His will to restore

Rx13

Rx WHERE THERE'S A WILL THERE'S A WAY

The 1960s were a troubled time. The Vietnam War divided the United States over patriotism and principle. Every evening, the news seemed to have updated information about the conflict, the controversy, and the commitment. One evening, I was watching a news broadcast when it showed a film clip taken overseas. This film bite showed a Buddhist monk who was protesting the war. This particular monk made the ultimate statement regarding his views concerning commitment and conflict. He sat down on the ground, folded his arms and legs, and then he had an assistant pour gasoline over his head and body and, finally, ignite it. I looked on in disbelief as this man postured his body and his will and never moved a muscle. Eventually, his charred remains fell to one side but even then, his body remained motionless.

Have you ever accidentally burned yourself? Probably. Did you remain motionless and silent? Not if you're like me, you didn't. The monk in the above incident had committed his will not only to give his life, but he willed to suffer a horrible, agonizing death with amazing dignity and control.

Some may say that this man threw his life away. Maybe. However, it showed me in very certain terms just how strong a person's will can be.

We know our reborn spirit is free from the power of sin.[1]

OUR SPIRIT IS FREE FROM SIN

> **No one who is born of God practices sin,** because
> *His seed abides in him; and he cannot sin, because he is born
> of God.*
> *1 John 3:9*

We also know that our body, our flesh, is our greatest problem.

I AM MY BIGGEST ENEMY

> **For the flesh sets its desire against the Spirit, and
> the Spirit against the flesh;** *for these are in opposition to
> one another, so that you may not do the things that you please.*
> *Galatians 5:17*

Mingled among our flesh and our spirit exists our soul. Our intellect, our emotions, and our will define the battlefield on which we live our lives. It is here, at command headquarters, where our will makes the decisions and commits our attitudes and actions to a lifestyle that allows us to experience the form of life that our Lord desires to provide. A totally healthy life style.

Matthew's gospel assembles a string of incidents that illustrate several different forms of battle that can take place for our will. Each of us has and will experience different obstacles that Satan uses to make it difficult to receive God's blessings. These obstacles can appear just as difficult to overcome as Goliath (1 Samuel 17: 4-11) must have appeared to the children of Israel. The important thing to remember is that we are in charge of our will. No one else is in charge of our will, and we are capable of making the right decision. Now

---

[1]   Henry Alford, *Alford's Greek Testament, Vol. IV, Part 2,* (Grand Rapids: Guardian Press, 1976), pp. 468-470.

let's look at chapter 8 of Matthew's gospel and attempt to imagine each individual's battle.

THE LEPER

> *And when He (Jesus) had come down from the mountain, great multitudes followed Him.* **And behold, a leper came to Him,** *and bowed down to Him, saying, "Lord, if You are willing, You can make me clean."* **And He (Jesus) stretched out His hand and touched him,** *saying, "I am willing; be cleaned." And immediately his leprosy was cleansed. And Jesus said to him, "See that you tell no one; but go, show yourself to the priest, and present the offering that Moses commanded, for a testimony to them."*
> *Matthew 8:1-4*

This passage is usually mentioned by those who teach that it's God's will to heal all.[2] Why? Simply because of Jesus saying, "I am willing, be cleansed." But this is not my point. What I would like us to consider is this: lepers were to remain separated from healthy society.[3] They were outcasts, and they were to shout out "Unclean!" whenever they came close to a clean individual.[4] Consider the stature of this leper's Goliath. His will had to look this giant square between the eyes and make a decision. His entire social and religious order demanded he keep away from Jesus. This leper did not allow these obstacles to keep him from forcing his way into Christ's presence. Can you imagine the healthy multitudes parting like the Red Sea to allow this believer an uncrowded *freeway* leading to a hearing by our Lord? Now, can you image how the jaws of the multitude dropped when Jesus not only stood His ground but also stretched forth His

---

[2]   W.E. Vine, *Expository Dictionary of New Testament Words, Vol. IV,* (Old Tappan: Fleming H. Revell Company, 1966), p. 54.

[3]   Herbert Lockyer, *All the Miracles of the Bible,* (Grand Rapids: Zondervan Publishing House, 1978), p. 172.

[4]   Matthew Henry, *Matthew Henry's Commentary in One Volume,* (Grand Rapids: Zondervan Publishing House, 1974), p. 126.

hand and touched the leper? The healing was obviously dramatic, but it was nearly anticlimactic compared to events that came prior. The will of this leper overcame his personal Goliath, and as his personal giant fell, victory arose in its place.

THE PARALYZED SERVANT

> ***And when He had entered Capernaum, a centurion came to Him***, *entreating Him, and saying, "Lord my servant is lying paralyzed at home suffering great pain." And He said to him, "I will come and heal him." But, the centurion answered and said, "Lord, I am not worthy for You to come under my roof, but just say the word, and my servant will be healed. For I too am a man under authority, with soldiers under me; and I say to this one, 'Go!' and he goes, and to another, 'Come!' and he comes, and to my slave, 'Do this!' and he does it." Now when Jesus heard this He marveled, and said to those who were following, "Truly I say to you, I have not found such great faith with anyone in Israel. And I say to you, that many shall come from east and west, and recline at the table with Abraham, and Isaac, and Jacob, in the kingdom of heaven; but the sons of the kingdom shall be cast out into the outer darkness; in that place there shall be weeping and gnashing of teeth." And Jesus said to the centurion, "Go your way; let it be done to you as you have believed." And the servant was healed that very hour.*
> Matthew 8:5-13

Unlike the leper, the centurion's social position assured him a hearing by Jesus. He had complete freedom to approach our Lord. That certainly wasn't his Goliath. However, his Goliath is equally formidable. First, the centurion was a Gentile and not one of the chosen children of Israel.[5] He was a different kind of outcast than

---

[5]   Albert Barnes, *Barnes' Notes on the New Testament*, (Grand Rapids: Kregel Publications, 1974), p. 38.

the leper. This Goliath would normally be sufficient to stop most people. In addition to not being a Jew, he was personally a symbol of the hated Roman Empire who occupied the Holy Land during that time.[6] He represented the enemies of God's people. His Goliath easily could have been these thoughts: Why should this Jew want to do anything for me or mine? Why should I give this carpenter's son an opportunity to publicly reject me? This centurion had a firm grasp of a far greater certainty. He recognized what God wanted for the entire human race, and he knew Jesus had the power and the authority to make it so. He recognized Jesus as the physical authority of the kingdom of God on earth just as his own presence represented the physical authority and power of the Roman Empire. This centurion was not going to let the suggestions of his Goliath stop him from receiving the benefits of God's kingdom.

MUST I ASK?

> *And when Jesus had come to Peter's home, He saw his mother-in-law lying sick in bed with a fever. And He touched her hand, and the fever left her; and she arose, and waited on Him.*
> *Matthew 8:14, 15*

Mark and Luke also record the healing of Peter's mother-in-law (Mark 1:29-31, Luke 4:38, 39). Although both accounts are equally brief, each adds something different and vital. Luke, a doctor, describes her fever as high. The Greek word he chose for *high* or *great* is the same word we use and translate as mega. *Mega* means a "thousand times" in the metric system, so it isn't difficult to understand Luke was saying she had a very high fever. She may not have been aware of the presence of Jesus. Now, Mark informs us that both Peter and his brother Andrew asked Jesus to help her. So where is the giant? Well, maybe there isn't a giant, but then again, maybe there is.

---

[6]   Ibid.

Unlike the centurion, Peter and Andrew were part of the *in-crowd*. The centurion asked for his servant whom Jesus hadn't seen or didn't know. On the other hand, Jesus knew Peter's mother-in-law, and He could observe the seriousness of her condition, yet He did nothing. And so the giant begins to speak to both Peter and Andrew: "Would you look at that! What's the matter with Jesus? Doesn't He see how sick Peter's mother-in-law is? Why doesn't He do something? He just healed that Gentile's servant. Doesn't He care about our family?" And so forth and so on. The giant continued his assault on the character of Jesus. Were the ears of Peter and Andrew deaf? I doubt it, but their victory came the moment they stopped listening and started talking. They both interceded for Peter's mother-in-law, and then Jesus clearly demonstrated His nature and rebuked the fever. Maybe this reminds you of another truth. That being no matter how well you know Jesus, it still begins with humility.

INCONVENIENCE

> ***And when evening had come,*** they brought to Him many who were demon-possessed; and He cast out the spirits with a word, and healed all who were ill in order that what was spoken through Isaiah the prophet, might be fulfilled, saying, "He Himself took our infirmities, and carried away our diseases."
> Matthew 8:16, 17

It is one thing for a single individual to dare and inconvenience another regarding a matter that could wait a few hours, but it is an entirely different matter for a group of individuals to impose a significant inconvenience upon another concerning the same type of need. The Goliath to this group, no doubt, spoke out with thoughtful consideration and said, "These matters can wait till morning. Don't bother Jesus now. Seek Him later at a more convenient hour." A noble sounding argument, but remember, timing is everything.

JESUS WANTS TO HELP NOW

> *For He says, "At the acceptable time I listened to you, and on the day of salvation I helped you"; behold,* **now is "the acceptable time," behold, now is "the day of salvation."**
> *2 Corinthians 6:2*

Satan would always have you delay in approaching Jesus, hoping your delay will last just long enough for you to slip into eternity.

FIVE THOUSAND TO ONE

> *And when He had come to the other side in the country of the Gadarenes, two men who were demon-possessed met Him as they were coming out of the tombs; they were so exceedingly violent that no one could pass by that road. And behold, they cried out saying, "What do we have to do with You, Son of God? Have You come here to torment us before the time?" Now there was at a distance from them a herd of many swine feeding. And the demons began to entreat Him, saying, "If You are going to cast us out, send us into the heard of swine." And He said to them, "Begone!" And they came out, and went into the swine, and behold, the whole heard rushed down the steep bank into the sea and perished in the waters.*
> *Matthew 8:28-32*

People wanted no contact with leprous individuals, and those who were afflicted separated themselves from the nonleprous community. However, demoniacs did not necessarily submit to the public's wishes. These two men would violently attack anyone who came their way. Their violent behavior was sufficient reason for the rest of society to avoid them. The Goliath that stood firmly between these men and Jesus meeting their need was the fact that people would flee from them out of fear for their very lives. They appeared helpless to escape their violent natures. Consider these two were outnumbered by numerous demons, yet they charged from the tombs toward Jesus, knowing in faith He would be the only One who would not run from them.

Just before they stormed from the tombs, I can imagine their Goliath snarling, "Don't be ridiculous. The moment you leave these tombs, those cowards are all going to turn and run. What makes you think this Jesus is any different?" The similar accounts in Mark and Luke (Mark 5:1-17, Luke 8:26-39) focus on one of these two individuals, an individual the Bible refers to as *Legion*. This man was afflicted by as many as five thousand demons.[7] If I were a single demon, I would use everything in my power and in my persuasion to keep the one I inhabited from getting anywhere near Jesus. Now, can you image the effort five thousand demons put up? Still, with the odds five thousand to one in their favor, all these demons where unable to overpower the will of the individuals from coming to Jesus.

Is Satan stronger than your will? Is he strong enough to prevent you from receiving what God wants you to have? Don't buy into that for a microsecond. It simply isn't true. Your will is stronger than the combined will of five thousand demons, and WHERE THERE IS A WILL, THERE IS A WAY.

THIS PRESCRIPTION PROVIDES
THE FOLLOWING BENEFIT

1. Confidence that any individual who commits his or her will to the revealed will of God will receive His promises

---

[7]   W.E. Vine, *Expository Dictionary of New Testament Words, Vol. II,* (Old Tappan: Fleming H. Revell Company, 1966), p. 3.

Rx14

And Jesus seeing their faith said to the paralytic, My son, your sins are forgiven.
Mark 2:5

WHAT DOES FAITH LOOK LIKE?

Is faith something we can see or do we just see the results of faith? Is faith mysterious or can we get *our heads* around it? Are we able to understand what we can do to bring about miracles, signs and wonders? If we can understand what occurred to bring about God's promises then maybe we can see these things take place more frequently in our lives. I believe we can make that discovery. Let's begin by looking at three incidents in the life of Christ where He describes faith. However before we start please allow me to paraphrase a definition of faith from the Bible.

A BIBLICAL DEFINITION OF FAITH

Now faith is the assurance of things hoped for, the conviction of things not yet seen.
Hebrews 11:1

May I paraphrase the above?

A PRACTICAL DEFINITION OF BIBLICAL FAITH

Faith is believing what God says and acting on His word (what He said).

A paraphrase . . . The Author

I will use this paraphrase throughout the next three incidents in the life of Jesus to show you that this is how He defined faith. We will be looking at *little faith*, *faith* and later, *faithless*.

HOW DID JESUS DEFINE "LITTLE FAITH"?

> *Now when Jesus saw great multitudes about Him,* **He gave commandment to depart unto the other side** *(v. 18). And when He was entered into a ship, His disciples followed Him. And, behold, there arose a great tempest in the sea, insomuch that the ship was covered with waves: but He was asleep. And His disciples came to Him, and awoke Him, saying, Lord save us: we perish. And He saith unto them,* **Why are ye fearful, O ye of little faith?** *Then He arose, and rebuked the winds and the sea; and there was a great calm (vv. 23-26). Matthew 8:18, 23-26 (KJV)*

What do you think the disciples thought when Jesus called them men of *little faith?* That must have hurt. Didn't they wake Him up because they believed He would save them? Of course they did. So what's this *little faith* business? Were they correct to presume Jesus would save them? He never said He would do that. I suppose they get an "A" for presumptive faith.

Which reminds me, did you ever bring home a report card from school, beaming with delight. You had A's and B's in all your subjects except one in which you received a C. When you did something like that did your parent(s) ever ask you why you got the C and failed to mention the A's and B's?

Jesus' disciples had presumptive faith but not the kind of faith that Jesus was referring to at that moment, which was faith in what He had said. Jesus could **see,** His disciples didn't believe they would get to the other side. Jesus doesn't order believers to fail. Believers fail because they don't follow His orders (His word).

Are you beginning to get the idea of how to determine if a person's life is showing if they believe what God has said?

Let's examine another situation.

HOW DOES JESUS DEFINE "FAITH"?

> *And behold, they were bringing to Him a paralytic lying on a bed; and Jesus **seeing their faith** said to the paralytic, "Take courage, my son, your sins are forgiven." And behold, some of the scribes said to themselves, "This fellow blasphemes." And Jesus knowing their thoughts said, "Why are you thinking evil in your hearts? For which is easier to say 'Your sins are forgiven' or to say 'Rise and walk'? "But in order that you may know the the Son of Man has authority on earth to forgive sins" - then He said to the paralytic - **"Rise, take up your bed and go home." And he rose, and went home.***
> *Matthew 9:2-7*

In this account we **see** not one but two examples of biblical faith. In the first instance, Jesus **sees** the faith of the paralytic's friends. They bring him to Jesus believing He would heal their friend. But wait a moment. Where did Jesus say He would do that? Actually Jesus said that in the previous chapter, Matthew 8.

JESUS SAID HE WILL HEAL PARALYSIS

> *And when he had entered Capernaum, a centurion came to Him, entreating Him, saying **"Lord, my servant is lying paralyzed at home, suffering great pain." And He (Jesus) said to him, "I will come and heal him."***
> *Matthew 8:5-7*

We **see** how the paralytic's friends were acting in faith but what about the paralytic himself? This is even easier. What did Jesus tell the paralytic? He told the paralytic, his sins were forgiven and then

He told him, "Rise, take up your bed, and go home." How did the paralytic respond to what Jesus said? Did he say "What's wrong with you? Can't you see that I am paralyzed?" Or did he hear Jesus' words, "Rise up and go home", and responded to those words in faith? I told you his faith would be easy to **see.** However, was it easy for the paralytic to do? I don't know but I can imagine he had to battle doubt and maybe fear as well. I know in a similar situation in my own life, I faced both fear and doubt (Case Study No. 2). Only by trusting God or believing what He said **and acting upon it,** was I victorious.

This situation provides us with two examples of individuals exercising biblical faith. All individuals involved chose to act on what Jesus had said and in a positive manner.

Now let's read a third account and **see** both *faith* and *little faith* in the life of one individual and each appearing only a second apart from each other.

FAITH: A NEVER ENDING BATTLE

> *And immediately He (Jesus) made His disciples get into the boat, and go ahead of him to the other side, while He sent the multitudes away (v. 22). And in the forth watch of the night He came to them walking on the sea. And when the disciples saw Him walking on the sea, they were frightened, saying, "It is a ghost!" And they cried out for fear. But immediately Jesus spoke to them, saying, "Take courage, it is I; do not be afraid." And Peter answered Him and said, "Lord, if it is You, command me to come to You on the water."* ***And He said, "Come!" And Peter got out of the boat, and walked on the water*** *and came toward Jesus.* ***But seeing the wind, he became afraid, and beginning to sink,*** *he cried out, saying, "Lord, save me!" And immediately, Jesus stretched out His hand and took hold of him, and said to him,* ***"O you of little faith, why did you doubt*** *(vv. 25-31)?"*
> *Matthew 14:22, 25-31*

Here we go again. Jesus described Peter's actions as *little faith*. What's up with that? When Peter thought he was in trouble, didn't he call out to Jesus to save him? Isn't that faith? Yes, but here Peter is exercising presumptive faith. It is true, Peter believed Jesus could save him. However, once again, Jesus never told Peter He would pull him out of the sea. Then there is that bit of Peter walking on the sea. What was that if not faith? Chopped liver? No. That was faith for sure, with a big fat "A". However that wasn't the faith Jesus was **seeing**. Jesus was **seeing** that Peter was now believing what his eyes were telling him instead of what Jesus had told him. Jesus **saw** that Peter had stopped believing what He had said, which was, "Come". That's what Jesus is defining as *little faith*. Jesus wants us to do what he tells us to do more than he wants us to assume what we believe He will do.

We are engaged in a spiritual war. Chess is a war game, kingdom vs kingdom. In spiritual warfare Satan's favorite weapons are fear and doubt. Together they are Satan's one-two punch. To Satan fear is *check* and doubt is *checkmate*.

It's time for a spiritual news break regarding, *Coming distractions*: "Fear and Doubt are coming soon to a situation near you."

Let's get very serious. If you are a Christian then sooner or later you will be engaged in spiritual warfare. We have seen Jesus define *faith* as well as, *little faith*; now let's **see** Him define *faithless*.

JESUS DEFINES "FAITHLESS"

And immediately, when the entire crowd saw Him (Jesus), they were amazed, and began running to greet Him. And He asked them, "What are you discussing with them (His disciples)?" And one of the crowd answered Him, "Teacher, I brought You my son, possessed with a spirit which makes him mute; and whenever it seizes him, it dashes him to the ground and he foams at the mouth, and grinds his teeth, and stiffens out. And I told your disciples to cast it out, and they could not do it." **And He answered them and said, "O unbelieving**

generation, how long shall I be with you? How long shall I put up with you. Bring him to Me!"
Mark 9:15-19

Notice, what Jesus said, "and He answered **them**, and not he answered **him**". In this particular situation Jesus describes (**sees**) the actions of His disciples as being *unbelieving*. What does *unbelieving* mean? The translators of the New American Standard Bible, which is the translation used almost exclusively in this book, chose to translate the original Greek word as *unbelieving*. However, their predecessors who translated the King James Version chose to translate the same word as *faithless*. Now according to *Strong's Exhaustive Concordance of the Bible, faithless* means: faithless, without faith or no faith.[1] Did that surprise you? Just kidding.

This is an excellent time to refocus our faith. The father in the above verses took his son initially to Jesus. We must remind ourselves, when we have a need for healing that Jesus is the healer, not man. We must always go to Him, not man. Jesus is the healer and man is the messenger, who tells us the benefits of the kingdom of God.

No matter what the name of the individual or how impressive his (her) ministry might appear, the results are because the person of the Holy Spirit, (not the individual), is confirming, with power and authority, the message of God's kingdom.

Why do I say Jesus was describing the actions of His disciples as being *faithless* rather that those of the boy's father? May I, ask a few questions. Did Jesus tell the boy's father that he would cast the demon out of his son? Did the boy's father say he was bringing his son to Jesus? Is it possible the boy's father believed Jesus would cast out the demon but he may not have had the same confidence in His disciples? However, it appears the father's faith was weakening.

---

[1] James Strong, Strong's Exhaustive Concordance of the Bible, Greek Dictionary of the New Testament,(Grand Rapids: World Publishing, 1986), p. 15.

LITTLE FAITH? PROBABLY. FAITHLESS? NO!

> *Immediately the boy's father cried out and began saying,*
> ***"I do believe**; help my unbelief."*
> Mark 9:24

Jesus said the problem was someone's lack of faith. Okay, but whose and why?

It was A. A. Allen who reminded us that God does not accept a sacrifice that has a blemish (Exodus 12:5).[2]

WOULD YOU LIKE A DYNAMIC MINISTRY?

> *I urge you therefore brethren, by the mercies of God to* ***present your bodies a living and holy sacrifice, acceptable to God,*** *which is your spiritual service of worship.*
> Romans 12:1

A dynamic ministry isn't always fun and games. It is easy to disqualify oneself. Let me be clear. I believe an improper attitude can effect our faith and our ministry, as much as, an obvious sin (Rx 21).

Now let's look at the above situation with this statement in mind for a possible explanation.

JESUS TOLD HIS DISCIPLES

> *And He called the twelve together, and gave them power and authority over **all** demons and to heal diseases.*
> Luke 9:1

Did Jesus tell these things to His disciples before they met the father and his son? Yes.[3]

---

2   A. A. Allen, The Price of God's Miracle Working Power, (Charleston: GreatSpace Independent Publishing, 2012), p. 110

3   Robert Thomas; Stanley N. Gundry, A Harmony of the Gospels, (Chicago: Moody Press, 1979), pp. 95, 121.

Obviously, His disciples were involved in spiritual warfare and the battle wasn't over. When His disciples saw Jesus returning did they run to Him and ask Him for help, or was it the boy's father who came running to Jesus (Mark 9:15)? Remember His disciples wasted no time in awakening Him in the boat. Remember Peter wasted no time in calling out to Jesus for help on the sea. In this instance Jesus didn't **see** His disciples coming to Him for help. Were they embarrassed? Whatever Jesus **saw,** He described as *faithless*.

Is it possible that the disciples' previous accomplishments had puffed up their pride, maybe just a little? If so, then I believe that could be considered a *blemish*.

NOW, HIS DISCIPLES COME TO HIM

> *And when He (Jesus) had come into the house, His disciples began questioning Him privately, "Why could we not cast it out?" And He said to them, "This kind cannot come out by anything but (fasting and) prayer".*
> Mark 9:28, 29

What Christian wants to be called *faithless,* especially by Jesus? Ouch! On the other hand what Christian wouldn't like to know how to avoid such an embarrassment?

So when Christ' disciples asked Him to explain why they had been unable to cast out the demon (Mark 9:28) any believer within hearing distance would have wanted to know Jesus' explanation. Wouldn't you?

We know the power of the person of the Holy Spirit hadn't grown weaker nor had the authority of God's word become lessened. So what was the cause of His disciples faithlessness?

This was Jesus' explanation, "This kind cannot come out by anything but fasting and prayer (Mark 9:29). Does that mean this kind of demon is capable of bringing about doubt in the minds of men?

Previously Jesus had given His disciples power (the presence of the person of the Hoy Spirit) and authority (the message of His kingdom) over all demons (Luke 9:1). As a result, His disciples followed His instruction and were successful in casting out demons (Luke 10:17).

Consequently His two words *this kind* cannot stand apart from His word *all.* Allow me to say this another way. This kind of demon doesn't require any more faith to cast out than any other kind of demon. However if a demon is able to bring about doubt in an individual's mind that would explain Jesus' answer. The purpose of fasting and prayer would be to strengthen or build up one's faith (Jude 20) rather than to add to that person's faith.

I consider humility or self denial as a form of fasting. I know from personal experience that when the message of the gospel is being accompanied by signs and wonders it is easy to get caught up in the moment and to overlook who is confirming God's word (Mark 16:20) and sometimes even why (John 3:16). If we overlook that fact then don't be surprised if the person of the Holy Spirit doesn't politely step aside and allow us to discover otherwise.

If you are a Christian then please consider this: if our message about the gospel of Jesus Christ fails to include His desire to heal the sick and make known the defeat of Satan's kingdom then the person of the Holy Spirit will have less to confirm and God's message to mankind will be incomplete and definitely less convincing. Then our message could easily be mistaken for another powerless religion instead of His will for the human race as revealed by a loving benevolent King.

Our role is to go boldly, in faith, proclaiming the good news of Jesus Christ and all the benefits of His kingdom. The role of the person of the Holy Spirit is to confirm or demonstrate the truth of Christ's message which we proclaim. In other words: get it right and see His might.

If Satan is powerless to disarm God, and he is, then why would we help him by omitting the truth of healing, signs and wonders (Acts 4:29-31)?

Who wants to be called *faithless*? Who wants to be called a Christian in name only? What!? No volunteers? If we would like to avoid needless defeat and embarrassment, then may I suggest we read His word daily (Romans 10:17) and couple that with routinely praying in the Spirit (Jude 20).

We have now seen Jesus describe or define *faith, little faith, and faithless or no faith*. All of these definitions can and will apply to the actions of every believer. That's a given. What is important is we be aware of when any of them might apply to us. If we understand that failure results from not acting on what Jesus has said, then maybe we will be able to correct our actions and believe Jesus regardless of what our situations are telling us. If we can make the necessary adjustments then Jesus will be more than pleased and our faith will bring forth His promises.

HOW TO FULLY PLEASE JESUS

> **And without faith it is impossible to please Him,**
> *for he who comes to God must believe that He is and that He is a rewarder of those who seek Him.*
> *Hebrews 11:6*

Before we move on to Section Two, may I give you a few other scriptures to read. **See** if you can identify what type of faith appears in each. Please read: Matthew 20:29-34, Mark 1:16-18, Luke 6:6-10, and Acts 3:1-8.

THIS PRESCRIPTION PROVIDES
THE FOLLOWING BENEFITS

1. Confidence to know how Jesus defines *faith*
2. Confidence to know how Jesus defines *little faith*
3. Confidence to know what Jesus defines as *faithless*
4. Confidence to be able to **see** the above without Jesus telling us

5. Confidence to be able to inspect our own lives to **see** if we are living in faith, and if not what could we do to correct our life

6. Confidence to know God is for us even when our actions suggest we have *little faith*

7. Confidence in knowing what to do to strengthen one's faith.

This concludes Section One on *Diagnosis*. Here, we discovered the etiology, or the origin, of all our sicknesses and diseases, which can be traced back to our exposure to sin (Rx 6 and 8). We also discovered the nature of the infective agent (Rx 7). In addition, we learned we have a reliable means of diagnosis (Rx 1). Then we were introduced to the miraculous cure for all our maladies (Rx 2-5). This cure and its broad-spectrum nature (Rx 11) have been thoroughly documented (Rx 12). However, we must be willing to accept treatment (Rx 13) and to understand there are certain areas of compliance that must be met. If compliance is overlooked, then recovery could be delayed (Rx 10). Finally, as so often is the case, certain lifestyle changes are recommended for complete, as well as longterm, recovery (Rx 9).

Now, let's turn our attention to Section Two on *Treatment* and see how healing in the kingdom of God takes place in the lives of ordinary, everyday people.

SECTION TWO

TREATMENT

The correct diagnosis determines what treatment will take place. This section outlines biblically prescribed forms of treatment, which will resolve our condition, without rejecting medical forms of therapy. It also informs us of some of the side effects, other things that might occur during treatment, which could discourage us. Hopefully, the following will encourage us to continue our therapy without interruption, so we can achieve the desired results. All *Case Studies* in this section are from actual experiences in the life of our family.

PRESCRIPTIONS 15-28

Prescription File No. 2

(Table of Contents)

Rx15

INSTRUCTIONS

John 3:16

Rx

**KINGDOM
VS
KINGDOM**

If you are a Christian, then what was it that attracted you to Christ? Was it possibly the above verse?

"FOR GOD SO LOVED THE WORLD

> *That He gave His only begotten Son, that whosoever believes in Him should not perish, but have eternal life."*
> *John 3:16*

It was during the last half of the twentieth-century that the influence of a well-known and worldwide evangelist made this verse the *poster child* for Christianity. You would see it written on signs appearing in large crowds. You would see it displayed at sporting events, as well as rallies. You would see it *everywhere*. It became so well-known that at times you would see just the reference, like above, and not the words. Which leads me to a fun question: How many times in the four biblical accounts of the life of Jesus would you guess He told the masses that God loved them? Five times, fifty times, possibly more? Would it come as a surprise to learn the correct answer is zero, nada, zip . . . never?

Please allow me to ask another question. The answer might be as equally surprising. How many times do you think Jesus mentioned the kingdom of God? The answer is close to one hundred times.

John 3:16 will always attract people to Christ, but let's look at how Jesus, through the biblical record, approached people concerning their need for forgiveness.

May I begin by asking if you have ever walked down a street and encountered an individual proclaiming, "Repent, the end is near" or maybe "Repent, for the kingdom of God is at hand"? Did the thought happen to cross your mind, *What a kook!* Or maybe you thought, *Right on! Preach it!?* Let's face it, *street preachers* are difficult to ignore.

The first New Testament street preacher might have been Jesus' cousin.

THE FIRST STREET PREACHER

> *Now in those days John the Baptist came, preaching in the wilderness of Judea, saying, "Repent for the kingdom of heaven is at hand."*
> *Matthew 3:1, 2*

Is this how God chose to announce His Son as Savior, coming King, or both? John was difficult to ignore, and his message drew crowds, including the religious leaders of the day. His message impacted people so much that many came to be baptized for repentance. Even Jesus came to be baptized.

JESUS ENDORSED JOHN'S MESSAGE

> **Then Jesus** arrived from Galilee at the Jordan **coming to John, to be baptized by him.**
> *Matthew 3;13*

John's message proclaimed the necessity for a change in life style, a change in the way an individual lives their life. It was a warning, as well as, a demand. It certainly was not a suggestion. It was a *heads up* about the consequences of ignoring what was contained in the message.

GOD ISN'T MESSING AROUND OR BLOWING SMOKE

> *"Therefore bring forth fruit in keeping with repentance; and do not suppose that you can say to yourselves, 'We have Abraham for our father'; for I (John the Baptist) say to you, that God is able from these stones to raise up children to Abraham. "And the axe is laid at the root of the trees; every tree that therefore does not bear good fruit is cut down and thrown into the fire."*
> *Matthew 3:8-10*

Earlier, I pointed out that Jesus endorsed John's message but:

WHAT DID JESUS THINK OF JOHN?

> *"Truly, I say to you, **among those born of women there has not arisen anyone greater than John the Baptist.**"*
> *Matthew 11:11*

Really? Not Abraham? How about Moses? Not even king David, who was a man after God's own heart? What was it about John that set him apart from these other impressive men of faith? Was it because he attended synagogue every Saturday? No. Was it because he was committed to tithing? No. Was it because he was so likable? Not likely, unless strangeness is your thing. So what was it? Although John was the son of a priest, that's right, he was a *preacher's* kid, he didn't work for a living or serve in the temple. In fact, he was homeless. With all due respect, John was just a tad strange. He wasn't the type of guy mom and dad would hope to see their daughter invite home for dinner.

The most impressive thing that can be said about John is the following:

HOW DID ISAIAH, THE OLD TESTAMENT PROPHET, SEE JOHN?

> *For this is the one referred to by Isaiah the prophet when he said, "The voice of one crying in the wilderness, **'Make ready the way of the Lord, make His paths straight!'"***
> *Matthew 3:3*

First, Isaiah saw Jesus as the approaching king of the Jews, their long-awaited Messiah-King. That made John the first New Testament forerunner. What is a forerunner? A forerunner, according to W. E. Vine, is "one sent before a king to see that the way is prepared".[1] A forerunner might read a proclamation from a scroll or simply announce the intentions and demands of the approaching king. Forerunners came with the authority of their king and they were backed up by his might.

HOW DID JOHN SEE HIMSELF?

> *The next day he (John) saw Jesus coming to him and said, "**Behold, the Lamb of God who takes away the sin of the world!**"*
> *John1:29*

John saw himself as the forerunner announcing the presence of the Savior of the world. However, John's proclamation meant Jesus also has to be our Healer.

---

[1] W. E. Vine, Expository Dictionary of New Testament Words (Old Tappan, Fleming H. Revell Company, 1966), p. 119.

JESUS: SAVIOR AND HEALER

> *Bless the Lord (King), O my soul, and forget none of His benefits;* **who pardons all your iniquities, who heals all your diseases.**
> *Psalms 103:2, 3*

So who was right? Isaiah or John? They both were right. Isaiah was seeing the second coming of Jesus, and John was alive at His first coming.

In addition, John also happened to announce the fact that Jesus was also to be the baptizer with the Holy Spirit.

JOHN HAD MORE NEWS ABOUT JESUS

> *"As for me (John), I baptize you with water for repentance, but He (Jesus) who is coming after me is mightier than I,* **He will baptize you with the Holy Spirit and fire."**
> *Matthew 3:11*

With that announcement, John became the first person to name all four major roles of Jesus: Savior, Healer, Baptizer with the Holy Spirit, and coming King. His last announcement refers, among other things, to the power and authority (Acts 1:6-8) that stands behind the forerunner and the message he proclaims.

After John was arrested, Jesus continued John's proclamation.

JESUS BECAME THE SECOND NEW TESTAMENT FORERUNNER

> *Now when Jesus heard that John had been taken into custody, He withdrew into Galilee (v. 12).* **From that time Jesus began to preach and say, "Repent, for the kingdom of heaven (God) is at hand (v. 17)."**
> *Matthew 4:12, 17*

Remember, the job of the forerunner is to prepare the way for the approaching king. The fact that Jesus continued John's message tells us the King of kings is still approaching.

Jesus obediently followed His own kingly declaration. Everywhere He was going to travel, He sent out His team of forerunners to bring the King's declaration, which amounts to the preamble of the good news of God's kingdom.

JESUS FIRST SENT OUT TWELVE FORERUNNERS (DISCIPLES)

> *And having summoned His twelve disciples, He gave them authority over unclean spirits, to cast them out, and to heal every kind of disease and every kind of sickness.* (v. 1). *"And as you go, preach saying, 'The kingdom of heaven (God) is at hand.'* (v. 7).
> *Matthew 10:1, 7*

> *And they went out and preached that men should repent.*
> *Mark 6:12*

However, more forerunners were to follow.

THEN JESUS SENT OUT SEVENTY MORE FORERUNNERS

> *Now after this **the Lord appointed seventy others, and sent them two and two ahead of Him to every city and place where He Himself was going to come.*** (v. 1). *"Whatever city you enter, heal those in it who are sick and say to them. '**The kingdom of God has come near to you.'*** (vv. 8, 9). "But whatever city you enter and they do not receive you, go out into the streets and say. For if the miracles had been performed in Tyre and Sidon which occurred in you, **they would have repented long ago.**" (vv. 10, 13).*
> *Luke 10:1, 8, 9, 10, 13*

I could go on with Peter's first message on the day of Pentecost (Acts 2:14-42) and Paul before King Agrippa (Acts 26:19).

Jesus may not have made a practice of telling people God loved them, but He showed them that God does love them and what the kingdom of God is like. However, He was constantly concerned about His followers awareness of the kingdom of God.[2]

HOW DID JESUS SPEND HIS LAST DAYS ON EARTH?

> *To these He also presented Himself alive after His suffering, by many convincing proofs, **appearing to them over a period of forty days and speaking of the things concerning the kingdom of God**.*
> *Acts 1:3*

It was extremely important that Jesus help His followers understand the Old Testament.[3]

Has God ceased to send out forerunners to prepare the way for His second coming? No. Is the kingdom versus kingdom conflict still taking place? Yes. Is the *King* of the first century also the *King* of this century? Absolutely. Has He arrived as King? Not yet. Has He changed His proclamation? If so, I haven't found it in the Bible, but I do see Him telling five of the seven churches in the book of Revelation that they need to repent. (Revelation 2:1-3, 22).

APPARENTLY JESUS HASN'T CHANGED HIS MIND

> ***Jesus Christ is the same** yesterday and **today and forever**.*
> *Hebrews 13:8*

---

2   Finis J. Dake, The Dake Annotated Reference Bible, The New Testament, (Dake Publishing Inc., 2014), p. 213.

3   F. F. Bruce, The Book of Acts, (Grand Rapids, Wm. B. Eerdman Publishing Co., 1977), pp. 34, 35.

Kingdom versus kingdom is serious stuff. It is no laughing matter. If you think the end of World War II left no doubt as to who was the most powerful nation on earth, then you haven't seen anything yet.

One thing is for sure. You want to be on the winning side.

May I give you a glimpse of how lop-sided it is?

KINGDOM VERSUS KINGDOM IS NO CONTEST

> *Then there was brought to Him a demon-possessed man who was blind and dumb, and He healed him, so that the dumb man spoke and saw. And all the multitudes were amazed, and began to say, "This man cannot be the Son of David, can he?" But when the Pharisees heard it, they said, "This man cast out demons only by Beelzebul the ruler of demons." And knowing their thoughts He said to them, "Any kingdom divided against itself is laid waste; and any city or house divided against itself shall not stand. **And if Satan casts out Satan, he is divided against himself; how then shall his kingdom stand** (vv. 22-26)? **But if I cast out demons by the Spirit of God, the Kingdom of God has come upon you** (v. 28)."*
> *Matthew 12:22-26, 28*

As I stated earlier, "Repent for the kingdom of heaven (God) is at hand" could be thought of as the preamble to the good news of God's kingdom. It also might be the bait that draws sinners to Jesus. Why not? It worked for John, Jesus, Peter, and Paul. Repentance must take place before anyone can make the great escape and enter the kingdom of God. Obviously, fish must be caught before they can be set free.

REPENT AND BE SET FREE

> *Jesus answered them, "Truly, truly, I say to you, everyone who commits sin is the slave of sin. The slave does not remain*

forever. ***So if the Son makes you free, you will be free indeed.”***
John 8:34-36

THIS PRESCRIPTION PROVIDES
THE FOLLOWING BENEFITS

1. Confidence that Christians are involved in a kingdom versus kingdom conflict
2. Confidence that all Christians are forerunners and witnesses of the coming King, Jesus
3. Confidence that as forerunners we have been given a specific proclamation
4. Confidence that King Jesus will equip His forerunners with more than enough power and authority to prepare the way for His coming

Rx16

THE GREAT ESCAPE

Have you ever heard someone say, "Everybody wants to go to heaven, but no one wants to die"? You might have even once or twice smirked in agreement.

On an August day in 1945, the inhabitants on the island of Honshu in the Pacific heard the sounds of three planes flying over head. They were flying higher and louder than any planes they had ever seen.

Unfortunately death is no guarantee of going to heaven.

THERE COULD BE A PROBLEM

> *And in as much as it is appointed for men to die once* ***and after this comes judgment.***
> *Hebrews 9:27*

Some of those on the island continued to look up and others returned to their daily routines.

Judgement might not be a pleasant thought, but it is unavoidable.

HOW WILL JUDGMENT TURN OUT?

> *For **all have sinned** and fall short of the glory of God.*
> *Romans 8:23*

The actual date was August 6, 1945, and the particular city was Hiroshima. One of those planes was a B-29 Super-fortress, named the Enola Gay.

HAVE YOU EVER HEARD OF NICODEMUS?

> *Now there was a man of the Pharisees, named* **Nicodemus a ruler of the Jews;** *this man came to Him (Jesus) by night and* **said to Him,** *"Rabbi, we know that you have come from God as a teacher; for* **no one can do these signs that You do unless God is with him."**
> *John 3:1, 2*

Just three loud planes flying over the largest island in the Japanese empire.

Obviously, the following scenario didn't occur, but what if it had? The time and the place are obviously different, but what if Jesus had been selling time shares? Okay, laugh. I get it; it's a stretch. Could He have said to Nicodemus something like the following: "So, Nicodemus, you like what you see. Great! And why not? It's truly unbelievable. Okay, let me explain it."

Then Jesus informed Nicodemus what he needed to do in order to have all the benefits he had seen and more. Nicodemus had to become a citizen of the kingdom of God. That's all. Okay. How does one do that?

YOU MUST BE BORN AGAIN

> *Jesus answered and said to him,* **"Truly, Truly, I say to you, unless one is born again he cannot see the kingdom of God.** *(v. 3). Nor can he enter into it (v. 5)."*
> *John 3:3, 5*

Japan had been at war with the United States since December 7, 1941, but by August of 1945, everyone knew that Japan was going to lose. It was only a matter of time and the loss of more lives on both sides.

It was about five days earlier that American planes had flown over Hiroshima, dropping leaflets written in Japanese informing the inhabitants that their city was going to be utterly destroyed and that they needed to evacuate. Japan had been bombed before, including the capital city of Tokyo in early 1942. Yet all their cities were still standing. Consequently, the warning might not have been taken too seriously. It easily could have been taken the same way many people look at a street preacher.

As the people on the ground looked skyward, they might have been thinking, *Only three planes. What damage can they do?* If they knew that those three planes were only going to drop one bomb, they might have thought, *What damage can one bomb do?* Well, it took less than a minute to find out.

August is the warmest month in Japan. The temperature can climb to around eighty degrees Fahrenheit, but at 8:15 a.m. on August 6, 1945, the temperature instantly skyrocketed to five thousand degrees Fahrenheit. That temperature is comparable to the temperature of our sun. Birds were vaporized in flight while humans were reduced to swirling streams of ashes. A city of over one million people was leveled to the ground in a matter of seconds. Still, Hiroshima will seem like a cartoon compared to hell itself. You could say that those who perished got the best of it.

To further describe what occurred that morning would be unnecessarily gross, but think about this: If you had been one of the curious people on the ground looking up and knew what was about to happen, do you think it is possible that you might have wished you had been born somewhere else? Anywhere else?

For over two thousand years God has been dropping leaflets on planet earth in all languages. Thanks to modern technology, *everyone* on earth can learn about the gospel, the good news about the kingdom of God. Maybe it's time to read God's leaflet, look spiritually upward, and consider what He is saying. A warning, no matter how unbelievable it might seem, can still be true.

HOW MUCH LONGER WILL GOD DROP LEAFLETS

'The gospel must first be preached to all the nations.'
Mark 13:10

Those on Hiroshima who took the leaflets seriously were the ones who truly got the best of it. Today it works the same way for those who take God's leaflet seriously.

WHY HELL WAS CREATED

*"Then He (God) will also say to those on His left, 'Depart from me accursed ones, **into the eternal fire which has been prepared for the devil and his angels.'"***
Matthew 25:41

America didn't want to bomb the Japanese citizens. The bomb was created to bring the Japanese leadership to its knees. Hell wasn't created for people but rather for the devil, and surprise, he won't be in charge.

God, through the sacrifice of His only begotten Son, Jesus of Nazareth, has made an escape available. The leaflet God drops, we call the New Testament, warns us of hell and tells us we can escape.

WHAT MAN CAN'T DO, GOD CAN DO

*And Jesus said to His disciples, "Truly, truly, I say to you, it is hard for a rich man to enter the kingdom of heaven. And again I say to you, it is easier for a camel to go through the eye of a needle, than for a rich man to enter the kingdom of God." And when the disciples heard this, they were very astonished and said, **"Then who can be saved?"** And looking at them, Jesus said to them, **"With men this is impossible, but with God all things are possible."***
Matthew 19:23-26

How does anyone enter the kingdom of God and become a citizen of that kingdom? Jesus told Nicodemus that the second birth is made possible by the Spirit of God with the cooperation of man.

BORN AGAIN BY THE SPIRIT OF GOD

Jesus said, "**Truly, truly, I say to you, unless one is born of water and the Spirit** *he can not enter into the kingdom of God.*"
John 3:5

All of us were physically born (of water) into the wrong kingdom. No offense, Adam. No offense, Eve. No matter how we turn out in life, we will still be captives in the wrong kingdom because of sin. No exceptions. All of us need to repent and unconditionally surrender to God and ask for His mercy and grace, or as John the Baptist said, "There will be unwelcome consequences (paraphrased)."

ONLY GOD CAN SOLVE OUR DILEMA

"*For God so loved the world, that He gave His only begotten Son, that whosoever (That's you and me) believes in Him shall not perish, but have eternal life.*"
John 3:16

Many who are reading this right now have accepted all of the above but, some might not **feel** like they are currently citizens in the kingdom of God. If you are one of them, you're not alone. It's more common than you might think.

FAITH, NOT FEELING

Now the just shall live by faith *but we are not of them who draw back unto perdition (disbelief); but of them that believe to the saving of the soul.*
Hebrews 10:38, 39 (KJV)

Remember, faith can be seen (Rx. 14). Faith is not feelings. Do you want to know for sure you are a child of God? Then simply follow this guarantee.

GOD'S GUARANTEE OF SALVATION

> ***If you confess with your mouth Jesus as Lord, and believe in your heart that God raised Him from the dead, you will be saved;*** *for with the heart man believes, resulting in righteousness, and with the mouth he (or she) confesses, resulting in salvation.*
> *Romans 10:9, 10*

That's God guarantee to you.[1] I don't care if you have ever done the above before or not. I've fought off doubt on more than one occasion by doing this. Let's do it together, okay? We have just demonstrated faith in God. Once you have done the above with honest sincerity, God guarantees you have been born again, this time of the Spirit. When you are born again, you have made the GREAT ESCAPE. That's even better than, "Beam me up, Scottie."

YOU ARE NOW IN THE KINGDOM OF GOD

> *For He delivered us from the domain (the authority) of darkness, and transferred us to the kingdom of His beloved Son, in whom we have redemption, the forgiveness of sins.*
> *Colossians 1:13, 14*

---

[1] R.C.H. Lenski: St. Paul's Epistle To The Romans, (Minneapolis: Augsburg Publishing House, 1961), pp. 655-657.

THIS PRESCRIPTION PROVIDES
THE FOLLOWING BENEFITS

1. Confidence that hell wasn't created for people, but rather for Satan
2. Confidence that when you are *born again*, you have entered the kingdom of God and have escaped Satan's domain
3. Confidence on how to be *born again* and be certain that you are
4. Confidence that once you are *born again,* you have escaped something far worse than an atomic bomb

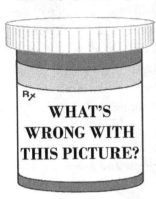

Rx17

For God is not a God of confusion but of peace . . .
1 Corinthians 14:33

WHAT'S WRONG WITH THIS PICTURE?

A new and unusual form of art appeared in the 1990s. I am not sure it's even been given a name. However, this form of art consists of a collection of multicolored dots and spots. When these dots and spots are viewed correctly, they reveal a very distinct picture, or so I've been told. But my response is "What's wrong with this picture? I simply can't see it." Nevertheless, I personally know and trust those who tell me they can see it. So I'm sure that it is there, and I'm confident that I could see it also, if I only took the time to consider it thoroughly.

Communication can be very much like this modern form of art. Daily communication is one of the most difficult processes we humans undertake. Maybe it was different before Babel, but unfortunately, that's the way it is today.

COMMUNICATION HASN'T ALWAYS BEEN A PROBLEM

> *"Come, let Us go down and there confuse their language*, that they may not understand one another's speech."
> *Genesis 11:7*

To help us understand how true this last statement is, let's reflect for a moment on our own lives. Did you ever have a problem communicating with your parents or maybe with your brothers or sisters? How about with a boyfriend or a girlfriend or other close friends? Teachers and coaches as well as employers and supervisors may have provided challenges in communication. Of course, there is the seeming ultimate challenge in communication: communicating with your husband or wife. I'm sure those of you who are married are shaking your heads in agreement at this very moment.

Communication is a two-way street, and problems in communication are a part of everyday life. So it should come as no surprise that communication was also a problem with Jesus and His disciples.

JESUS WASN'T ALWAYS EASY TO UNDERSTAND

> *And Jesus said to them, "Watch out and beware of the leaven of the Pharisees and Saducees." And they (His disciples) began to discuss among themselves, saying, "It is because we took no bread (vv. 6, 7)."* ***"How is it that you do not understand that I did not speak to you concerning bread?*** *But beware of the leaven of the Pharisees and Saducees." Then they understood that He did not say to beware of the leaven of bread, but of the teaching of the Pharisees and Saducees (vv. 11, 12).*
>
> *Matthew 16:6, 7, 11, 12*

This problem in communication occurred even though Jesus was physically present with His disciples. Just think, His disciples could hear the loudness of His voice, its tone, even His inflection and His emphasis. They could also see His gestures and observe His body language. In addition, they were able to experience the communication of His touch. And still, with all these benefits, there were times when they did not understand the meaning of His words.

Today none of these physical benefits are available to His church. Now, consider this. If *the twelve* could be confused by His words when He was still among them, is it possible that we could also misunderstand His meaning in His absence? His disciples had another benefit going for them. Jesus was able to personally clear up their confusion.

JESUS WANTS TO BE UNDERSTOOD

> *But Jesus, aware of this, said, "You men of little faith*, *why do you discuss among yourselves that you have no bread* (v. 8)? *How is it that you do not understand that I did not speak to you concerning bread? But* **beware of the leaven of the Pharisees and Saducees." Then they understood that He did not say to beware of the leaven of bread, but of the teaching of the Pharisees and Saducess** (vv. 11, 12).
> *Matthew 16: 8, 11, 12*

We can see that our level of faith is a factor in our ability to understand what God is saying. However, this is a factor we can control to a considerable degree.

WE CAN INSURE OUR FAITH PROGRESSES

> *So faith comes from hearing* and hearing by **the word of Christ.**
> *Romans 10:17*

We can expect our faith to increase as we become more familiar with what God says in His Word.

Another thing we can see from these verses in Matthew is that Christ wants us to understand what God is saying to us. He was present with *the twelve*, and they allowed Him to help them understand what He said. Jesus doesn't want the Bible, God's word, to be a mystery to any of us.

JESUS PERSONALLY HELPS US UNDERSTAND

> *Now He said to them, "These are My words which I spoke to you while I was still with you, that all things which are written about Me in the Law of Moses and the Prophets*

*and the Psalms must be fulfilled." **Then He opened their minds to understand the Scriptures.***
Luke 24:44, 45

We do not have the benefit of Christ's physical presence, but Jesus did not leave us helpless. He promised to send us a helper, someone who would take His place while He was physically absent.

THE HOLY SPIRIT GIVES US UNDERSTANDING

*"If you love Me, you will keep my commandments. And I will ask the Father and He will give to you another Helper that He may be with you forever (vv. 15, 16). **But the Helper, the Holy Spirit, whom the Father will send in My name, He will teach you all things,** and bring to your remembrance all that I said to you (v. 26)."*
John 14:15, 16, 26

But when He, the Spirit of truth, comes, He will guide you into all the truth; *for He will not speak on His own initiative, but whatever He hears, He will speak; and He will disclose to you what is to come.*
John 16:13

Here, Jesus gives us some great promises of assurance, promises whose fulfillment began no later than fifty days after His crucifixion.

THE HOLY SPIRIT IS HERE THIS VERY MOMENT

And when the day of Pentecost had come, *they were all together in one place (v. 1). **And they were all filled with the Holy Spirit** and began to speak with other tongues, as the Spirit was giving them utterance (v. 4).*
Acts 2:1, 4

According to Christ's promise the person of the Holy Spirit from that moment onward came to be our helper forever. Although He came to be our helper and to guide us into all the truth, still there remain things, that are difficult to understand.

THE HOLY SPIRIT REQUIRES OUR COOPERATION

> As also in all his (Paul's) letters, speaking in them of these things, **in which are some things hard to understand**, which the untaught and the unstable distort, as they do also the rest of the Scriptures, to their own destruction.
> 2 Peter 3:16

Consequently, it is important for each of us to be familiar with the word of God, but not to allow that familiarity to create a false security within us that tells us we know it all, but rather to allow the Holy Spirit to use that familiarity with God's word to teach us all things and to guide us into all the truth.

So let's quickly review what we have just learned:

1. Misunderstanding what God has said can occur. It occurred with Jesus and His disciples, and it can occur today.
2. Jesus does not want His word to be misunderstood.
3. Today His invisible presence is available in the person of the Holy Spirit to help us understand the truth.
4. The Holy Spirit uses Christ's (God's) word to remove confusion and to clear up misunderstandings.
5. When we allow the person of the Holy Spirit to accomplish His purpose our understanding will increase.

Some of us may have recognized what appears to be a contradiction between what God has said in the Old Testament and what Jesus reveals God's nature to be in the New Testament. This very moment, we may be asking ourselves, WHAT'S WRONG WITH THIS PICTURE?

We know misunderstandings can and do occur, so with this fresh in our minds, let's examine some verses that could result in confusion and a potential misunderstanding.

Moses informed the children of Israel that God promises to put sickness upon the disobedient among His people.

DISOBEDIENCE AND SICKNESS GO HAND IN HAND

"But it shall come about, if you will not obey the Lord your God, to observe to do all His commandments and His statutes which I charge you today, that all these curses shall come upon you and overtake you (v. 15). If you are not careful to observe all the words of this Law which are written in this book, to fear this honored and awesome name, the Lord your God, then the Lord will bring extraordinary plagues on you and your descendants, even severe and lasting plagues, and miserable and chronic sickness. And He will bring back on you all the diseases of Egypt of which you were afraid, and they shall cling to you. Also every sickness and every plague which, not written in the book of this law, the Lord will bring on you until you are destroyed (vv. 58-61)."
Deuteronomy 28:15, 58-61

On the other hand, the New Testament informs us that it is the devil's will, not God's will, to oppress us and to make us sick. God's plan has always been for us to be healthy.

OUR BODIES DECLARE GOD'S WILL

"For since the creation of the world His (God's) invisible attributes, His eternal power and divine nature, have been clearly seen, being understood through what has been made, (our bodies), so that they (we) are without excuse."
Romans 1:20

JESUS VISIBLY DEMONSTRATES THE WILL OF THE INVISIBLE CREATOR

And He (Jesus) is the radiance of His (God's) glory and **the exact representation of His nature.** *Hebrews 1:3*

JESUS CAME TO DO GOD'S WILL

Jesus said to them, **"My food is to do the will of Him (God) who sent me,** *and to accomplish His work."* *John 4:34*

JESUS CAME TO PUT THE DEVIL OUT OF BUSINESS

The Son of God (Jesus) appeared for this purpose, **that He might destroy the works of the devil.** *1 John 3:8*

JESUS CAME TO REVERSE THE WORKS OF THE DEVIL

"The thief (the devil) comes only to steal, and kill, and destroy. **I (Jesus) came that they might have life, and might have it abundantly."** *John 10:10*

JESUS HEALED ALL THOSE WHO WERE OPPRESSED BY DEVIL

You know of Jesus of Nazareth, how God anointed Him with the Holy Spirit and power and how **He went about doing good, and healing all who were oppressed by the devil, for God was with Him.** *Acts 10:38*

GOD'S PURPOSE IS TO RESTORE AND NOT TO DESTROY

> *And knowing their thoughts* **He (Jesus) said to them,**
> **"Any kingdom divided against itself is laid waste; and**
> **any city or house divided against itself shall not stand.**
> *And if Satan casts out Satan he is divided against himself;*
> *how then shall his kingdom stand?"*
> *Matthew 12:25, 26*

These last six verses would at first seem to be in conflict with Deuteronomy 28. Did God change His mind?

GOD DOES NOT CHANGE

> *"For I, the Lord, do not change; therefore you, O sons*
> *of Jacob, are not consumed."*
> *Malachi 3:6*

This appears to be an excellent time to remind ourselves that God does not desire for us to be confused.

GOD DESIRES ORDER AND UNDERSTANDING

> *For you can all prophesy one by one, so that all may*
> *learn and all may be exhorted; and the spirits of prophets are*
> *subject to the prophets;* **for God is not a God of confusion**
> *but of peace, as in all the churches of the saints.*
> *1 Corinthians 14:31-33*

God's word informs us that if we are confused or if we misunderstand His word our *faith* is fruitless.

DOUBT CANCELS OUT FAITH

*But let him ask in faith without doubting, **for the one who doubts is like the surf of the sea driven and tossed by the wind. For let not that man expect that he will receive anything from the Lord**, being a double-minded man, unstable in all his ways.*
James 1:6-8

God wants to clear up these types of situations. It's of help to understand that the word *unstable* refers to faith that isn't fully developed.[1]

GOD REWARDS SINCERE-SEEKING HEARTS

*And without faith it is impossible to please Him, for **he who comes to God must believe that He is, and that He is a rewarder of those who seek Him.***
Hebrews 11:6

If we are confused, or if we don't understand God's words, we can still know that He will take care of the matter when we seek Him through His word and expect the help of His Spirit. So we seek.

An examination of the Bible reveals a certain belief was common to all humanity for at least four thousand years. It was widely accepted that wrong or sinful actions could bring about adverse physical consequences that affected the health of the guilty individual. This view can be found beginning with the very first book of the Bible.

---

[1]   W. E. Vine, Expository Dictionary of New Testament Words, (Old Tappan, Fleming H. Company, 1966), p. 175.

GOD-FEARING PEOPLE RECOGNIZED
THE CONSEQUENCES OF SIN

> *And Abraham said of Sarah his wife, "She is my sister." So Abimelech King of Gerar sent and took Sarah. But God came to Abimelech in a dream of the night, and said to him, **"Behold you are a dead man because of the woman whom you have taken, for she is married."***
> *Genesis 20:2, 3*

The Law of Moses and the statutes and ordinances made it very clear to the nation of Israel that there is a connection between sinful actions and physical well-being. Thus, in the time of Christ, we see this belief voiced by Christ's own disciples.

THE PEOPLE OF GOD HELD THIS BELIEF

> *And His disciples asked Him, saying, **"Rabbi, who sinned, this man or his parents, that he should be born blind?"***
> *John 9:2*

It should be considered that Jesus didn't say the individual's condition wasn't the result of sin but rather that the works of God might be displayed in him (John 9:3).

Finally, we see in the time of Paul this same view was held by those on the island of Malta.

THE HEATHEN ACCEPTED SIN AND ITS CONSEQUENCES

> *But when Paul had gathered a bundle of sticks and laid them on the fire, a viper came out because of the heat, and fastened on his hand. And when the natives saw the creature hanging from his hand, they began saying to one another, **"Undoubtedly this man is a murderer, and though he***

*has been saved from the sea, justice has not allowed him
to live."*
Acts 28:3, 4

We have seen this belief among the people of God (John 9:2), among the God-fearing (Genesis 20:2, 3), and among the ungodly (Acts 28:3, 4). This view was voiced throughout the biblical world. It is a view that did not seem to disturb anyone. It is a view that simply acknowledged that God or *justice* had their own way of dealing with wrong or sin. But as Christians we must know the will of God. We cannot have faith regarding a situation until we know the will of God. We cannot be wondering if it is or isn't God's will that we do or not do a certain thing, or if God will or won't do a certain thing. Once we know God's will, what God says about something, then the result becomes predictable. Why? Because His will does not change.

GOD WILL NOT CHANGE HIS WILL

Forever, O Lord, ***Thy word is settled in heaven.***
Psalm 119:89

When we know God's will, we no longer need to include the phrase, *If it be Thy will.* So let us continue to seek for and search out God's will.

THIS PRESCRIPTION PROVIDES
THE FOLLOWING BENEFIT

1. Confidence that obedience and forgiveness promotes good health

The following is the first of 12 case studies. One study will appear at the conclusion of Rx 17 through Rx 28. Each study is an factual event, and it will be immediately followed by a Q & A (question and answer) section designed to assist the reader in discovering what faith looked like in each case study.

CASE STUDIES

NO.1

WHO'S THE HEALER?

I was in my first semester at LIFE Bible College in Los Angeles. It was a Friday, and we were having chapel. That day we had a guest evangelist, who was telling us about our miracle-working God. At the end of the chapel time, the dean stepped forward and announced if there was anyone present with a physical need they could remain for prayer and ministry. I didn't have a need, but I decided to stay. Several miracles occurred, and then I noticed a classmate of mine had also remained. He was a veteran who walked with a noticeable limp.

When it was his opportunity to speak to the evangelist, he was greeted with, "You have one leg shorter than the other!" I immediately thought, *now, that didn't require a prophet.* Then the evangelist quickly added, "I'm going to pray for you, and the Lord is going to restore your leg. Sit down!" My classmate sat on a chair, and then he was asked to extend his legs. One leg was clearly two inches shorter than the other leg. But what happened next was the biggest shock I had experienced in my life, up to that point.

Before the evangelist said another word, or had a chance to lay a hand on my classmate and pray, the shorter leg moved forward until it was equal to the other leg in length. I was no more than four feet removed from him, and he just sat there with both legs extended and equal in length. The remaining student body, and the faculty as well, all watched in amazement, and then everyone spontaneously broke out in praise to God.

Q & A (questions and answers)

1. Do you **see** any of the three definitions of **faith** as pointed out in Rx 14? Explain your answer

2. Read or review: Rx 11

3. Read, consider, and discuss (if possible): Exodus 15:26, Psalms 107:20, Romans 10:17.

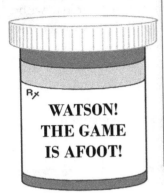

Rx18

INSTRUCTIONS

He made known to us the mystery of His will, according to His kind intention which He purposed in Him.
Ephesians 1:9

I was about ten years old when I made a discovery that impacted my life forever. Surprise, it wasn't Jesus. Bigger surprise, it wasn't girls either. It was nothing less than the incredible Sherlock Holmes. One evening I was watching TV, and I stumbled across a Sherlock Holmes mystery staring Basil Rathbone as Holmes and Nigel Bruce as the lovable Dr. Watson. I was hooked instantly. I not only became a fan of Sir Arthur Conan Doyle's Sherlock Holmes, but I also became acutely aware of the fact that most of us have a *gift* for overlooking very obvious clues in our lives. This is a *gift* our third grandchild, Dara didn't seem to receive. She doesn't miss a thing.

The Bible uses the word mystery on several occasions. It normally refers to something that was once hidden but is now revealed.[1] The mystery of divine healing or the fact that God wants to heal all of us has been revealed in His word, but the clues that reveal that truth can easily overlooked. However, once they are discovered, it is hard to imagine how they could have been overlooked for so long. With that in mind, let us examine the life of Job for clues to that end.

The life of Job provides us with several important clues to open our understanding. But before we discover these clues, let's reacquaint ourselves with the book of Job. It is generally accepted that Job lived

---

1   W. E. Vine, *Expository Dictionary of New Testament Words*, (Old Tappan, Fleming H. Company, 1966), p. 97.

before the time of Moses.[2] Consequently, he was not familiar with the laws, statues, and ordinances of God. Job did not live under the Law, nor was he aware of the stipulated blessings and curses mentioned in the Law. Nevertheless, it is obvious he recognized God and lived and worshipped in a manner pleasing to God.

LIVING ACCORDING TO THE LAW WITHOUT KNOWING THE LAW

> *For when Gentiles who do not have the Law do instinctively the things of the Law, these, not having the Law are a law to themselves, in that they show the work of the Law written in their hearts,* their conscience bearing witness, and their thoughts alternately accusing or else defending them.
> Romans 2:14, 15

It is important to realize that even though God had not yet manifested His will through the means of the Old Testament to Israel, His will nonetheless was being demonstrated in Job's life. God had not revealed to Job through His spoken or written word the consequences of different attitudes and actions or different ways of worshipping God. Yet God was still the same unchanging God. He still was rewarding those who sought and feared Him. Thus, a review of Job's life will enlighten us to several important truths that were in operation in his day, and in our day as well. Remember that this was before the time of Moses. These revelations of the truth concerning God and His nature will help us have a better understanding of some of God's words as we see them in the Law. They should remove some of the seeming contradictions between the God of the Old Testament and the God of the New Testament, who are the same God.

The first thing we learn is that Job was a very special person.

---

[2]   Finis Dake, Dake's Annotated Reference Bible, The New Testament, ((Lawrenceville, Dake Publishing, Inc., 2014), p. 805.

A MAN CAN LIVE A BLAMELESS LIFE

> *There was a man in the land of Uz, whose name was Job, and **that man was blameless, upright, fearing God, and turning away from evil.***
> *Job 1:1*

Next, we learn that such an individual troubles Satan greatly because he is unable to touch him.

GOD PROTECTS THOSE WHO LIVE RIGHTEOUSLY

> *And the Lord said to Satan, "Have you considered my servant Job? For there is no one like him on the earth, a blameless and upright man, fearing God and turning away from evil." **Then Satan answered the Lord, "Does Job fear God for nothing? Hast Thou not made a hedge about him and his house and all that he has, on every side?** Thou hast blessed the works of his hands, and his possessions have increased in the land."*
> *Job 1:8-10*

We can also see that Satan hates every blessing God provides to us because the only way Satan can rob a person who turns away from evil is by obtaining God's permission.

SATAN NEEDS GOD'S PERMISSION
TO TOUCH THE BLAMELESS

> *"But put forth Thy hand now and touch all that he (Job) has; he will surely curse Thee to Thy face." **Then the Lord said to Satan, "Behold, all that he has is in your power only do not put forth your hand on him."** So Satan departed from the presence of the Lord.*
> *Job 1:11, 12*

If you are not convinced of this last statement, then consider this:

DEMONS HAD TO ASK FOR JESUS' PERMISSION TO ENTER PIGS

> *And behold, they (the demons) cried out, saying, "What do we have to do with You, Son of God? Have You come here to torment us before the time?" Now there was at a distance from them a herd of many swine feeding. And **the demons began to entreat (implore) Him, saying, "If You are going to send us out, send us into the herd of swine."** And He said to them, "Begone!" (permission granted). And they came out, and went into the swine, and behold, the whole herd rushed down the steep bank into the sea and perished in the waters. Matthew 8:29-32*

Satan realizes that God puts a hedge of protection around the blameless. Satan knows God's power is capable of defending that perimeter against any penetration. Satan understands there is no way he can touch Job as long as God's power is protecting him, so Satan tries to tempt God to do the very thing Satan desires to do. God wants us to know that He does not turn His power against the blameless. It is not His will or the purpose of His kingdom to harm His own. God wants us to know who is our real enemy. He wants us to understand that it is Satan and his kingdom that desires us harm. It is Satan's kingdom that such harm serves. So God makes an exception as well as an example of Job. God draws back His protective hedge and power around Job to prove a point once and for all time. Now Satan is forced to expose and express his will for mankind. What decision does he make? Satan strips Job of all his material blessings, including his sons and daughters (Job 1:13-19). However, Satan has something more sinister in mind than just robbing Job of his possessions.

SATAN WANTS JOB (US) TO BLAME GOD

*"**Through all this Job did not** sin or did he **blame God**."*
Job 1:22

Satan enjoyed every second of the plundering that occurred in Job's life. Why did Satan attack Job so viciously? Was it simply to remove God's blessings? Most certainly not! Satan is aware of our weaknesses. He realizes the impact that stress and grief has on mankind. He is counting on the overwhelming stress and grief that Job is experiencing to produce what Satan desires most. Satan won't be satisfied until Job or God's children curse God for their adversity. Satan wants us to think that our adversity is God's fault. Yes, God's will.

Now we come to an extremely important piece of information. It was Satan's will that stripped Job of his family and possessions, but it was God who accepted the responsibility for the loss.

GOD SAYS HE WAS RESPONSIBLE FOR JOB'S ADVERSITY

*And the Lord said to Satan, "Have you considered My servant Job? For there is no one like him on the earth, a blameless and upright man fearing God and turning away from evil. And he still holds his integrity, **although you incited Me against him,** to ruin him without cause."*
Job 2:3

God has proven His point. He didn't make Satan touch Job. That was Satan's will. Nevertheless, God accepted the responsibility because He granted Satan permission.

If Satan needs God's permission before he can touch a blameless man's possessions, it should come as no shock that he needs God's permission before he can ever touch the body or mind of a person who is blameless and upright and fearing God and turning away from evil.

SATAN DOESN'T GIVE UP EASILY

> *And Satan answered the Lord and said, "Skin for skin!* *Yes, all that a man has he will give for his life. However, put* *forth Thy hand, now and touch his bone and his flesh; He* *will curse Thee to Thy face."* **So the Lord said to Satan,** **"Behold, he is in your power, only spare his life." Then** **Satan went out from the presence of the Lord, and smote** **Job with sore boils from the sole of his foot to the crown** **of his head.**
> *Job 2:4-7*

Here we see Satan tempting God to turn His power against His own. Satan cannot exercise his power against the blameless, and God always refuses to be the servant of evil.

GOD CANNOT BE TEMPTED

> *Let no one say when He is tempted, "I am tempted by* *God;" for* **God cannot be tempted by evil,** *and He Himself* *does not tempt anyone.*
> *James 1:13*

Yet one more time, God does not remove but rather retracts His protection around Job, so Satan *according to his own words* can take his "best shot." Satan knows that man values his life and his health above all that he has. Satan also knows that deep down in the hearts of all men they recognize the reality of a creative God. This is something that Satan never overlooks. However, he will always take the risk, given the opportunity, thinking man will curse or blame God rather than turn to God in his moment of greatest need. Satan also knows that those we love and those who love us are the ones we expect to have the most understanding. Consequently, they are the ones who can disappoint us the most. How does Job react to Satan's all-out attack?

JOB REFUSES TO CURSE GOD

> *Then his (Job's) wife said to him, "Do you still hold fast your integrity? Curse God and die!" But he (Job) said to her, "You speak as one of the foolish women speaks. Shall we indeed accept good from God and not accept adversity?"* **In all this Job did not sin with his lips.**
> *Job 2:9, 10*

Job may not have understood why things were the way they were, but he recognized it would be foolish for his character and his testimony to be dependent upon his condition.

Satan loves to have others do his work for him. Here, Job's wife was a potential accessory. Instead of encouraging her husband, she attempted to have him do the very thing Satan wanted him to do, curse God. Tell God that He's responsible for your condition, and do it with an attitude. Then just die! Give up! What's the point! Where God refuses to be the servant of Satan, others do so unaware.

But the truth we need to firmly establish in our hearts and minds is that Satan is responsible for Job's physical condition, as well as, his adversity. God does not turn His power upon His own. When this truth has taken root in our being, we will be very careful how we use the phrase "If it be God's will." Does our testimony depend upon our condition, be it sick or healthy, or does it depend upon God's word?

We must remember, Job was not aware of Moses or the Ten Commandments. Job was not aware of God's promised blessings or curses in response to obedience or disobedience to God's word. However, Job did accept the all-powerful Creator, and he understood his position in relationship to such an awesome God. With his limited knowledge and understanding, Job, in essence said, "How can I accept health from God and not sickness?" In his own way, and with his limited understanding, Job was saying, "If it's God's will, then I will be healed." This makes it easier to understand why Job's example troubled God so greatly.

GOD REALIZED JOB'S LIMITED UNDERSTANDING

And he (Job) still holds his integrity, although you incited
*Me against him, to ruin him **without cause.***
Job 2:3

Where there is no sin, where one is blameless, then there is no cause or reason for an individual to suffer loss or sickness. Satan needs a reason before he can touch a Christian.

Today, unlike Job, we have available the full revelation of God's written word as it appears in the Christian Bible. Our understanding does not have to be limited. Our integrity should be at least equal to that of Job's, and we should not sin with our lips. That is, whatever is happening to us should not change who we are. Our testimony should always echo God's will as revealed in His word. Unfortunately, many of us have innocently used the phrase, *If it's God's will, then I will be healed. If it's God's will,* is a valid expression in circumstances where God's will has not already been revealed, however, we should never find ourselves using it in regards to healing. We have clearly seen in God's word that it is His will that we be healthy and prosper in body, soul, and spirit. Thus saying, "If it's God's will, then I will be healed" is like saying, "If it's God's will, then I will confess my sin," or saying "If it's God's will, then I will repent of my sin," or saying "If it's God's will, then I will ask for forgiveness." The phrase, *If it's God's will, then I will be healed* should sound just as ridiculous as these other phrases.

I have no problem imagining Satan presenting himself before God and saying, "Did You hear your kid, God? He just blamed you for his adversity. He just said, 'If it's God's will, then I will be healed.' Your kid actually believes it's Your will he is (still) sick. I win, you lose God! There is nothing You can do about it, because he is convinced it must be Your will that he continues to suffer. Let me tell You, God, I really like it. I mean, I really, really like it! If I could, I would love it! You know what I mean, God? Ha. Ha, Ha!"

If you are a Christian, that is, if you have accepted the sacrifice of Jesus Christ as payment in full to God for your sinful nature and actions, then God has a marvelous plan for your life and your everlasting future. But guess what! Satan also has a plan for your life. Only, Satan's plan is not the plan you would knowingly choose.

I learned the three R's when I was in grade school. You know, Reading, wRiting and aRithmatic. Well, in Satan's kingdom, there are the three P's: Power, Pain, and Permission. Satan has all the power he needs to produce more pain and suffering than any of us want to experience. Unfortunately, many of us have already experienced a portion of that suffering, and some of us at this moment are experiencing that pain. What many of us have not realized is that when we became a blood-bought, born-again Christian, *a praise the Lord*, thank You Jesus, change occurred. We entered God's kingdom, and God's final judgment regarding our qualification to spend forever with Him has been stamped *blameless*. You're now in the same category as Job, only God doesn't need any more exceptions or examples.

CONDEMNATION HAS BEEN REMOVED

"But now having been freed from sin and enslaved to God, you derive your benefit, resulting in sanctification, and the outcome, eternal life."
Romans 6:22

There is therefore now no condemnation for those who are in Christ Jesus.
Romans 8:1

A Christian is *blameless* and belongs to God. A Christian is the property of God.

You asked, "What's wrong with this picture?" Well, it needed to be focused. We simply have a tendency to concentrate on what appears as distortion. Of course, when we do that, we can miss the big picture. Our diseases result from our disobedience and Satan's opportunistic designs, and not God's direct action. In a manner of speaking, through disobedience we place the order, and Satan delivers the goods.

SINFUL ACTIONS BRING THE CURSES OF SICKNESS

> *"**But it shall come about, if you will not obey** the Lord your God, to observe to do all His commandants and His statutes with which I charge you today, that **these curses shall come upon you and overtake you.**"*
> *Deuteronomy 28:15*

It leaves me speechless to realize that God accepts the responsibility for Job's sickness (etc.), even though, He personally does not put sickness upon His children. Rather, He put all the diseases His children could ever bear upon His unique Son, Jesus.

JESUS SUFFERED OUR CURSES AND SICKNESSES

> ***Christ redeemed us from the curse of the Law, having become a curse for us*** - *for it is written, "Cursed is everyone who hangs on a tree."*
> *Galatians 3:13*

When Jesus was crucified on a wooden cross fashioned from a tree, He bore the curse of the Law. Do you want to carry your sins around with you the rest of your life and into eternity? Of course not! Jesus' blood makes it possible to be free from our sin.

JESUS' BLOOD CLEANSES FROM SIN

> *If we say that we have fellowship with Him and yet walk in darkness, we lie and do not practice the truth; But if we walk in the light as He Himself is in the light, we have fellowship with one another, and **the blood of Jesus His Son cleanses us from all sins.***
> *1 John 1:6, 7*

None of us want to carry our sins around, so why would anyone want to carry the consequences of those sins around? Why would any of us want to bear our sickness? Jesus was cursed for us. His body bore the curses that would (or have) come upon us and overtake (or have overtaken) us? None of us have to bear them.

JESUS TOOK OUR SINS AND OUR SICKNESSES

> *But He was pierced through for our transgressions, He was crushed for our iniquities; the chastening for our well-being fell upon Him, and **by His scourging we are healed**.*
> *Isaiah 53:5*

God decided that His Son would be the final sacrifice. Jesus would bear the sin and the sickness of the world.

JESUS THE FINAL SACRIFICE

> *The next day he (John the Baptist) saw Jesus coming to him, and said, **"Behold, the Lamb of God who takes away the sin of the world."***
> *John 1:29*

The authority for sickness emanates from sin, but when sin is no longer present, sickness no longer has any authority or right to remain.

A PARDON FROM SIN AND A RIGHT TO BE HEALED

> ***Bless the Lord, O my soul,*** *and forget none of His benefits;* ***Who pardons all your iniquities; who heals all your diseases.***
> *Psalm 103:2, 3*

God's plan is to completely restore our lives from the adverse effects of sin. This is something our faith can use as an anchor.

GOD WILL NOT CHANGE HIS PLAN

Forever, O Lord, ***Thy word is settled*** *in Heaven.*
Psalm 119:89

It has been previously stated that Satan has all the power and all the pain he requires to make man's life miserable. But for those of us who have repented of our sins and accepted Jesus as our curse-bearer, Satan's authority or right has been canceled. Asking for daily forgiveness frustrates Satan to the max because sin is his permission slip. Satan requires permission to touch our minds or our bodies. On the other hand, Satan does not have to ask for permission to touch a non-Christian. A nonbeliever is not playing on a level playing field versus Satan. One must realize that Satan is far more powerful than mere man. Satan can touch a non-Christian's mind or body when-ever he chooses. So if anyone thinks "mind over matter" works, then they are saying either Satan doesn't exist or that they are capable of overpowering Satan's kingdom's designs. Lots of luck!

How long could any of us resist Satan in our own power? But then maybe someone is thinking, "I don't even believe in a God or Satan. I don't believe the Bible is God's word, and I especially don't believe Jesus is the Son of God or that He died for my sins or that He rose from the grave, and guess what? I've never had a sick day in my entire life!" If these kinds of thoughts are running through your mind, I would like to ask you if you have ever seen a cat *toy* with a mouse? I mean this kindly, but if you are thinking something like the above, then you are acting like your name is Mickey, and you spend a great deal of time in Anaheim, California, or wherever else Disneyland exists.

The only way any of us can be victorious over the devil is to have the help of someone who is more powerful. A Christian has the power and authority of God available to him in the name of Jesus and in the person of the Holy Spirit. We have seen that Jesus promised the same Holy Spirit who was with Him would be present with us forever.

THE HOLY SPIRIT IS ALWAYS WITH US

> *If you love Me, you will keep My commandments. And* ***I will give you another Helper, that He may be with you forever.***
> *John 14:15, 16*

THE SPIRIT OF JESUS IS MORE POWERFUL THAN SATAN

> *And amazement came upon them all, and they began discussing with one another, saying, "What is this message?* ***For with authority and power He commands the unclean spirits and they come out."***
> *Luke 4:36*

Maybe you're not certain you are a Christian, but you're certain of one thing: you want to be a Christian. When we become a Christian, it is something far more than a decision to join a particular religious movement. It is a life-creating experience that occurs in our spirit, and it is brought about through the person of the Holy Spirit.

THE HOLY SPIRIT BRINGS NEW LIFE

> *"That which is born of flesh is flesh, and* ***that which is born of the Spirit is spirit."***
> *John 3:6*

It is a very special moment that occurs between you and the living God. It is a moment all heaven eagerly awaits.

ALL HEAVEN IS ON YOUR SIDE

*"In the same way, I tell you, **there is joy in the presence of the angels of God over one sinner who repents.***"*
Luke 15:10

It is a moment in time that every Christian has experienced. Each of us experiences a moment of physical birth, so each Christian experiences a specific moment of spiritual birth. When we experienced physical birth we left the darkness of our mother's womb and entered the light of day, but when we experience the moment of our spiritual birth, we leave the darkness of this world and Satan's kingdom, and enter the kingdom of God and His light. Now we have a bright new future, and our former life is behind us.

A CHRISTIAN HAS A NEW LIFE

Therefore if any man is in Christ, *he is a new creature; the old things passed away;* ***behold new things have come.***
2 Corinthians 5:17

One's moment of physical birth could have occurred without any outside help. It could have happened with just our mother and ourself being present. However, for most of us there was likely someone else present to assist. Maybe your moment of spiritual birth is at hand. If so, I would like to offer you what I have found to be some simple but helpful suggestions. I trust they will assist you through your own personal life-transforming, power-releasing, new birth experience.

A SPIRITUAL MIDWIFE'S ADVICE

1. Be honest with yourself and admit you have sinned against God.

2. Now admit to God that you have sinned against Him.

3. Tell God you recognize Jesus received the punishment you deserve for your sin.

4. Let God know you realize the blood of Jesus cleansed you from all your unrighteousness and that His body bore the curses of your sickness.

5. Inform God that you are truly sorry for your former life and that you repent of it. Tell Him your heart is in agreement with His will for your life and that you desire a life that is free from the power of sin and the curses of sickness.

6. Ask God to forgive your sin and to deliver you from the power of sin and to heal you fully (both mentally and physically).

7. Tell God you receive His forgiveness, His deliverance and His healing, in Jesus name.

8. Ask Him to send you the person of the Holy Spirit with all the power and authority of the kingdom of God to enforce your request and God's will for your life.

9. Thank Him for His forgiveness, His deliverance, His healing and the presence of His Spirit.

10. And most of all, thank Him for making you one of His children.

God cherishes your prayer of repentance and your request for His outside help. He certainly has initiated a new birth in your spirit. Now, what kind of mother would leave her newborn alone? Your Heavenly Father isn't going to leave you alone. You need His nurturing and care to become all you are to become in Him. Talk to Him all the time. Know His Spirit is with you always. Maintain your thankful heart. Get to know Him better each day as you read your Bible. If you don't have a Bible, get one as soon as possible.

Now, you also have a new spiritual family. Meet your new brothers and sisters in Christ. Find a church home where you know you are learning God's word. The abundance of denominations within the Christian church testifies that groups of believers slightly disagree on what God has said in His word. This fact serves to illustrate the problem of communication and understanding mentioned in a previous prescription. So be careful not to let anyone persuade you that God isn't all you have come to believe Him to be. Your heavenly Father has a great future for you beginning now. Listen to the person of the Holy Spirit. He is God's presence with you. He will personally teach you God's word and help you discover God's plan for your life. And remember the person of the Holy Spirit will never tell you anything that cannot be found in the Bible.

Share your new life with your friends and acquaintances. God loves them also, and He has an exciting plan and future for them. Tell them what God has done for you and how He has changed you. If they knew you before, they will notice the change. They will want to know what brought about your physical or emotional changes. Remember, Jesus made the difference and continues to make the difference.

CHRISTIANS HAVE SOMETHING TO SAY

> *I will give thanks to the Lord with all my heart;* ***I will tell of all Thy wonders.***
> *Psalm 9:1*

THIS PRESCRIPTION PROVIDES
THE FOLLOWING BENEFIT

1. Confidence that we need to be forgiven of daily sin
2. Confidence that Satan not God uses sin as a *permission slip* to attack us
3. Confidence that daily forgiveness cancels out Satan's permission slip

CASE STUDIES

NO.2

CAN GOD ANSWER A SELFISH PRAYER?

It was the spring of my freshman year at Bible College, and I had decided to try out for the school baseball team. There I was a twenty-eight year-old freshman competing with young men, like Dale Downs, who were in their late teens and early twenties. I hadn't played hardball in nearly ten years. I knew this wasn't going to be easy, but I really wanted to play, and I wanted to be a starter. I was fielding third base one day during batting practice when the hitter lined a shot that exploded in the dirt directly in front of my right leg. I was unable to react in time to glove the ball, and it slammed against my shinbone. I hit the ground with a *thud* and rolled off the field rubbing my leg. I was in considerable pain, and I could feel a knot swelling on my leg. I knew a blood clot of this nature would mean I would be out for as long as two weeks.

So I began to pray out loud. I repeated over and over, "By His stripes I've been healed." I kept rubbing, but there was no change. In fact, the knot seemed to be getting larger. Then a thought entered my mind, *Do you really believe that?* I knew that thought wasn't coming from me. I thought about it for a moment, and then I realized that if I did believe it, I would have to act like I believed it. However, I also knew if I stood up and the clot was still there, the pain would be unbearable. Could this have been fear? Well, it was rubber-meets-the-road time, and I had to make a decision. Would it be doubt or faith? I couldn't find the courage or faith to stand up in the normal manner. That would take too long, so I laid on my back, raised both legs, arched by back, and kicked to my feet. My eyes were fixed on my leg as I landed with both feet on the ground. My soul erupted with joy as I watched the clot instantly shrink and then disappear. I felt no pain at all. There was only a small red mark left as a reminder of the incident.

Q & A (questions and answers)

1. Do you **see** any of the three definitions of **faith** as pointed out in Rx 14? Explain your answer.

2. Read or review: Rx 12

3. Read, consider, and discuss (if possible): Hebrews 11:1

Rx19

**WHO GOOFED?
I'VE GOT
TO KNOW**

**Be angry and do not sin . . .
And do not give the devil an
opportunity.
Ephesians 4:26, 27**

Some of you who have been Christians for some time might be thinking, "Wait a minute. Slow down. When I accepted Jesus as my personal Savior, I was declared blameless, right? Now, if I was declared blameless, doesn't that mean Satan needs permission before he can ever touch me, mentally or physically? Well then, something is definitely wrong, because I am suffering! I thought that Satan couldn't touch the blameless. Am I really a Christian? **WHO GOOFED? I'VE GOT TO KNOW!**

If you happen to be suffering, be it mentally or physically, and you don't seem to be recovering, that doesn't mean you are not a Christian. Can you say or have you said that, "Jesus is Lord?" Do you really believe God raised Him from the dead? If so, then:

YOU ARE A CHRISTIAN

> *If you confess with your mouth Jesus as Lord, and believe in your heart that God raised Him from the dead, you shall be saved;* for with the heart man believes, resulting in righteousness, and with the mouth he confesses, resulting in salvation.
> Romans 10:9, 10

"Okay, I'm certain that I am a Christian, but would someone please explain how I can be blameless and still not recover from my illness?"

This is precisely the question as well as the seeming conflict that must be resolved. Let us begin by paraphrasing the words of Sherlock Holmes: "When all other solutions have been eliminated, whatever remains, no matter how improbable, must be the answer."

I have very fond memories of my youth. I recall that between the ages of eight and eleven a few of the kids on our block would frequently go to the Saturday matinee. Believe it or not, admission was only nine cents for kids under twelve-years old. In addition, we saw a double feature. Anyway, it was shortly after World War II, and the Korean conflict had just begun. So as you can imagine, war movies were still popular. Needless to say, we saw our fair share of them. However, it was some years later that I saw such a movie titled *Kelly's Heroes*. This was a secular movie, but it actually helped me answer the question, "How can a Christian become afflicted and not recover?"

Hopefully, it will help you as well. *Kelly's Heroes* takes place in Europe after D-day, and it contains a scene where a squad of American soldiers works its way into a clearing only to find themselves in the midst of a German minefield. As you know, a minefield is a deceptive and silent, yet very deadly form of warfare. To the casual observer, there doesn't appear to be any danger, however, the next step could result in loss of limb or life. In this movie, one unfortunate GI stepped on a mine, and immediately every other soldier was aware of their precarious situation.

In many ways, the Old Testament serves notice to the Christian of the presence of danger, just as the detonated mine served to the GIs in *Kelly's Heroes*.

SIN WILL DETONATE SPIRITUAL MINES

For I do not want you to be unaware, brethren, that our fathers were all under the cloud, and all passed through the sea; and all were baptized into Moses in the cloud and

in the sea (vv. 1, 2); *Nevertheless, with most of them God was not well-pleased; for they were laid low in the wilderness.* **Now these things happened as examples for us, so that we should not crave evil things, as they also craved** (vv. 5, 6). **and they were written for our instruction, upon whom the ends of the ages have come** (v. 11).
1 Corinthians 10:1, 2, 5, 6, 11

The land mines that were used during World War II obviously didn't care if you were American or German, friend or foe, Christian or non-Christian. If you stepped on a mine, it accomplished its purpose.

THE PURPOSE OF THE ENEMY

The thief (our enemy, Satan) comes only to steal, and kill, and destroy.
John 10:10

We know that Satan is our enemy and he must not be overlooked.

WATCH OUT FOR THE ENEMY

But whom you forgive anything, I (Paul) forgive also; for indeed what I have forgiven, if I have forgiven anything, I did it for your sakes in the presence of Christ. **In order that no advantage be taken of us by Satan;** *for we are not ignorant of his schemes.*
2 Corinthians 2:10, 11

Unfortunately, Satan isn't our only problem. There is another opponent, that dwells even closer.

THE HUMAN RACE LIVES IN A MINE FIELD

For the flesh sets its desires against the Spirit, and the Spirit against the flesh; for these are in opposition to one another, so that you may not do the things that you please. Galatians 5:17

But I see a different law in the members of my body, waging war against the law of my mind, and making me a prisoner of the law of sin which is in my members. Romans 7:23

The descendants of Adam, the human race, you and I, are *magnetized* toward sin. The sin of Adam, the original sin, not only brought about spiritual death and separation from God it also made us citizens of Satan's kingdom. It in addition left us with bodies that crave just the opposite of God's laws for a sound, healthy body. The nature of our flesh is such that it can never co-exist with God eternally.

DEATH: THE ONLY SOLUTION FOR REBELLIOUS FLESH

Then the Lord God said, "Behold the man has become like one of Us, knowing good and evil; and now, lest he stretch out his hand, and take also from the tree of life, and eat, and live forever (v. 22)." So, He drove the man out; and at the east of the garden of Eden He stationed the cherubim, and the flaming sword which turned every direction, to guard the way of the tree of life (v. 24). Genesis 3:22, 24

This flesh we live in is the very reason we must die, but as we have already seen, physical death does not require the assistance of Satan or his sicknesses. Of course, he always welcomes permission and the opportunity to lend his expertise for our moment of physical death.

All of us realize we have stepped on our fair share of spiritual mines before we received Jesus as our personal Savior.

ALL OF US HAVE SINNED

> **For all have sinned** and fall short of the glory of God.
> Romans 3:23

And we know our flesh is capable of sin after we become Christians.

CHRISTIANS CAN STILL SIN

> **If we say that we have no sin, we are deceiving ourselves,** and the truth is not in us.
> 1 John 1:8

Whenever sin is committed, the *blameless* light is turned off. Satan couldn't touch Job without God's permission. Job was blameless according to God. But when we sin Satan is given an opportunity. The *permission granted* light is then turned on, and Satan loves to personally inform God of our current status.

SATAN: THE ACCUSER OF CHRISTIANS

> And the great dragon was thrown down, the serpent of old, which is called the devil and Satan, who deceives the whole world; he was thrown down to the earth, and his angels were thrown down with him. And I heard a loud voice in Heaven, saying, "Now the salvation, and the power, and the kingdom of God and the authority of His Christ have come, for **the accuser of our brethren has been thrown down, who accuses them before our God day and night."**
> Revelations 12:9, 10

If the *permission granted* light is on, Satan will accuse us and obtain the permission required to touch our minds and bodies. This is a light we have frequently turned on in the past and maybe even in the not-so-distant past. It is a light that must be turned off. This is a subject that we will deal with specifically in Rx 21 and 22, I HATE IT WHEN THEY DO THAT and IF AT FIRST YOU DON'T SUCCEED, FOLLOW INSTRUCTIONS.

WHO GOOFED? I'VE GOT TO KNOW! Unfortunately you, and I goof every time we violate God's laws. In the movie *Kelly's Heroes*, one brave soldier recognized what had to be done, so he very carefully advanced from his position and clearly marked each mine he encountered. Finally, he avoided each mine and safely escaped danger. Soon the remaining members of his squad followed his trail, and everyone escaped danger.

God's incredible love and desire for us to be healthy in every way, spiritually, emotionally, and physically, motivated Him to clearly mark and identify each threat to our well-being. Our earthly bodies, which amount to spiritual mine fields, if left undisciplined, would work against our best interest. However, as members of *God's squad*, we are able to follow God's trail to safety.

THE TRAIL TO SAFETY

> *Thy word is a lamp to my feet, and a light to my* *path.* *I have sworn, and I will confirm it, that I will keep thy righteous ordinances.*
> *Psalm 119: 105, 106*

THIS PRESCRIPTION PROVIDES
THE FOLLOWING BENEFIT

1. Confidence that if we follow our physician's (Jesus') instructions, we will avoid a lot of problems

CASE STUDIES

HAS GOD'S MINISTRY CHANGED?

NO.3

My wife and I during our early ministry had become acquainted with an evangelist by the name of Albie Pearson. We learned he was going to be the guest speaker at a youth service not far from where we lived. So we decided we would attend, and perhaps we would get a chance to see him afterward.

Two weeks before this service, I had been reading in the gospels, and I found myself focusing on instances where Jesus would cast out a demon. Finally, I asked God to allow me to see this happen.

The evening of the service, Albie spoke from the Old Testament about idolatry, witchcraft, drugs, etc. The service didn't seem to last very long, and only one person, a young boy, went forward in response to the message. He and Albie appeared to be talking when the boy fell to the floor like his legs had been cut out from underneath him. Soon Lu and I found ourselves in a rear room of the church along with the boy and two gentlemen we had never seen before. One gentleman was on each side of the boy, who was rolling franticly back and forth on the floor. At first, I thought the gentlemen were speaking to the boy, who was only twelve years-old, but then I became aware of the fact that they were addressing an evil presence and commanding it to leave in Jesus's name. Forty-five minutes, later nine different evil spirits had been identified. Each one had gained access to the boy's life through unrecognized and unrepentant sin. Soon I found myself waring right beside my Christian brothers and using the name of Jesus. One by one, each spirit surrendered to that name, and when all nine were gone, the boy appeared totally free and able to praise God.

Q & A (questions and answers)

1. Do you **see** any of the three definitions of **faith** as pointed out in Rx 14? Explain your answer.

2. Read or review Rx 7 and 15.

3. Read, consider, and discuss (if possible): Matthew 4:17, Matthew 12:28, Mark 16:17, 18, Romans 6:16

Rx20

Rx

HEY, DOC!
WHO'S SIDE
ARE YOU ON?

I had the opportunity to obtain a degree in both theology and pharmacy; however, most of my professional life has been spent in the latter endeavor. Consequently I've had the good fortune to get to know many different physicians. I certainly hold their profession with the utmost respect. The motivation and efforts of these individuals, as well as all those in the health field is to see people restored to good health and to remain sound mentally and physically. Their expertise is to assist in healing and the prevention of disease.

Who could argue that these motivations and efforts do not align with God's own motivation and ministry?

GOD'S WILL IS THAT YOU BE HEALTHY

*You know of **Jesus of Nazareth**, how God anointed Him with the Holy Spirit and with power, and how He **went about doing good, and healing all who were oppressed by the devil; for God was with Him.***
Acts 10:38

The medical profession and technology have advanced greatly over the last one hundred years. Today, if a mental or physical condition has a name, then there is a specialist to treat that condition. Yet with all the improvements this last century has seen, people still suffer and die from numerous conditions and diseases that have no known cures. In this regard the twentieth-century was very similar to the first-century.

PHYSICIANS CAN ONLY DO SO MUCH

> *And a woman who had a hemorrhage for twelve years,*
> **And had endured much at the hands of many physicians,**
> **and had spent all that she had and was not helped at all,**
> *but rather had grown worse. After hearing about Jesus, came up*
> *in the crowd behind Him, and touched His cloak* (vv. 25-27).
> *And immediately the flow of her blood was dried up; and she*
> *felt in her body that she was healed of her affliction* (v. 29).
> *Mark 5:25-27, 29*

Every time I read about this incident in the life of Christ, I remember the words of one of my pharmacy professors. This professor would love to tongue-in-cheek expound upon the benefits of being a dermatologist. A dermatologist is a doctor who treats skin conditions. I would like to apologize in advance to anyone in the field of dermatology who may be reading this chapter. I'm sure you've heard this many times before. This professor seemed to delight himself in saying, "The patients of a dermatologist never die, nor do they become healed." I sometimes think he regretted not becoming such a specialist. Of course, he was being humorous, but his point was well made. The predicament that many who suffer from skin conditions have is that their condition is chronic, that is, it never completely goes away. They have to pay to visit the doctor. Then they have to pay for their medication. Their condition may improve or it may not improve. Often it will reoccur. Thus the cycle repeats itself. It is a very frustrating and disappointing scenario. One can easily understand why the thought occurs, HEY DOC! WHOSE SIDE ARE YOU ON?

True, a skin condition generally is not as serious as cancer or other typically life-threatening conditions, but regardless how serious our condition might be, God desires to remove it. If your doctor told you the only way to save your life was to have major surgery, or radiation, or chemotherapy, would you do it? Is that a *yes* I hear? These forms of treatment take place everyday. They take place to the redeemed, as well as, the unredeemed. Christians receive these forms of treatment everyday of the year. They are costly, sometimes painful, and not always successful. But if our doctor says we need to do it, then we do it. But what if our doctor told us to go wading in a dirty river, would we do it? I doubt it! We would probably change doctors immediately. But if the word of God said to do it, would we do it? In order to receive God's healing we must respond to His word (Rx 14), regardless of our feelings. Belief is one thing, acting on what we say we believe is something else. That is faith.

GOD'S WORD ISN'T ALWAYS EASY TO FOLLOW

> *Now Naaman, captain of the army of the king of Aram, was a great man . . . but he was a leper (v. 1). And Elisha sent a messenger to him saying,* **"Go and wash in the Jordan seven times, and your flesh shall be restored to you and you shall be clean** *(v. 10)." So he went down and dipped himself seven times in the Jordan,* **according to the word of the man of God; and his flesh was restored** *like the flesh of a little child, and he was clean (v. 14).*
> *2 Kings 5:1, 10, 14*

Naaman struggled greatly with God's diagnosis, as well as the prescribed therapy, but finally he submitted and was healed (2 Kings 5:11-14). How we respond to God's word will determine if we receive God's benefits.

GOD PROVIDES A COMPLETE CURE

> **He sent His word and healed them,** *and delivered them from their destructions.*
> *Psalms 107:20*

215

Bless the Lord, O my soul, and forget none of His benefits; Who pardons all you iniquities; *Who heals all your diseases;*
Psalms 103:2, 3

Few Christians would deny that all healing has its source in God. If our healing is assisted by the efforts of a medical team, it is still our minds and bodies that God has designed to respond to the prescribed treatment. However, it is very easy to fail to recognize that a mind or body that remains unhealthy probably exists because of something we or our ancestors did that was contrary to God's laws. Our failure to address this root cause of our condition could eventually prove fatal.

WE NEED THE LORD'S DIAGNOSIS

*And in the thirty-ninth year of his reign, Asa became diseased in his feet, his disease was severe, **yet even in his disease he did not seek the Lord, but the physicians.** So, Asa slept with his fathers, having died in the forty-first year of his reign.*
2 Chronicles 16:12, 13

Most of us are more like King Asa than we would like to admit. If something is wrong with us, we either run down to the local drugstore and purchase a nonprescription remedy, or if something is more serious, then we see a doctor. How often is it that we go before the Lord and discuss our situation with Him before we do anything else? How often do we approach our problem in the same exact manner as the ungodly? If doctors and drugs help us overcome our condition and restore us to normal health, are we fully healed? Do we even bother to take a brief moment to consult with our Lord, the Great Physician? Do we ask Him if we contributed to our problem? If we neglect to consult with God, how are we any different than the patient of the skin doctor we mentioned earlier? That patient frequently gets better only later to become worse.

If we find ourselves with a serious mental or physical problem, hopefully we will realize that we can approach our Lord.

DISCUSS YOUR PROBLEM WITH GOD

> *For we do not have a high priest who cannot sympathize with our weaknesses, but one who has been tempted in all things as we are, yet without sin.* **Let us therefore draw near with confidence to the throne of grace, that we may receive mercy and may find grace to help in time of need.**
> *Hebrews 4:15, 16*

The Lord will reveal the root cause of our condition, and He will prescribe the treatment that will completely eliminate the problem, physically and spiritually.

A Christian can go to the Lord for an accurate diagnosis and for correct therapy. This is an advantage a Christian has available to him or her that is not available to the non-Christian. The non-Christian only has the finest man can offer, that is if he can afford it, or if his insurance will allow it. However, God provides the ultimate health plan with zero premiums and no deductible. *Office visits* are easy to schedule; there is no waiting. In addition, God is able to impart to His children more than comfort and encouragement. He is able to give absolute confidence as to the outcome of their condition.

CONFIDENCE FROM KNOWING GOD'S WILL

> *And* **this is the confidence** *which we have before Him,* *that* **if we ask anything according to His will, He hears us. And if we know that He hears us** *in whatever we ask,* **we know that we have the requests which we have asked from Him.**
> *1 John 5:14, 15*

We must consciously make the Lord the head of our medical team. He is to be the very first member chosen. If we choose Him first and consult with Him appropriately, then no other members may be required. If we overlook the importance of Him being the head of our medical team, or if we delegate Him to a subordinate role, the results could be devastating. However, when we consciously select Him to be our Great Physician our prognosis immediately becomes excellent.

LISTEN TO OUR GREAT PHYSICIAN

*"But you shall serve the Lord your God, and He shall bless your bread and your water; And **I will remove sickness from your midst**. There shall be no one miscarrying or barren in your land; **I will fulfill the number of your days**."*
Exodus 23:25, 26

*And He said, "If you will give earnest heed to the voice of the Lord your God, and do what is right in His sight, and give ear to His commandments, and keep all His statues, I will put none of these diseases on you which I have put on the Egyptians; **For I, the Lord am your Healer**."*
Exodus 15:26

THIS PRESCRIPTION PROVIDES
THE FOLLOWING BENEFIT

1. Confidence that we should discuss our situation with our Great Physician (God/Jesus)

CASE STUDIES

NO.4

REMISSION OR A PROMISE KEPT?

One evening during a midweek service at the church where we were attending, a close friend of ours, Gary Gelish, shared with those in attendance that his mother, Agnes, had been diagnosed as having a cancerous tumor. He said she was scheduled for surgery the next morning. I can remember some of us who were seated nearby gathering ourselves around him and asking God to remove the cancer and heal his mother.

The next morning, her presurgery x-rays failed to reveal the presence of a tumor. Additional tests were performed, but they only confirmed the tumor was no longer present. Surgery was no longer necessary.

We later learned his mother experienced a warm sensation moving over her body at the same time we were praying for her.

The world of medicine explains this type of occurrence as *spontaneous remission*, however, believers have another explanation.

Q & A (questions and answers)

1. Do you **see** any of the three definitions of **faith** as pointed out in Rx 14? Explain your answer.

2. Read or review Rx 12.

3. Read, consider, and discuss (if possible): Psalms 107:20, Matthew 8:5-13.

Rx21

INSTRUCTIONS

In those days Hezekiah became mortally ill . . .
Then Hezekiah turned his face to the wall, and prayed to the Lord.
Isaiah 38:1, 2

If you grew up with a brother or a sister, you no doubt remember what it was like to have your brother or your sister run to your mom or dad and tell them every time you did something wrong. You remember those fun times, don't you?

Personally, I grew up without any brothers or sisters, so tattling was a joy of childhood I missed. However, I was only temporarily deprived. I met my future wife when I was in my late twenties, and we soon became engaged and married. Guess what happened next? We had two beautiful children. I wasn't going to be denied the joy of tattling any longer! If you had brothers or sisters or if you are a parent of more than one child then you also know the joy of tattling.

Whenever such a situation arose, my children soon discovered which of daddy's buttons to push. Frankly, it always got to me when the guilty child would confess to doing the dastardly deed and with crocodile tears in their eyes say, "Daddy, I promise I'll never do it again. Please don't punish me!" About this time, you could see the other child's eyes roll and you just knew that child was thinking, I HATE IT WHEN THEY DO THAT! Both children knew that dad took no pleasure in having to serve in this aspect of fatherhood. On occasion dad would allow the crime to go unpunished with a guarantee given that it would not happen again. Incidentally, I would not recommend this as standard operating procedure for any parents' manual.

Our heavenly Father cannot overlook our crimes against Him. The original sin of Adam created a debt that no man could repay. The original sin of Adam spiritually separated the human race from God. We can see that the results of Adam's fall were his fear of and his separation from God.

GOD AND MAN BECAME SEPARATED

> *Then the Lord God called to the man, and said to him,* ***"Where are you?"*** *And he (the man) said,* ***"I heard the sound of Thee in the garden, and I was afraid because I was naked so I hid myself."***
> *Genesis 3:9, 10*

This separation from our heavenly Father left us with little protection from Satan and his kingdom of darkness. In fact, Adam's fall left us living in a physical being that actually desires to do the very things that are opposed to its best interests. Mankind's natural physical being desires to serve Satan's kingdom and its interests far more than God's kingdom and His interests. Every member of the human race from Adam onward is born into Satan's kingdom.

WE ALL BEGIN LIFE AS SLAVES TO SIN AND DEATH

> *I find then the principle that evil is present in me, the one who wishes to do good. For I joyfully concur with the law of God in the inner man, but I see a different law in the members of body, waging war against the law of my mind, and* ***making me a prisoner of the law of sin*** *which is in my members.*
> *Romans 7:21-23*

> *Do you not know that when you present yourselves to some one as slaves for obedience, **you are slaves of the one whom you obey**, either sin resulting in death, or of obedience resulting in righteousness?*
> *Romans 6:16*

Here is where God deserves a standing ovation. Thanks be to God! He sent Jesus to pay the debt resulting from the fall of Adam and to free all mankind from the consequences of the law of sin and death that exists in our members.

JESUS PAID OUR DEBT

> ***Knowing that you were not redeemed with perishable things*** *like silver or gold from your futile way of life inherited from your forefathers, **but with** precious blood, as of a lamb unblemished and spotless, **the blood of Christ**.*
> *1Peter 1:18, 19*

Jesus' blood, and only Jesus' blood can redeem us from our debt to God. Once we are redeemed, God can offer eternal life as a gift to be received in the person of Jesus Christ.

FACT: ETERNAL LIFE IS A GIFT

> *"For God so loved the world, that **He gave** His only begotten Son, that whoever believes in Him should not perish, but have **eternal life**."*
> *John 3:16*

God's word provides us with another fact, a fact that lets us know we will be saved.

FACT: BELIEVE, CONFESS, BE SAVED

> *If you **confess** with your mouth Jesus as Lord, and **believe** in your heart God raised Him from the dead, you shall be **saved**.*
> *Romans 10:9*

Did you notice that there is no mention of sin in either of these verses? Eternal life is a gift from God, a gift made possible by the sacrifice of His Son, Jesus.

FAITH A GIFT

> *For by grace you are saved through **faith** and that not of yourselves, it **is the gift of God**.*
> *Ephesians 2:8*

Every Christian is familiar with this portion of the gospel, and that is why it is so interesting to note the glaring contrast. The very first word that came forth from the mouths of John the Baptist, Jesus Christ, His disciples, Peter on the day of Pentecost, and Paul to those unfamiliar with the gospel, was, *repent* (Rx 15).

REPENT: JOHN THE BAPTIST

> *"**Repent**, for the kingdom of heaven is at hand."*
> *Matthew 3:2*

REPENT: JESUS THE CHRIST

> *"**Repent**, for the kingdom of heaven is at hand."*
> *Matthew 4:17*

REPENT: THE TWELVE DISCIPLES

And He summoned the twelve and began to send them out in pairs (v. 7). And they went out and preached that men should **repent** *(v. 12).*
Mark 6:7, 12

REPENT: PETER ON PENTECOST

*"**Repent**, and let each of you be baptized in the name of Jesus Christ for the forgiveness of your sins."*
Acts 2:38

REPENT: PAUL TO THE MEN OF ATHENS

"Therefore having overlooked the times of ignorance, God is now declaring to men that all everywhere should **repent.** *"*
Acts 17:30

Repent means far more than the mere acceptance of a biblical fact. Repent means a change of thinking that results in repentance, which is a change in lifestyle. Repentance means to turn around. Repentance requires actions, not just mental assent. Repentance is visible. So if eternal life is a gift from God and of course it is, then why is *repent* given such priority by the most significant people in the New Testament? Why is *repent* expressed as a command?[1] We are all responsible for the death of God's only son, and it was brutal. Keeping that in mind, repentance in exchange for forgiveness, restored health, eternal life, and being counted among God's children seems like the smallest demand imaginable. Doesn't it?

These are two intriguing questions. Let's remind ourselves of the two major consequences of Adam's fall. First, we became spiritually separated from God. Second, that separation left us defenseless

---

[1] Nathan E. Han, A Parsing Guide to the Greek New Testament, (Scottdale, Herald Press, 1975), p. 3.

against Satan. Our bodies became permanent enemies of God; they crave all that is opposed to God's overall plan for our lives. Our bodies have received a death sentence because they could never again be brought to a place where they, by themselves, would serve God. We became slaves to our bodies and to Satan. Sickness followed as a natural consequence.

Our heavenly Father sent Jesus to take care of both consequences. Jesus' sacrifice made it possible to be spiritually reunited with God. However, in the process, Jesus experienced the feeling of being separated from God.

JESUS FELT OUR SPIRITUAL SEPARATION

> *And at the ninth hour Jesus cried out with a loud voice, "Eloi, Eloi, Lama Sabachthani?" Which is translated,* **"My God, My God, why hast Thou forsaken me?"**
> *Mark 15:34*

Jesus took upon Himself the feeling of spiritual separation from His heavenly Father, a fact the entire human race has lived with since Adam. Jesus suffered that separation for all mankind, and now all mankind can be reunited with their heavenly Father. Jesus took care of the spiritual separation created by the fall of Adam. But Jesus did even more. Jesus' body felt and suffered every abuse Satan can impose upon our bodies.

JESUS' BODY SUFFERED OUR SICKNESSES

> *Surely our griefs (sickness) He Himself bore, and our sorrows He carried; yet we ourselves esteemed Him stricken, smitten of God and afflicted. But He was, pierced through (wounded) for our transgressions, He was crushed for our iniquities; the chastening of our well-being fell upon Him,* **and by His scourging we are healed.**
> *Isaiah 53:4, 5*

Our spiritual separation from God resulted from an action by Adam, an action you and I could not control. On the other hand, our griefs, our sickness, result, more than not, from our actions. We, not Adam or the actions of our ancestors, for the most part, are responsible for our condition. Therefore, *repent* is a command. Jesus suffered our griefs and our sicknesses, which we no longer need to suffer. In fact, we are commanded not to suffer for something Jesus had already suffered. Repentance is the first step in being separated from that suffering, be it mental or physical. Actually, repentance is the first step toward being born again, and this time, into the kingdom of God.

WE ARE NOT TO OBEY SIN

> *For the death that He (Jesus) died, He died to sin, once for all; but the life that He lives, He lives to God. Even so consider yourselves to be dead to sin, but alive to God in Jesus Christ.* **Therefore, do not let sin reign in your mortal body that you should obey its lust.**
> *Romans 6:10-12*

We know sin is our problem. We know if left alone, it would rule in our bodies, and we know our diseases result from the opportunity sin offers the enemy.

The Old Testament informs us that King Hezekiah was a very special king, a king who followed God's laws.

HEZEKIAH OBEYED GOD

> *He (Hezekiah) did right in the sight of the Lord, according to all that his father David had done (v. 3). He trusted in the Lord, the God of Israel; so that after him there was none like him among all the kings of Judah, nor among those who were before him. For* ***he clung to the Lord; he did not***

depart from following Him, but kept His command-
ments, which the Lord had commanded Moses (vv. 5, 6).
2 Kings 18:3, 5, 6

Now this was a special guy, but even he became mortally ill.

HEZEKIAH BECOMES MORTALLY ILL

In those days Hezekiah became mortally ill. And Isaiah
the prophet the son of Amoz, came to him and said to him,
"Thus says the Lord, 'Set your house in order, for you shall
die and not live.'"
Isaiah 38:1

Why did Hezekiah become mortally ill? Didn't he keep the commandments given to Moses? Where did Satan get an opportunity and permission to attack him? It is not uncommon to see a saint suffer. Such as, a man or woman of God who has served God so diligently for so many years, and yet he or she is suffering from some awful condition. How can that be? Look at Hezekiah. It was happening to him. How did Hezekiah react to the news of his impending death?

HEZEKIAH TURNS TO GOD AND PRAYS

Then Hezekiah turned his face to the wall, and
prayed to the Lord, and said, "Remember now, O Lord,
I beseech Thee, how I have walked before Thee in truth and
with a whole heart, and have done what is good in Thy sight."
And Hezekiah wept bitterly.
Isaiah 38:2, 3

Isn't Hezekiah also asking in his prayer, "How can this be? Why am I going to die so early in life? Haven't I served and obeyed You?" Did Hezekiah ask these or similar questions? If so, it is not stated clearly. However he cried bitterly. Was this simply because he didn't want to die? Maybe.

THE LORD RESPONDS TO HEZEKIAH'S PRAYER

> *Then the word of the Lord came to Isaiah, saying: "Go and say to Hezekiah, 'Thus says the Lord, the God of your father David, I have heard your prayer, **I have seen your tears; behold, I will add fifteen years to your life**. And I will deliver you and this city from the hand of the king of Assyria; and I will defend the city.'"*
> Isaiah 38:4-6

Obviously, the Lord not only heard Hezekiah's prayer but also responded favorably. Could the Lord have revealed to Hezekiah something that required repentance? The Lord's answer included the nation as well as Hezekiah. We will see this wasn't a coincidence.

ATTITUDES AND ACTIONS ARE EQUALLY RESPONSIBLE

> *Give glory to the Lord your God, before He brings darkness and before your feet stumble on dusky mountains, and while you are hoping for light He makes it into darkness, and turns it into gloom. But if you will not listen to it **my soul will sob in secret for such pride; and my eyes will bitterly weep and flow down with tears, because the flock of the Lord has been taken captive.***
> Jeremiah 13:16, 17

Hezekiah did not become mortally ill until after the Lord had provided an unexpected victory over the Assyrian army. Of course this victory brought about an obvious celebration.

VICTORY OR SUCCESS CAN REVEAL PRIDE

So the Lord saved Hezekiah and the inhabitants of Jerusalem from the hand of Sennacherib the king of Assyria, and from the hand of all others, and guided them on every side. And many were bringing gifts to the Lord at Jerusalem and choice presents to Hezekiah king of Judah, so that he was exalted in the sight of all nations thereafter (vv. 22, 23). **But Hezekiah gave no return for the benefit he received (national or personal), because his heart was proud;** *therefore wrath came on him and on Judah and Jerusalem (v. 25).*
2 Chronicles 32:22, 23, 25

We know Hezekiah had a problem with pride. It is a temptation that the gifted and the successful must face. However, the glory for being gifted and successful is God's and not the individual's. Pride is something that requires repentance.

GOD HATES PRIDE

*The fear of the Lord is to hate **evil; pride and arrogance and the evil way, and the perverted mouth, I hate.***
Proverbs 8:13

Did Hezekiah repent of his pride when he prayed to God concerning his illness? Did Hezekiah humble himself?

HEZEKIAH BOWS HIS KNEE TO GOD

However, Hezekiah humbled the pride of his heart, *both he and the inhabitants of Jerusalem, so that the wrath of the Lord did not come on them in the days of Hezekiah.*
2 Chronicles 32:26

Here, we can see that attitudes (pride and arrogance) can be just as responsible for our sickness as our actions. Humility and repentance are required for both attitudes and actions. What can be fun is to imagine Satan rolling his eyes at the moment of our humility and repentance and his saying with absolute disgust, I HATE IT WHEN THEY DO THAT!

Oh yes, he does!

THIS PRESCRIPTION PROVIDES THE FOLLOWING BENEFIT

1. Confidence that our attitudes as well as our actions can require repentance before our recovery will take place.

CASE STUDIES

NO.5

COULD YOU PREFORM A MIRACLE?

My wife awoke me one evening not long after our introduction to spiritual warfare and asked me to pray for her. She said she wasn't feeling well. I was only *half-awake,* but I rolled over and laid my hands on her and dispassionately asked the Lord to heal her. Then I promptly rolled back on my side of the bed and attempted to go back to sleep. I soon heard her say, "I don't feel any better." I replied with little sympathy, "Well God has healed you!" The next thing that came out of my wife's mouth fully awoke me. She growled, "I hate you!" Wrong! I knew my wife loved me: therefore, someone else was speaking to me. In a moment, we found ourselves engaged in a spiritual conflict. This was the first time Lu and I had experienced *hand-to-hand* combat with demons without others being present. When the battle was over, four evil spirits had left when commanded to do so in the name of Jesus. It was then that we personally knew the power and authority that resides with us in the person of the Holy Spirit when used in conjunction with the name of Jesus.

Q & A (questions and answers)

1. Do you **see** any of the three definitions of **faith** as pointed out in Rx 14? Explain your answer.

2. Read Rx 36.

3. Read, consider, and discuss (if possible) Matthew 10:1, Mark 9:38, 39, Luke 10:1, 9, 17.

Rx22

Rx
IF AT FIRST YOU
DON'T SUCEED,
FOLLOW
INSTRUCTIONS

Some of us have spent endless hours attempting to put together a *zillion*-piece puzzle. Sure, we have a picture that shows us what it will look like when it's completed, but I've yet to find a puzzle that comes with a sheet of instructions. Puzzles are like mysteries. They present a challenge, but when they are completed, they offer personal satisfaction as the reward. However, no clues are included, except the picture on the face of the puzzle's box. What kind of a challenge would a puzzle offer if it came with a numbered skeleton outline showing each piece in place with each individual piece correspondingly numbered? No challenge, no satisfaction, no sale!

On the other hand, the mystery of divine healing, the puzzle of how to receive healing, begs for a sheet of instructions. If an outline of the solution were provided for each mental or physical problem we encountered, who would complain? Who would miss the challenge? Who needs the challenge? Who wants the challenge? The answer is universal. Nobody! However, there are some interesting similarities between the ordinary puzzle and divine healing. The first thing most people attempt in solving a puzzle is to assemble the border. The border clearly indicates the puzzle has an end. It can only go so far and no farther. Once the border is assembled, the one facing the challenge has a handle on the task at hand. They know it will be completed, and victory will be seen.

One must also have a handle on divine healing. The individual must know the problem is contained; it can only go so far. There is an answer. That is why the eleventh prescription in this book, READ MY LIPS, assembled the border of the puzzle we refer to as divine healing. We must know God wants all of us healthy, and if we are not healthy we must know God wants us to return to a healthy state. When we have accepted these truths, we have assembled in our minds and hopefully in our hearts, the essential border needed to ensure a positive course toward receiving full and complete health.

Have you ever spent several hours, maybe even days, attempting to put a puzzle together only to discover you are missing one or two pieces? Frustrating, right?

There are countless Christians who have a handle on divine healing. They have the border intact. They know God wants to heal them, but there seems to be one or two pieces missing. We all know it only takes one missing piece to keep a puzzle from being complete. Failure to act on one overlooked truth is all that keeps us from returning to full health. If we have a handle on a situation but we fail to see the anticipated results, then it is easy to become frustrated and eventually accept the situation instead of the answer. God forbid! On the other hand, can you imagine how you would feel if you discovered the missing piece, the piece that completed your healing? You discovered the overlooked truth that put it all together for you. Would you shout with joy? Thank You, Jesus! Would you praise Him? Hallelujah! Would you serve Him with renewed enthusiasm? Hopefully.

Do you have any idea what will happen in the realm of spiritual darkness when you set in place that final piece? Sure, you do! A horrible scream of defeat will be heard coming from every conquered demon,

"I HATE IT WHEN THEY DO THAT!"

Everyone will want to know what you did to become well. What was the missing piece of the puzzle? What brought this all about?

The years go by, but some things don't really change very much. They are just packaged differently. All of us realize that sometime in our life, we have given an ear to an unholy suggestion. A suggestion similar to this:

THE LIE: SIN HAS NO ILL CONSEQUENCES

> *And the serpent said to the woman, **"You surely shall not die!** For God knows that in the day you eat from it your eyes will be opened, and you will be like God, knowing good from evil."*
> *Genesis 3:4, 5*

And somehow, consciously or unconsciously, we believed the lie. We have convinced ourselves, "No one is going to be hurt if I do this or that. I don't see any problem." Do those type of thoughts sound familiar?

THE FALLACY: WHAT COULD GO WRONG?

> ***When the woman saw that the tree was good for food, and that is was a delight to the eyes, and that the tree was desirable to make one wise,*** *she took from it's fruit and ate; and she gave also to her husband with her, and he ate.*
> *Genesis 3:6*

Approximately four thousand years later, the apostle John restated this fallacy.

THE FALLACY RESTATED

> *For all that is in the world, **the lust of the flesh and the lust of the eyes and the boastful pride of life, is not from the Father,** but is from the world.*
> *1 John 2:16*

The insatiable cravings of our flesh and of our eyes to acquire are coupled with the arrogance of a deceived understanding, together they produce a persona that is totally unacceptable to God.

Satan was right about one thing, but he didn't tell the whole truth. Our eyes have been opened to see everything but from the wrong perspective. They have been blinded toward seeing the things of God.

EYES THAT ARE OPEN

> ***Then the eyes of them (Adam and Eve) were opened,*** *and they knew that they were naked; and they sewed fig leaves together and made themselves loin coverings.*
> *Genesis 3:7*

BUT EYES THAT ARE BLINDED

> *And even if our gospel is veiled, it is veiled to those who are perishing.* ***In whose case the god of this world has blinded the minds of the unbelieving,*** *that they might not see the light of the gospel of the glory of Christ, who is the image of God.*
> *2 Corinthians 4:3, 4*

We who are Christians understand that Jesus is the image of God, that He is the Word of God, and that He is the light of God's truth to us.

JESUS IS THE LIGHT

> *In the beginning was the Word, and the Word was with God, and the Word was God (v. 1). And the Word became flesh (Jesus), and dwelt among us, and we beheld His glory as of the only begotten from the Father, full of grace and truth (v. 14).* ***In Him was life, and the life was the light of men.***

And the light shines in the darkness, and the darkness did not comprehend it (vv. 4, 5).
John 1:1, 14, 4, 5,

Jesus is the light of God's truth. We know that darkness can never extinguish light, but rather, light pushes out darkness. Consequently, the more intimate we are with Jesus, God's word, the more darkness is forced out of our lives. We see things in our lives we didn't realize were there.

AWARE OF OUR ERROR

*For that which I am doing, I do not understand; for **I am not practicing what I would like to do**, but I am doing the very thing I hate.*
Romans 7:15

When we are aware of the fact that there are actions and attitudes present in our life in which we no longer have agreement, we want to be free from their control.

THE CRY FOR FREEDOM

But if I am doing the very thing I do no wish. I am no longer the one doing it, but sin which dwells in me (has control) (v. 20). *Wretched man that I am! **Who will set me free from the body of this death*** (v. 24)?
Romans 7:20, 24

Now that brings us to the two words that Satan absolutely hates to hear us utter: *repent* and *forgiveness*. When we tell God we repent of a certain action or attitude, then Satan knows that we are aware of the fact that we have been in agreement with his desires instead of God's will. Satan knows when we repent that we have fallen out of agreement with him. We have completed *the border* of the puzzle.

We recognize the lusts of our flesh, eyes, and mind. He knows that nothing can stop the puzzle of our healing from coming together. One of the most important missing pieces has been discovered and set into place. Satan will no longer be able to prevent our health from being restored.

Please allow me to use an illustration from my background in pharmacy. A pharmacist is required by law to counsel all patients concerning their medications. There is one classification of drugs called nonsteroidal anti-inflammatory drugs (NSAIDs). They are commonly used to relieve the pain of arthritis. Whenever a pharmacist dispenses this type of medication, he needs to inform the patient to avoid aspirin while taking this drug. These medications and aspirin work at the same location in the body. However, aspirin will arrive at the site of action first, and consequently, it will block the beneficial action of the other drug. This truth has a spiritual correlation. The presence of unrepentant and unforgiven sin acts in a similar way: that is, it blocks the benefit provided by the suffering Jesus' body endured on the cross.

HEALTH FROM CHRIST'S WOUNDED BODY

*And He Himself bore our sins in His body on the cross, that we might die to sin and live to righteousness; **for by His wounds you were healed**.*
1 Peter 2:24

REPENTANCE BRINGS THE PROMISE

*The Lord is not slow about His promise, as some count slowness, but is patience toward you, not wishing for any to perish **but for all to come to repentance**.*
2 Peter 3:9

That brings us to another word Satan hates and to another essential piece of the puzzle: *forgiveness*! Repentance and forgiveness appear to be two halves of the same piece. Repentance and forgiveness combine to deliver a sure one-two knockout punch against Satan and his demons of disease. The scenario is something like this:

Satan and his demon hordes suggest and seduce our weak minds and bodies to be in agreement with their character and to sin against God. Sin provides the opportunity they need to gain permission and access to our minds and bodies. Satan, who represents the prosecuting attorney in this scenario, hears the complaint(s) of his client(s), the demons, who witnessed our sinful attitude(s) and/or action(s). Next, Satan comes before God, the judge (1 Peter 4:1-5).

GOD JUDGES THE LIVING AND DEAD

> *But they shall give account to **Him (God) who is ready to judge the living** and the dead.*
> *1 Peter 4:5*

Satan, representing his personal interests, as well as, the interests of his demon eyewitnesses, presents his accusations against us before God.

SATAN IS OUR ACCUSER

> *And I heard a loud voice in heaven, saying, "Now the salvation, and the power, and the kingdom of our God and the authority of His Christ have come, for **the accuser of our brethren** has been thrown down, who accuses them before our God day and night."*
> *Revelation 12:10*

God listens to Satan's accusation(s) against us, and then it is our turn to speak on our own behalf. If we have not promptly repented of our sin and asked God's forgiveness, what will we say? Repentance is the responsibility of man. It's our part, our half, of the missing piece.

Forgiveness is God's part. If we have discovered and set this piece in place, then this is what will occur:

GOD FORGIVES AND FORGETS

> *"But this is the covenant which I (God) will make with the house of Israel (God's people) after those days, declares the Lord, I will put My law within them, and on their heart I will write it; and I will be their God, and they shall be My people." **"For I will forgive their iniquity, and their sin I will remember no more."***
> *Jeremiah 31:33, 34*

What Jeremiah stated, approximately six hundred years before the birth of Jesus, applies to the church as well as the nation of Israel. This becomes very clear when we read the New Testament book of Hebrews. Some thirty years after the crucifixion and the resurrection of Jesus,[1] the author of Hebrews, who is appealing to Jewish thought, restates the words of Jeremiah and he applies them to the church.

JEREMIAH RESTATED FOR THE CHURCH

> *But He (Jesus), having offered one sacrifice for sins for all time, sat down at the right hand of God (v. 12) . . . for by one offering He has perfected for all time those who are sanctified (Christians). And the Holy Spirit also bears witness to us; for after saying, "This is the covenant that I will make with them after those days says the Lord: I will put My laws upon their hearts, and upon their minds I will write them." He then says, **"And their sin and their lawless deeds I will remember no more** (vv. 14-17)."*
> *Hebrews 10:12, 14-17*

---

[1] Finis Dake, The Dake Annotated Reference Bible, New Testament, (Lawrenceville, Dake Publishing Inc., 2014), p. 448.

A Christian stands before God well represented. We have our own defense counsel.

OUR ATTORNEY IS JESUS CHRIST

> *My little children, I am writing these things to you that you may not sin. And if anyone sins,* **we have an Advocate (an attorney) with the Father, Jesus Christ the righteous.** *1 John 2:1*

We already know a great deal about our defense attorney, but let's look at just two things the above verses informs us regarding His credentials. First, He is with the Father, God, who is the judge, and employs Him. The Judge, the One who is going to decide our case, is providing our counsel and paying for our defense. Second, our attorney is righteous. He is always right. He has never lost a case, and He never will lose a case.

Jesus, our attorney, stands before God, the Judge. and states that His client (that's us) has filed the necessary motions of repentance and a request for forgiveness. Now, with the courts permission, the defense would like to see the evidence of the specific crimes in question (our sinful attitudes or actions). The Judge then asks the prosecutor, Satan, to provide the requested evidence. Satan responds that it has been filed in the heavenly record. The Judge then asks for the heavenly record to be reviewed. Guess what? There is no record of any such crime being committed. The prosecutor and the eyewitnesses are outraged and demand a thorough reexamination of the heavenly records. This time, the Judge, God, rises from the bench and with a stern, penetrating glare directed toward the desk of Satan, the prosecutor, and his demon clients, declares: "There is no evidence against this defendant (you and me)." In addition, God states, "I have no memory of any such events having occurred. Therefore, I find your clients (Satan's demons) guilty of being false witnesses, and I revoke all authority to hold the defendant any longer. You are instructed (commanded) to release the defendant from bondage. Any other action on your part will be interpreted as contempt of court (trespassing). This is My verdict."

YOU AND JOB ARE TWO OF A KIND

> **And the Lord said to Satan, "Have you considered My servant (fill in you name)?** *For there is no one like him (or her) on the earth, a blameless and upright man (or woman), fearing God and turning away from evil."*
> *Job 1:8*

In addition, God says to Satan, "My verdict is that your demons are false witnesses, and I don't need to remind you of what the law says regarding false witnesses."

THE PENALTY FOR BEING A FALSE WITNESS

> *If a malicious witness rises up against a man to accuse him of wrongdoing, then both the men who have the dispute shall stand before the Lord, before the priests and the judges who will be in office in those days. And the judges shall investigate thoroughly; and* **if the witness is a false witness and he has accused his brother falsely, then you shall do to him just as he had intended to do to his brother, thus you shall purge the evil from among you.**
> *Deuteronomy 19:16-19*

I can, and maybe you can also, imagine God, the Judge, continuing with His verdict, "And since you demons are guilty of being false witnesses and since the defendant has filed the necessary motions with the court, you will release the prisoner (again, you and me) immediately, and you will no longer oppress or torment his mind or body, so long as he remains innocent without any unforgiven accusations."

BEING BLAMELESS BRINGS FREEDOM

> *If (when) we confess our sins, He is faithful and righteous to forgive us our sins **and to cleanse us from all unrighteousness.***
> 1 John 1:9

God's verdict in both the Old and the New Testament is the same. The evil, the unrighteousness, the sickness, etc., must go. We are to be cleansed and purged of our oppression. What is the name of the one who is oppressing you? Is it cancer, arthritis, depression, lack of forgiving others or does it have another name? No matter. When we meet God's conditions, it must depart. Ask for forgiveness. If needed, call it by name and order it to leave in the name of Jesus of Nazareth.

AUTHORITY IN JESUS' NAME

> *"And these signs will accompany those who have believed: **in My name they will cast out demons. They will lay hands on the sick, and they will recover.**"*
> Mark 16:17, 18

In closing, may I give you a hint regarding those last couple of pieces to the puzzle? Frequently, the last two missing pieces are the following: (1) failing to ask for forgiveness for a particular sin or sins. That's something you know God will provide. However, this next piece (2) can be slightly more difficult to put into place. If someone has offended (sinned against) you, then you need to forgive them. That could be more difficult, right?

If you're having difficulty doing either of these, you might also be having difficulty seeing your healing become apparent.

One more hint, by doing these two things it is very likely an individual will avoid the yo-yo prayer syndrome: prayer followed by relief, followed by relapse, followed by prayer, etc. Sin, in all forms, must always be dealt with.

THIS PRESCRIPTION PROVIDES
THE FOLLOWING BENEFIT

1. Confidence that we are proceeding in the right direction

CASE STUDIES

NO.6

IS THE DOCTOR THE FINAL WORD?

Charity-Rae is the name of our firstborn. She was an answer to prayer. Shortly after her birth, we *gave* her back to God through the ceremony of dedication. Brother Ralph Moore performed the dedication. My wife and I both recognized she truly belonged to God.

Charity was a handful from the beginning. When she was about two-years old we were living in Torrance, California. One day, she fell on the exposed corner of a sharp metal object. It punctured a hole through the skin directly underneath her lower lip. It was obvious the injury was going to require stitches, so we rushed her to a nearby pediatrician, Lawrence Park, who was also located in Torrance.

About two hours later, we discovered her tongue had also been sliced. Somehow all of us had missed this injury. We called the doctor and explained the situation. The doctor said it would not have made any difference even if we had noticed the tongue, because you don't put stitches in a tongue. He said it would heal quickly but a ridged scar area would likely result where the two sides of the tongue finally aligned and healed. He also said that our daughter might have a slight speech impediment. The thoughts of our daughter having an abnormally ridged scar on her tongue and possibly a speech impediment were not pleasant thoughts for either of us. So we held her in our arms and asked God to heal her tongue properly.

A couple of weeks later, everyone was delighted to learn her tongue had healed without leaving a trace of injury, and her speech was never affected. She still chattered incessantly. All glory to God!

Q & A (questions and answers)

1. Do you **see** any of the three definitions of **faith** as pointed out in Rx 14? Explain your answer.

2. Read or review Rx 20

3. Read, consider, and discuss (if possible): Mark 11:24, John 14:13, 14, 1 Peter 2:24.

Rx23

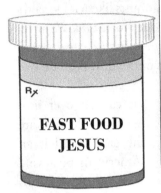

Rx

**FAST FOOD
JESUS**

The first real job I ever had was working at a nearby McDonald's restaurant. I was eighteen years old, and drive-thrus didn't exist yet. I really enjoyed my job, and I learned to work at each station: the window, the fries, the grill, etc. I enjoyed working the window and the grill more than the other stations. I can remember how good it made me feel the first time I was able to cook and prepare forty-eight burgers all by myself, and in only five minutes. Oh yeah! I thought I was really something.

When I began at McDonald's, burgers only cost eighteen cents, fries were twelve cents, and drinks were ten and fifteen cents. Incidentally, I was paid seventy-five cents an hour. Those of us who worked the window would love to have races to see who could register the most customers or the most sales during peak hours. I was very competitive at that time, so I memorized the menu and the tax table, and that allowed me to total an entire order in my mind. Thus I was able to make only one entry on the register. Obviously, that saved time. For instance, a burger, fries and a large drink would be forty-seven cents, tax included.

Since the 1950s, fast-food has developed into a full-blown industry. It seems the impact of this industry has had considerable influence on the thinking of our nation. This industry, coupled with the overall advances in technology, are changing people's mental outlook around the world. The attraction to restaurants like McDonald's is that they are quick, fast, and convenient, while at a *reasonable* price, or at least reasonable at one time. These are very attractive features to those who live in an economy that demands both adult members of a household be employed.

Unfortunately, the fast-food mentality has carried over into other areas of our lives. Americans have become a people who are increasingly intolerant of delays. Obviously, the credit card is an outstanding illustration of how little patience Americans possess: *I want it, and I want it now!* This thinking has even overflowed into Christianity. My wife has said, "Americans expect a FAST FOOD JESUS."

In many ways, our concept of God has evolved from that of a Santa Claus into that of ultimate service. We no longer pray and wait. Now we ask, and if we don't receive before Christmas, we either change *God*; or else, we *change* God. Don't let this play on words confuse you. Please allow me to explain. We face three basic decisions when God doesn't respond in the manner we hope He will respond. First, we can decide to change what or who we worship as God. But then, what or who will we worship? Can we change or alter the Bible's definition of God? No. Could there be another God who will meet our needs and expectations? The religious people who lived in Athens during the time of the apostle Paul recognized the fact that a god may exist whom they had not yet encountered. They left the door open to allow for other gods.

ANOTHER GOD

> *And Paul stood in the midst of the Aeropagus and said, "Men of Athens, I observe that you are very religious in all respects. For while I was passing through and examining the objects of your worship, I also found an altar with this inscription, 'To an unknown god' what therefore you worship in ignorance this I proclaim to you."*
> *Acts 17:22, 23*

Certainly, Christians are not looking for another God. We already know the one and only true God.

JESUS: THE ONLY TRUE GOD

> *He who eats My flesh and drinks My blood has eternal life, and I will raise him up on the last day* (v. 54). *As a result of this many of His disciples withdrew, and were not walking with Him anymore, Jesus said therefore to the twelve, "You do not want to go away also, do you?" Simon Peter answered Him, "Lord, to whom shall we go?* **You have the words of eternal life** (vv. 66-68)."
> *John 6:54, 66-68*

God has made some statements in His word that are very difficult to hear or understand. There are statements that seem unreasonable. Still, Peter, the twelve, and we as well recognized that only Jesus has the words of eternal life.

The second decision we can make is to change God. Religious, God-fearing people have for centuries exhibited the tendency to change or to adapt their God, or to interpret the message of their God so that it conforms to their concept of the truth.

THE GOSPEL CAN BE DISTORTED

> *I am amazed that you are so quickly deserting Him who called you by the grace of Christ, for a different gospel; Which is really not another; only* **there are some who are disturbing you, and want to distort the gospel of Christ.**
> *Galatians 1:6, 7*

There is a third decision that one can make, and that is to accept and to believe God's word just as it is written. Incidentally, God issues a serious warning to any who attempt to change what He has said.

THE WARNING IN REVELATION

I testify to everyone who hears the words of the prophecy of this book: **If anyone adds to them,** *God shall add to him the plagues which are written in this book;* **And if anyone takes from the words of the book of this prophecy,** *God shall take away his part from the tree of life and from the Holy City, which are written in this book.*
Revelation 22:18, 19

God is very specific about the consequences of altering the book of Revelation, and He does not hesitate to advise against altering the good news of Jesus Christ.

THE WARNING IN GALATIANS

But even though we, or and angel from Heaven, should preach to you a gospel contrary to that which we have preached to you let him be accursed. As we have said before, so I say again now, **if any man is preaching to you a gospel contrary to that which you received let him be accursed.**
Galatians 1:8, 9

We can see God is very specific about changing the gospel.

If the author of the gospel of Mark were writing his account of the life of Christ today, he would be thinking of America and Americans and not Rome and Romans. Two thousand years ago the might of Rome ruled the world. The Romans were a spoiled, impatient, and demanding people. Do they remind you of any contemporary nation or people? I don't know about you, but I kind of see myself as a modern day Roman. That explains why the gospel of Mark is loaded with miracles that were *immediately* visible. This type of miracle would naturally appeal to the Roman mind.

The typical American of the 1980s and the 1990s was very much like the typical first-century Roman. However, it is very important for us to realize that none of the four authorized biographies of Jesus of Nazareth are comprehensive.

THE GOSPELS: ENOUGH BUT NOT ALL

> **And there are also many other things which Jesus did,** which if they were written in detail, I suppose that even the world itself would not contain the books which were written.
> John 21:25

Therefore, we must guard ourselves from inadvertently accepting that all divine healing is manifested immediately. This type of reasoning has opened many to disappointment and frustration. Can God heal instantly? Just read Mark's gospel. However, does God state He will always heal instantly? Or does God simply promise to restore our health?

GOD IS OUR HEALER

> And He said, "If you will give earnest heed to the voice of the Lord your God, and do what is right in His sight, and give ear to His commandments, and keep all His statues, I will put none of the diseases on you which I have put on the Egyptians; for **I, the Lord, am your Healer.**"
> Exodus 15:26

GOD HEALS EVERY DISEASE

> **Bless the Lord,** O my soul, and forget none of His benefits; who pardons all your iniquities; **who heals all your diseases.**
> Psalms 103:2, 3

GOD'S WORD HEALS

> **He sent His word and healed them,** and delivered them from their destructions.
> Psalms 107:20

JESUS IS THE WORD OF GOD

> *In the beginning was the Word, and the Word was with God, and the Word was God. And the Word became flesh (Jesus), and dwelt among us,* and we saw His glory, glory as of the only begotten from the Father, full of grace and truth.
> John 1:1, 14

IT'S OFFICIAL: BELIEVERS ARE HEALED

> And when evening had come, they brought to Him many who were demon-possessed; and **He cast out the spirits with a word, and healed all who were ill.** In order that what was spoken through Isaiah the prophet might be fulfilled, saying, **"He Himself took our infirmities, and carried away our diseases."**
> Matthew 8:16, 17

There is only one decision for a believer to make: know God's word, believe God's word, act on God's word, and confess (speak) God's word. A believer who is accepting God's healing for their mind or body should say to those who inquire about that believer's health the same thing that God says regarding that believer's health.

We in the medical field realize that two people can experience the same trauma, and yet they can recover at different rates. For instance, two brothers may both have the flu. One brother may fully recover in three days, but it may require three weeks for the other brother to fully recover. Yet no one doubts that both will eventually recover. However, when it comes to divine healing, that is, healing that results from believing God's word, prayer, and ministry, we silently anticipate that healing will always be visible immediately. This type of thinking is something we have allowed to develop, sort of like *the apple Adam ate* or *the three wise men*. The fact is, the gospel's records varying rates of healing for the same condition.

IMMEDIATE RECOVERY

> *And a leper came to Him, beseeching Him and falling on his knees before Him, and saying to Him, "If you are willing, you can make me clean." And moved with compassion, He stretched out His hand, and touched him, and said to him, "I am willing; be cleansed."* **And immediately the leprosy left him and he was cleansed.**
> *Mark 1:40-42*

Here, as we might expect, Mark records the *instantaneous* healing of a leper. Now let's look at the gospel of Luke.

PROLONGED RECOVERY

> *And as He entered a certain village, ten leprous men who stood at a distance met Him; And they raised their voices, saying, "Jesus, Master, have mercy on us!" And when He saw them, He said to them, "Go and show yourselves to the priests." And it came about that* **as they were going, they were cleansed.**
> *Luke 17:12-14*

Mark wanted to impress the Roman mind with what Jesus could do.[1] On the other hand, Luke, who was a physician, was familiar with the fact that people heal at different rates. Time wasn't what impressed Luke. Luke was impressed by who Jesus was, and this is what he wanted the recipient of his (Luke's) gospel to understand.

I personally have seen healing that took place in nine seconds, healing that took nine hours, and healing that wasn't visible for ninety days. However, the bottom line is, God's healing was manifested in all of them. When we meet God's conditions, and when we do the will of God, we will receive God's promises.

---

[1]   Herbert Lockyer, All The Books and Chapters of the Bible, (Grand Rapids, Zondervan Publishing House, 1977), p. 226.

BELIEVE IT AND YOU'LL SEE IT

*For you have need of endurance, **so that when you have done the will of God, you may receive what was promised.***
Hebrews 10:36

DON'T BE LIKE ADAM

The next few paragraphs did not appear in the initial printing of this book. Since then, I have inserted "A Word About COVID" as well as having decided to include these paragraphs. However, I must apologize. In this section I did not print out the Bible passages which I referenced. I understand how convenient that feature can be; I am truly sorry. I hope you read them. God will use them to increase your faith.

You may have never thought about it, but God tells us immediately in His word that miracles can occur over a period of time... at least relative to man's concept of time. Right now, you might be thinking, "Really? I must have missed that. Where does God say that?" In Genesis chapter one. He states this truth implicitly when He informs us that He created the heavens and earth in six days (Genesis 1:31). I consider creation to be the greatest miracle of all. On the other hand, I don't consider six days to be instantly. Do you think He might have had a reason for telling us He did it over a period of time? Could the reason have been He isn't capable of doing it instantly...or maybe He got fatigued...then of course He could have had second thoughts about His design. No laughing allowed. Although, those thoughts are amusing. That kind humor exposes how we really perceive God. He is Almighty! Seriously, could it be that *time* to God and *time* to man are not necessarily the same thing? Please allow me to explain. I have no problem accepting that what occurs in the mind of God takes place immediately. Why not? While what takes place in the mind of man takes a little longer to materialize. For instance, to say, "Let there be light (Genesis 1:3)" and to create a light bulb are two different things. One occurred instantly and the other took thousands of years to come into being.

If God would have told us that He had created the heavens and the earth instantly, then we would have a problem. We would no longer have any reason to think or believe any promise in the word of God could take place other than instantly.

However, God explicitly informs us that His promises can take place over a period of time, as well as instantly. That's the very next thing He tells us. Consider this. God warned Adam that on the day he ate from the tree of the knowledge of good and evil he would surely die (Genesis 2:16, 17). Did that actually happen? Maybe you have wondered why Eve didn't drop over dead after eating the forbidden fruit. I am rather certain Adam wondered. The Bible tells us Eve was deceived by Satan (1 Timothy 2:14), but Adam wasn't deceived. He had heard the warning directly from God. So, he could have thought, why is Eve still alive? Thus, Adam was given an opportunity to doubt the word of God. Have you ever been given an opportunity to doubt Him? DON'T BE LIKE ADAM and believe what your eyes tell you or listen to what others say about your particular condition *instead* of what God says about it. You don't need to stop seeing your health professional but don't stop believing God either.

Adam died *spiritually* on that very day (John 3:3), then 930 years later his *physical* body hit the ground and completed the process (Genesis 5:5). Listen to what Jesus tells us about *spiritual* and *physical* death. He uses the word *dead* both figuratively and literally in the same sentence (Matthew 8:21, 22). In other words, spiritually and physically can coexist together.

I could go on and tell you about Abraham (Genesis 12:2) having to wait 25 years before he got to see the son God had promised him. You may recall Abraham was 100 years old when Isaac was born, and his wife Sarah was 90 years old. No miracle there. Tongue in check.

The bottom line is to relax (Of course, now why didn't I think of that) and simply accept *by faith* that when God says something, there is no doubt about it. It has already been recorded in the annals of heaven as having taken place (Matthew 16:19). To God it's history…history that man may *or may not* have experienced (yet) in his concept of time.

Maybe we all could learn a lesson from nature. In a rainstorm we might see lighting miles away streaking across the sky. Then moments later, we experience the crackling sound from that discharge and hear the boom from the resulting thunder. Did I say, a moment or two later? *Didn't they both occur at the same time?*

Maybe a more relevant question might be: Did we see the light? No pun intended. If you have read His promise regarding your condition, then you have read the heavenly record. So, we can be confident of what is to follow. If you believe in thunder, then believe God's word. God is not a man that He should lie (Numbers 13:19).

God always allows man an opportunity to doubt Him as well as to believe Him. Faith, *acting on what God has said* (Rx 14), is the key to the results you will see. If or when our situation *appears* to be hopeless, we should remember what our Lord said to Sarah when she laughed about His promise to give her a child, *"Is anything too difficult for the Lord?"* (Genesis 18:10-14).

THIS PRESCRIPTION PROVIDES THE FOLLOWING BENEFITS

1. Confidence that we have the best treatment available in Jesus
2. Confidence that there is no time limit for our healing to be manifested or seen.

CASE STUDIES

NO.7 CAN YOU ALWAYS TRUST YOUR FEELINGS?

One day I received a call from one of the men in the church, Vern L. He said he had been periodically experiencing severe chest pain. He mentioned that he had been to a doctor and was told his heart was fine. Then he added that when he went to church and asked for prayer the pain would subside, or even leave. However, as soon as he left church, the pain would return. He had hardly finished with his story when the Holy Spirit gave me the confidence to tell him, "God will heal you!"

My wife and I went to his home, and soon we were all seated. I told him to ask God to heal him. He had just begun to pray when he raised his head and exclaimed, "They're over there! They're over there!" as he pointed to the right side of the room. The Spirit of God within me said, "Oh no they're not. They are right next to you." Again, a spiritual conflict broke out, and this time, the demons were more intimidating than ever. The brother reached down and picked up a floor-heating grate and approached me with hate in his eyes. I was sure it would be no trouble at all for him to make me look like a waffle. But again, the spirits trembled at the name of Jesus; and when they were commanded to put the grate right back where they had found it, they obeyed. Eventually, the brother was freed, and one of the spirits that left called itself *fear*. It had gained access to the man's life when he was just a young boy. His father had dunked his head in a water trough, and the fear he experienced at that moment troubled him the remainder of his life. However, on that day, the true cause of the man's symptoms was uncovered and his health was restored.

Q & A (questions and answers)

1. Do you **see** any of the three definitions of **faith** as pointed out in Rx 14? Explain your answer.

2. Read or review Rx 13.

3. Read, consider, and discuss (if possible): Matthew 8:28-32, Matthew 10:1, Luke 10:19.

Rx24

INSTRUCTIONS

For with the heart man believes, resulting in righteousness, and with the mouth he confesses, resulting in salvation.
Romans 10:10

I can remember being a senior at LIFE Bible College in Los Angeles. Once again, I had decided to try out for the varsity baseball team. This time I was, a thirty-five year old, man attempting to compete with teenagers and young men in their late teens and early twenties. I had pulled a hamstring muscle during the final week of spring training, but since I was a senior walk-on I continued to play instead of allowing the leg to heal properly. Then in the second week of our season, we had a three-game road trip to northern California. Our first game was at night in Visalia. It was early March, and it was cold. I can remember how my leg ached during the pregame warm-ups. I knew it was going to be a long evening but I had no idea just how long it was going to be. When Visalia's team came to bat in the bottom of the sixth inning, the score was something like 14 to 0 in Visalia's favor. I was playing second base, and the ground I had to cover was beginning to look and feel more like a runway at LAX than second base. We had a play at second base that half inning and after the play I told our shortstop that my leg was killing me. He looked my way, pounded his fist into his glove, and said, "HANG IN THERE, BABY!"

"Hang in there, baby" is an expression used in America to encourage a person to keep going and not to quit. Some years back, a similar expression was used in certain Christian circles. That expression was *pray through*. *Pray-through* or *praying-through* was used to encourage an individual to remain before the Lord in prayer and expectation when healing wasn't yet visible.

How long does one *hang in there* or *pray-through*? If you are anything like me, you may recall asking your mom, "When will dinner be ready?" And if your mom was anything like my mom, she would reply, "Dinner will be ready when it's ready." The good news concerning Jesus Christ is *dinner is ready.* Now is the day of salvation.

SALVATION (HEALING) IS NOW

> *And working together with Him, we also urge you not to receive the grace of God in vain. For He says, "At the acceptable time **I listened to you**, and on the day of salvation, **I helped you; Behold NOW is the day of salvation.**"*
> *2 Corinthians 6:1, 2*

Salvation is deliverance from the consequences of sin. Sickness is one of the consequences of sin. Paul uses the expression *the day of salvation,* to refer to all the benefits provided to man by God in the person of Jesus Christ through the person of the Holy Spirit. Consequently, this expression could have been translated in a far more limited, but just as accurate way by saying, "Now is the day of your healing. Today you are healed."

Some of us are thinking, *That's easy for you or Paul to say, but you don't know the pain or agony that I'm suffering. You have no idea what it's like to be in my situation!* Maybe not, but Jesus does. In fact, Jesus suffered pain and agony for each of us so He could provide our *day of salvation,* our *day of deliverance,* our *day of healing and health.*

JESUS SUFFERED EVERYONE'S ILLNESSES

> *Surely He has borne our sickness and carried our sorrows; yet we regarded Him as a stricken one, smitten of God, and afflicted. But He was pierced for our transgressions; He was bruised for our iniquities; the punishment which pro-*

cured our peace fell upon Him, **and with His stripes we are healed.**
Isaiah 53:4, 5 (Berkeley)

Well, there it is. We just read it. The Bible says, we are healed! God says, Jesus took care of our sin and our sickness. Do we believe God? If we believe God's word in our hearts, then we will discover that faith allows that word to come out of our mouths. When that word comes from our mouth then we can rest assured we will experience the full benefits of salvation.

CONFESSION BRINGS POSSESSION

But what does it say? The word is near you, in your mouth and in your heart, that is, the word of faith which we are preaching, That **if you confess with your mouth** *Jesus as Lord, and believe in your heart that God raised Him from the dead,* **(then) you shall be saved; For with the heart man believes, resulting in righteousness, and with the mouth he confesses, resulting in salvation (forgiveness, deliverance and healing).**
Romans 10:8-10

Consider this: If we believe Jesus provides us with salvation and in our hearts we know that salvation includes His healing, yet we have not openly declared that belief with our mouths, then have not we silently denied His full work on the cross? Does this thought trouble you? Maybe it provokes you. If this thought troubles you, maybe God is using His word to make a positive change in your life. On the other hand, if this thought provokes you, then it may be because you are an individual who has verbally but innocently denied this portion of God's deliverance for all mankind. The apostle Paul, a man thoroughly schooled in the Old Testament, was also provoked by the truth of Jesus Christ, and he innocently denied His purpose. Then a time came when Paul had his special encounter with Jesus, and it is my prayer that anyone provoked by the above statements will also receive personal ministry by our Lord through His Spirit.

JESUS EVEN LOVES THOSE WHO DENY HIM

> *Now Saul (Paul), still breathing threats and murder against the disciples of the Lord, went to the high priest, and asked for letters from him to the synagogues at Damascus, so that if he (Paul) found any belonging to the Way (Christians), both men and women, he might bring them bound to Jerusalem. And it came about that as he journeyed, he was approaching Damascus, and suddenly a light from heaven flashed around him; and he fell to the ground, and heard a voice saying to him,* **"Saul, Saul, why are you persecuting Me (Jesus)?"**
> *Acts 9:1-4*

Notice, Jesus didn't seem to be angry or upset with Paul. Instead, He asked Paul, "How can someone who loves Me so much, say and do the things you are doing to Me and My church?" Paul loved God. Paul was very sincere, but Paul was mistaken. We previously learned that it is possible to misunderstand the thing our Lord has told us. The Lord could easily be saying to each of us, "You know My will is that none should perish."

THE LORD DESIRES NONE SHOULD PERISH

> *First of all, the, I urge that entreaties and prayers, petitions and thanksgivings, be made on behalf of all men (to God) (v. 1),* **who desires all men to be saved and to come to the knowledge of the truth** *(v. 4).*
> *1 Timothy 2:1, 4*

*The Lord is not slow about His promise, as some count slowness, but is patient toward you, **not wishing for any to perish but for all to come to repentance.***
2 Peter 3:9

It is not difficult to imagine Jesus saying, "Why do you say or even think I won't heal you? You love Me, and I love you." Jesus isn't angry because our understanding of Him isn't perfect. He simply wants to lead us into His way. It's for His glory and our own well-being.

However, Satan, our accuser, doesn't care where we're coming from. He will gladly take either form of confession, repressed denial, or expressed denial directly to our God and remind Him of His word. Where we fail to take God at His word, Satan expects God to keep His word.

TOO BAD GOD, YOU CAN'T HELP

But he who denies Me** (Jesus and His work) before men **shall be denied** (outside help) **before the angels of God.
Luke 12:9

Again, we see what it means to give Satan an opportunity. First, we give him an opportunity to afflict us, by our sin, unconfessed and unrepentant; then we allow him to continue that affliction by not confessing that the good news of Jesus Christ applies to us. God has given us some sensational opportunities. God has provided us with incredible benefits. Why would anyone of us choose to ignore them?

HEALING: A BENEFIT IN JESUS

*Bless the Lord, oh my soul, and forget none of His benefits; Who pardons all your iniquities; **Who heals all your diseases.***
Psalms 103:2, 3

All heaven rejoiced the moment you believed in your heart Jesus died for you and your sins; and believe me, Satan cursed the moment you declared with your mouth that Jesus is your Lord and Savior and that God raised Him from the dead.

HEAVEN REJOICED

*"I tell you that in the same way, **there will be more joy in heaven over one sinner who repents,** than over ninety-nine righteous persons who need no repentance."*
Luke 15:7

Have you ever declared with your mouth that Jesus is your Healer? All heaven is anxiously awaiting that recognition and declaration as well. You were eternally separated from God an instant before you received Jesus as your personal Savior. Then in less than a microsecond of time, with your belief and your confession, you became His child. Up until that point, God was limited by your lack of belief and of course, by your lack of confession. The moment we recognize and confess Jesus is also our Healer, then God is no longer limited in this area of our lives. He can then enforce our claim to this benefit

SORRY, SATAN, GOD WILL HELP

*And I (Jesus) say to you, everyone who confesses Me (My word and my benefits), before men, **the Son of Man shall confess him also before the angels of God**. (who then will be dispatched to his aid).*
Luke 12:8

Some of us have attempted the above because of the urging and insistence of other well-meaning brothers and sisters in Jesus. We went through the motions in our flesh but not in our spirit. Unfortunately, the results were dismal. The following will probably cover some of the feelings that each of us may have experienced. "Do you know how I feel when I confess what **you** say is God's Word, and my body and my mind seem to be no different? **I feel** like a fool. **I feel** like a hypocrite. **I feel** like I'm the only person on the face of the earth who is trying to believe this. **I feel** like everyone is looking at me as if I were some kind of fanatic, or possibly that I'm even mentally unbalanced. **I feel** some people tolerate me and others laugh at me. **I feel** very uncomfortable, and **I feel** all alone. What's the use? Why try to hang in there?" Well, the first thing **you** need to understand is that **your** situation will be influenced more favorably by what **you** believe rather than by what others say or believe. **You** are to believe what **God says** and not what others say.

GOD'S POWER IS RELEASED BY AGREEING WITH HIS WORD

> *For I am not ashamed of the gospel of Christ: for it is the power of God unto salvation (or healing) to everyone who believes, to the Jew first and also to the Greek. For in it the righteousness of God is revealed (our healing is seen) from faith to faith; as it is written.* ***"But the righteous man shall live by faith*** *(confessing what we believe, not what we feel)."* Romans 1:16, 17

We should never feel uncomfortable or ashamed when we tell others that God's word applies to us personally. For instance, God's word says, that by Christ's stripes (whipping), we have been healed. Maybe those you work with don't agree with you, **but Jesus does**. Maybe your family doesn't agree with you, **but Jesus does**. Maybe your brothers and sisters in the Lord don't agree with you, **but Jesus does**. Maybe your pastor and church elders don't agree with you, **but Jesus does**. Maybe the dean of one of the most respected institutions of theological training doesn't agree with you, **but Jesus still does**, because He always agrees with His own word. Jesus always says "amen" to His word, and amen means: *so let it be*. Thank You, Jesus.

JESUS ALWAYS AGREES WITH HIS WORD

> *And I (Jesus) say to you, everyone who confesses Me (My words, My benefits), before men, the Son of Man shall confess (say the same thing about) him also before the angels of God.*
> *Luke 12:8*

Every time I remind myself of these truths, these promises, I discern the momentum changing in my own life. No matter how bad I may look or feel, why would I ever want to say anything other than, "God's promises apply to me!" Does that mean the battle is over? No! However, it does mean the victory is assured. Don't stop confessing God's word. They are the words that assure the victory of the Lord. HANG IN THERE, BABY!

VICTORY IS ASSURED

> *My son, give attention to my words; incline your ear to My sayings. Do not let them depart from your sight; Keep them in the mist of your heart. **For they are life to those who find them, and health to all their whole body.*** *Proverbs 4:20-22*

If Jesus says, let all the above be so, and we know He does; then who or what can keep it from happening?

NOTHING CAN STOP GOD FROM HEALING US, BUT US

> *What then shall we say to these things? **If God is for us, who is against us** (v. 31)? For I am convinced that neither death, nor life, nor angels, nor principalities, nor things present, nor things to come, nor powers, nor height, nor depth, nor any other created thing, shall be able to separate us from the love of God, which is in Christ Jesus our Lord (vv. 38, 39).*
> *Romans 8:31, 38, 39*

THIS PRESCRIPTION PROVIDES
THE FOLLOWING BENEFIT

1. Confidence that trusting the word of God is the thing to do.

CASE STUDIES

WHO SAID, "BE FRUITFUL AND MULTIPLY?"

NO.8

Greg and Nancy S., a young couple we knew, had been attending a weekly Bible study and fellowship at our home. They had been married a few years, but the Lord had not blessed them with children. Although they had been trying for some time, they were now becoming discouraged. One evening they revealed this fact to those who happened to be at the fellowship. They said they had been seeing a doctor, but nothing seemed to help. They were naturally concerned, and they requested prayer for their situation. The first thing we did was to determine if it was God's will for them to have children. Once you know God's will regarding a situation, then you can pray with confidence. When we agreed it was God's will for a couple who desired children to expect that blessing, we attempted to discover what was frustrating God's will. We discovered that Nancy had been an adopted child. When she learned of this fact, she allowed bitterness and unforgiveness into her life. The dangers of unforgiveness were pointed out, and that situation was resolved. Prayer, ministry, and deliverance then followed, and after a few months the two were on their way to becoming proud parents.

Q & A (questions and answers)

1. Do you **see** any of the three definitions of **faith** as pointed out in Rx 14? Explain your answer.

2. Read or review Rx 17 and 19.

3. Read, consider, and discuss (if possible): Genesis 1:28, Genesis 9:1, Psalms 128:1-6, Matthew 18:21-35.

Rx 25

THE UNANSWERED PRAYER

How many times have you prayed and felt God didn't answer your prayer? Me too! Maybe a well-intentioned Christian tried to encourage you by telling you something like this: "God answers all prayers. His answer was just, 'No.'" Or maybe your friend's advice was more instructional, and it went something like this: "Don't feel so bad. You may have asked with the wrong motive."

A SURE "NO" ANSWER

> *You ask and do not receive, because you ask with wrong motives,* so that you may spend it on your pleasures.
> *James 4:3*

In certain situations, the above may be sound advice; but if our situation is the need for healing, then neither explanation applies.

JESUS DESIRES TO HEAL ALL

> *"You know of Jesus of Nazareth,* how God anointed Him with the Holy Spirit and with power, and how *He went about doing good, and healing all who are oppressed by the devil; for God was with Him."*
> *Acts 10:38*

However, there is a biblical account that we can not escape. It is the sickness and the resulting death of Lazarus.

LAZARUS'S SICKNESS

Now a certain man was sick, Lazarus of Bethany,
the village of Mary and her sister Martha.
John 11:1

Mary, Martha and Lazarus were good friends of Jesus, so Mary and Martha naturally sent for Him.

JESUS INFORMED

The sister's therefore sent to Him, saying, **"Lord, behold, he whom You love is sick."**
John 11:3

Now think about this for a moment. You're not feeling well; in fact you're very sick. That's the bad news. However, the good news is, Jesus loves you, and He has been notified by your sisters of your sickness. That would certainly improve my attitude concerning my situation. How about yours? However, Lazarus has something, that makes his situation look even better.

JESUS LOVED MARY AND MARTHA

Now Jesus loved Martha and her sister, and Lazarus.
John 11:5

Of course, Lazarus didn't know how Jesus initially responded, but if he had he would have even felt better about his situation.

JESUS' RESPONSE

> *But when Jesus heard it, He said,* **"This sickness is not unto death,** *but for the glory of God, that the Son of God may be glorified by it."*
> *John 11:4*

All Lazarus had to do was sit back and wait for Jesus to hurry back to Bethany and take care of his sickness. He had healed countless others before. He had even healed strangers; and Lazarus was a close friend whom Jesus loved. No problem. Right? Well not exactly.

JESUS DELAYED

> *When therefore He heard that he was sick,* **He stayed there two days longer in the place where He was.**
> *John 11:6*

It was during this delay that Lazarus died; and that's when Jesus decided to go to Lazarus. If Lazarus had known that was going to happen, he might have said, "I didn't see that coming."

JESUS HEADS FOR LAZARUS

> *and after that He said to them, "Our friend Lazarus has fallen asleep; but I go, that I may awaken him out of sleep." The disciples therefore said to Him, "Lord, if he has fallen asleep, he will recover (vv. 11, 12)."* **Then Jesus therefore said** *to them plainly,* **"Lazarus is dead, and I am glad for your sakes that I was not there, so that you may believe;** *but let us go to him (vv. 14, 15)."*
> *John 11:11, 12, 14, 15*

Lazarus died! What went wrong? Mary and Martha sent for Jesus. They prayed. Jesus heard about Lazarus in time to do something. In fact, Jesus said, "This sickness is not unto death." How could Jesus, who is God in the flesh, make such a mistake? If Jesus didn't answer the prayers of Mary and Martha, whom He loved, then what are our chances? Don't let these questions bother you. We will soon see that Jesus didn't make a mistake and that Mary and Martha's prayer was not THE UNANSWERED PRAYER. And don't let the enemy trick you. Jesus loves you just as much as He loved Mary, Martha, and Lazarus.

Remember Job? Remember how it troubled God when He allowed Satan to touch His blameless servant?

GOD WAS TROUBLED

> And the Lord said to Satan, "Have you considered My servant Job? For there is no one like him on the earth, a blameless and upright man fearing God and turning away from evil. And he still holds fast his integrity, **although you incited Me against him,** to ruin him without cause."
> Job 2:3

God had His own reason for allowing this to occur to Job, but Job certainly hadn't provided the reason. God used Job to illustrate that the blameless do not have to be concerned about potential sickness, nor do they have to remain in a state of sickness or disease.

If I may say so, Lazarus is the New Testament counterpart of Job. He also is a singular illustration. In fact, Lazarus is the ultimate illustration of God answering the prayer of the sick. "How can that be?" you ask. Actually, people die everyday in hospitals throughout the world only to be brought back to life through the efforts of doctors, devices, and drugs. How long they were dead is of no concern to them. The only thing that really matters to them is that they are once again alive. Remarkably, that was not the mindset of those who lived during the time of Christ. The concept of death held by the first-century Jew was as follows. At death, the spirit of the individual left the body, but it remained around the deceased for approximately three days.[1] As you can easily see, that view was considerably different than the view or views held today. The definition of death today can vary greatly. For instance, today we have two major medical definitions. One is *physical death*, where the heart fails to function, and another is *brain dead*, where the brain waves cease to exist. Of course, God has His own definition, and He revealed part of that definition to Martha.

JESUS DEFINES DEATH

Jesus said to her, **"I am the resurrection and the life; he who believes in Me shall live even if he dies,** *and everyone who lives and believes in Me shall never die. Do you believe this?"*
John 11:25, 26

As far as Jesus was concerned, Lazarus had never died. Therefore, Jesus was not mistaken when He said, "This sickness is not unto death." However, Jesus was in the process of revealing a major truth. That truth is that there is a resurrection of the physical body after what we consider as death. There was only one way He could prove that point and that was by meeting the definition of death held by the Jewish culture. Consequently, Jesus had to be sure Lazarus was considered dead for three days.

Now let's return to our other problem. Lazarus was sick, Jesus was informed, but Lazarus died. When Mary was notified that Jesus was approaching, she immediately went to Him.

MARY GOES TO JESUS

Therefore, when Mary came where Jesus was, she saw Him and fell at His feet, saying to Him, **"Lord, if You had been here, my brother would not have died."**
John 11:32

---

[1]   Albert Barnes, Barnes' Notes On The New Testament, (Grand Rapids, Kregel Publications, 1974), p. 319.

Here, Mary echoes the words of her sister, Martha. Listen to Martha.

MARTHA'S WORDS EXACTLY

Martha therefore said to Jesus, ***"Lord if you had been here, my brother would not have died."***
John 11:21

Jesus loved Mary, Martha, and Lazarus. If I were standing next to Jesus, I am sure I would have heard something like this: "Jesus, why didn't you come? Why were you not here in time to heal our brother?" Jesus was about to make one of the most important statements in all of His word, but there was no way He could remove Himself from the human emotion of that moment. The very thought that God is somehow separated and independent of our feelings would be totally incorrect. God is deeply involved in our situations. God has a very personal relationship with each of His children.

JESUS FELT THE SORROW

When Jesus therefore saw her weeping, and the Jews who came with her, also weeping, He was deeply moved in spirit, and was troubled. *And said; "Where have you laid him?" They said to Him, "Lord come and see."* ***JESUS WEPT.***
John 11:33-35

Jesus wept is the shortest verse in all the Bible, and a discussion concerning those two words could easily fill an entire chapter. Mary was weeping, and so were the Jews who were with her. Have you ever had your emotions released by seeing the emotions of others being poured out? Mary and the Jews were grieving with wailing and other loud sounds of expressions, but not necessarily tears. However, their sorrow triggered our Lord's deep felt emotions, and tears streamed down His face. Don't lose track of the fact that this is your Creator, your God, crying over the death of one of His children.

GOD IS INVOLVED IN ALL OUR LIVES AND DEATHS

> *Precious in the sight of the Lord is the death of His godly ones.*
> *Psalms 116:15*

Here, Jesus was about to demonstrate the reality of the resurrection, but the prerequisite for that moment was the loss of the life of Lazarus, His friend, through sickness. It was a loss of life that appeared to occur because He did not respond as anticipated. His seeming lack of response brought forth the normal questions.

MAN ALWAYS QUESTIONS GOD

> *But some of them said, "Could not this man, who opened the eyes of him who was blind, have kept this man also from dying?"*
> *John 11:37*

This type of question again deeply moved Jesus. He fully understood the implications. Consequently, Jesus proceeded to the tomb, had the cover removed, and . . .

"HEALED" LAZARUS

> *And when He had said these things, He cried out with a loud voice,* ***"Lazarus, come forth." He who had died came forth,*** *bound hand and foot with wrappings; and his face was wrapped around with a cloth. Jesus said to them, "Unbind him, and let him go."*
> *John 11:43, 44*

Sure, Jesus proved there is a resurrection of our physical bodies, but He also *proved* that when a believer asks God to heal him or her, God will respond accordingly. Did anyone wonder if Lazarus was still sick? That thought never occurred. Did it occur to you? Jesus restored a decaying Lazarus. He restored a dead man. He didn't just heal a dying man.

It troubled Jesus greatly that it appeared He had ignored the prayers of Mary and Martha. It brought tears to His eyes when He experienced their sorrow and grief, but it never has to happen again. There doesn't have to be another Lazarus. God has made His position very clear on both subjects: the resurrection and healing.

So what's the bottom line? Death is not a deadline for faith, and God is omnipresent.

Mary and Martha believed Jesus wanted to heal Lazarus, but they didn't understand His omnipresence. God is everywhere. Distance is never a problem.

MARY AND MARTHA DIDN'T UNDERSTAND

> *Therefore, when **Mary came where Jesus was**, she saw Him and fell at His feet, **saying** to Him, "**Lord, if you had been here . . .**"*
> *John 11:32*

> ***Martha** therefore **said** to Jesus, "**Lord if you had been here . . .**"*
> *John 11:21*

They didn't understand Jesus is God, and God is everywhere.

JESUS IS ALWAYS WITH US

> *"Go therefore and make disciples of all nations, baptizing them in the name of the Father, and the Son, and the Holy Spirit, teaching them to observe all that I commanded*

you; and lo, **I am with you always, even to the end of the age.**"
Matthew 28:20

We individually need to realize that when we ask God to heal us, we are asking for something that God also desires. God wants us to be healthy. We are asking for something in His will. We are not asking selfishly.

A SURE "YES" ANSWER

And this is the confidence which we have before Him, that, **if we ask anything according to His will, He hears us. And if we know that He hears us in whatever we ask, we know that we have the requests which we have asked from Him.**
1 John 5:14, 15

THIS PRESCRIPTION PROVIDES THE FOLLOWING BENEFIT

1. Confidence that we can ask for healing from any condition or disease.

CASE STUDIES

WHAT IS A PERSON SUPPOSED TO BELIEVE?

Our second child, Leon Troy, was born six weeks premature. He was also born with severe physical problems. He was left with only partial function of his sole surviving kidney. He also experienced three major surgeries in the first fifteen months of his life.

His resulting physical condition dictated that if he survived his teen years, he would be considerably shorter in stature than if he had not experienced these difficulties. In addition, neither his mother nor his father is very tall. And as could be expected, he was always among the smallest, if not the smallest, in his peer group.

He had his fourth and final surgery when he was eight years old. On an ensuing follow-up exam, x-rays were taken to evaluate his kidney. When my wife, who is a registered nurse, viewed them, his kidney reminded her of a scrambled egg and not anything like a kidney bean. Troy's past, present, and future were staring her right in the face. It was on her way home from the doctor's visit that she realized she had a decision to make. Either the x-rays were conclusive or God's word was the final say. Later that same evening she told me what had transpired, and that she chose to believe God. She said she considered the x-rays the best shot Satan had to keep her from having faith in God's word. So she decided the x-rays were the lie, and God's word was the truth.

We continued to see that Troy had the best medical attention we could provide, but his physical condition didn't appear to change medically over the course of the next ten years. However, the miraculous thing is our son is now five foot ten inches tall and weighs nearly two hundred pounds. Both of those statistics are greater than his dad's by nearly ten percent.

Q & A (questions and answers)

1. Do you **see** any of the three definitions of **faith** as pointed out in Rx 14? Explain your answer.

2. Read or review Rx 14.

3. Read, consider, and discuss (if possible): Mark 3:1-5, Luke 6:6, 7.

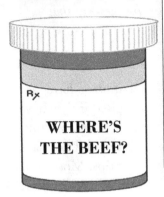

Rx26

INSTRUCTIONS

For this reason I endure all things for the sake of those who are chosen, that they also may obtain the salvation which is in Christ Jesus and with it eternal glory.
2 Timothy 2:10

There was an expression that became very popular in the 1980s. That expression was WHERE'S THE BEEF? A well-known fast-food chain used this expression in a series of TV commercials. These commercials showed a little old lady examining her hamburger and then demanding, "WHERE'S THE BEEF?" The implication was that there wasn't sufficient ground beef inside her sandwich. I assume the chain was attempting to inform its audience that if they happened to go somewhere else for burgers they could run the risk of being dissatisfied. In other words, "You'll find what you are looking for inside of our burgers."

Today many Christians have not been informed healing is included in their salvation, and still others don't personally inspect Christ to discover all that is in Him. If any of us fall into either of the above two categories or both, it doesn't mean there is something wrong with us or that we are second-rate Christians? Absolutely not! It simply means that we are uninformed, but this isn't anything new. Uninformed Christians have been around since the first-century.

UNINFORMED CHRISTIANS

Therefore, if the whole church comes together in one place, and all speak with tongues, and there come in those

*who are **uninformed** or unbelievers, will they not say that
you are out of your minds?*
1 Corinthians 14:23 (KJV)

How can someone believe God's promises if they have not
heard about them, and how can someone become gifted if they have
not heard about the gifts God has for them? Today, if we are uninformed, that's a sorry situation. Why? The early church did not have
the advantage of a written Bible at everyone's finger tips. Most of us
can own a Bible, or at least we have access to one. We really don't
have an excuse for remaining uninformed. What is even more unfortunate is that the uninformed and the ungifted Christian is the one
who is most likely to miss out on experiencing the miracles of God.

I certainly do not want to be labeled as a Christian who is uninformed. Do you? And I don't want to be a Christian who doesn't
expect or inspect the things of God. If you are like me, then you want
to have everything that's available *in* Jesus Christ. Now that is just the
point. Is healing included *in* Jesus?

I have a marvelous wife. She is truly a wonderful blessing from
the Lord. Christmas, birthdays, showers, and other occasions that
provide an opportunity to offer gifts are times my wife has really
excelled. Frequently, she will present a larger gift box that contains
many other smaller gift boxes inside. Every time she does something
like this, she reminds me of our heavenly Father.

JESUS IS GOD'S LARGEST GIFT BOX

*"For God so loved the world that **He gave His only
begotten Son**, that whoever believes in Him should not perish, but have eternal life."*
John 3:16

Who would want to refuse such a gift? Or stated in other words,
who wouldn't want to receive such a gift?

JESUS IS TO BE RECEIVED

> ***But as many as received Him,*** *to them He gave the right to become children of God, even to those who believe in His name.*
> *John 1:12*

The moment we received Jesus as God's biggest gift, our personal Savior, we became part of God's family. God said you have the right; yes, the authority to say He is your Father. You are now His child. I can remember when I was just six-years old that I received a cowboy outfit for Christmas. Mom helped me get all dressed up, and then Dad pinned a sheriff's badge on my shirt. That badge meant I was no longer just another cowboy. One day, the above verse took on a special meaning to me. I realized my heavenly Father had pinned a badge on me that read, *God's kid.*

Now that we have received the big package that is Jesus, what else is inside?

A VERY SPECIAL GIFT

> *For the wages of sin is death, but **the free gift of God is eternal life IN Christ Jesus** our Lord.*
> *Romans 6:23*

Here, we see that we not only get to be a child of God, but also included *in* Jesus Christ is eternal life. My wife would occasionally do the multiple-gift thing with our children. I can remember them opening the big package and then one smaller gift after another. Once in a while they would open a gift that really captured their attention, and for a moment, you wondered if they would ever finish opening the remaining gifts. They would get so excited about a certain gift that all the other gifts didn't seem to matter. Eternal life can be such a gift. We can become so excited and so grateful that our heavenly Father could easily wonder if we are ever going to discover everything else He has for us *in* Jesus. Of course, He is God and He does know, but as for us, do we continue to discover all that is *in* Christ Jesus, or does our inspection slow down or even stop? Is there anything else *in* Jesus? Oh yes, probably more than any of us in this lifetime will ever discover, but let's continue to inspect as well as expect.

So what else do we find *in* Jesus?

SALVATION IS IN JESUS

> *For this reason I endure all things for the sake of those who are chosen, that they also may obtain* **the salvation which is IN Christ Jesus** *and with it eternal glory.*
> *2 Timothy 2:10*

The right to call ourselves God's kids, have eternal life, and now salvation are *in* the person of Jesus. However, just what is salvation? Salvation is a big subject, so maybe the question should be, "Can we expect healing to be included in salvation?" If we expect healing, to be a part of salvation, then we need to inspect salvation or a least discover if healing is linked to this bigger subject.

It would be easy for us to conclude that only a panel of scholars would be able to make such a determination. What makes scholars so privileged? May I explain? Isn't our all-capable and infallible God able to reveal the truth to each of us as individuals through His word and by His Spirit, or must we be dependent upon other fallible people such as ourselves? I explained earlier that the Bible is the word of God. God personally selected every word and inspired the human authors in such a way that each author himself chose to use the word that God had selected. In addition, each author was able to do this without his personality being altered in any way. Does this explanation seem difficult to imagine? It shouldn't. After all, God is the potter of each of us.

GOD IS THE POTTER AND MAN IS THE CLAY

On the contrary, who are you, O man, who answers back to God? **The thing molded will not say to the molder,** *"Why did you make me like this," will it?*
Romans 9:20

This knowledge and confidence that each word in the Bible was selected and put there by God is our greatest comfort, along with knowing what follows.

GOD HELPS BELIEVERS UNDERSTAND HIS WORD

And beginning with Moses and with all the proph-ets, **He (Jesus) explained to them the things concerning Himself in all the Scriptures** *(v. 27). And they said to one another, "Were not our hearts burning within us* **while He was speaking to us on the road, while He was explain-ing the Scriptures to us** *(v. 32)?"* **Then He (Jesus) opened their minds to understand the Scriptures** *(v. 45).*
Luke 24:27, 32, 45

It is also comforting to know that very ordinary people were able to understand God's message and to receive the ministry of our Lord. In fact, the *down-and-outers* received Jesus just as easy as the *in-and-outers.*

GOD HELPS NONBELIEVERS UNDERSTAND HIS WORD

And it happened that as He was reclining at the table in the house, **behold many tax gathers and sinners came and were dining with Jesus** *and His disciples. And when the Pharisees saw this, they said to His disciples, "Why is your Teacher eating with tax collectors and sinners?" But when He*

heard this, He said, **"It is not those who are healthy who need a physician, but those who are sick."**
Matthew 9:10-12

The people who were the religious *in crowd*, the Pharisees, had more trouble understanding Jesus' message and ministry than those whom the Pharisees felt were inferior. It is interesting to note that Jesus in His reply likened those who come to Him as those who need healing. Since God personally selected each word in the Bible, this certainly is no mere coincidence.

Unfortunately, the above scenario reoccurs throughout church history, and we see it again mentioned to the church at Corinth.

WE ALWAYS NEED JESUS

For consider your calling, brethren, that there were not many wise according to the flesh, not many mighty, not many noble; but God has chosen the foolish things of the world to shame the wise, and God has chosen the weak things of the world to shame the things which are strong, and the base things of the world and the despised, God has chosen, the things that are not that He might nullify the things that are, that **no man should boast before God.**
1 Corinthians 1:26-29

There is one additional comment I would like to make before we return to the question, "Is healing included in salvation?" The Old Testament was originally written in Hebrew with some Aramaic portions;[1] the New Testament was written in Greek.[2] However, the group of men who translated the Bible into the language of the people, the English language, spoken at the time of King James I of

---

[1]   Benjamin Davidson, The Analytical Hebrew and Chaldee Lexicon, (Grand Rapids, Zondervan Publishing House, 1975), Preface.

[2]   Robert H. Gundry, A Survey of the New Testament, (Grand Rapids, Zondervan, Publishing House, 1976), p. XV.

England, where the best scholars of their day. I happen to believe God also molded those men to perform that very task so the common people of that day could easily understand the message of our Lord. That means the words they selected in their translations accurately communicated the Lord's message to the English speaking world of their day. Someone who lived at that time and who was able to read and understand the language would not need an interpreter to help him or her understand the message of our Lord. In other words, an individual would not have the need for a personal scholar to insure they knew the truth. The same can be said for us today. If any of us need outside help to better understand God's simple written-word, then we can count on Him personally to provide such through the agency of the person He calls the Holy Spirit. The Holy Spirit will reveal God's truth to us. It is one of His jobs.

THE HOLY SPIRIT: OUR TEACHER AND GUIDE

*Now we have received, not the spirit of the world, but the Spirit who is from God, **that we might know the things freely given to us by God**.*
2 Corinthians 2:12, 13

*But the Helper, the Holy Spirit, whom the Father will send in My name, **He will teach you all things,** and bring to your remembrance all that I said to you.*
John 14:26

*But when **He**, the Spirit of truth comes, **He will guide you into all the truth**; for **He** will not speak on **His** own initiative, but whatever **He** hears, **He** will speak; and **He** will disclose to you what is to come.*
John 16:13

I took the time to say the above, because I believe if we can read our Bible with only a basic understanding of English, and if we are willing to ask the person Holy Spirit to reveal God's truth to us, we can know the things God has freely given to us. Tax collectors and sinners had no problem and neither should we. So let's proceed to read God's word, and let's see if we can determine an answer to our question, "Is healing included in salvation?"

THIS PRESCRIPTION PROVIDES
THE FOLLOWING BENEFIT

1.   Confidence that everything we need is available in Jesus

CASE STUDIES

NO.10

HOW IMPORTANT IS DAILY FORGIVENESS?

I began to pastor a pioneer church soon after graduating from Bible college. One Sunday, we had a family of three join us for our morning worship service. When the service was concluded, the congregation got to meet them, and I had an opportunity to speak to the husband, whose name was Gary. He was remarkably open about himself. He informed me he had been in therapy for some time because he exhibited a suicidal tendency. He was already a believer, so he recognized this tendency was inappropriate. Just before they left, I gave him a book to read, *Pigs in the Parlor.* I asked him to tell me what he thought of it when we saw each other the next Sunday.

The following Sunday, he and his family returned, and he told me he could relate to what he had read. Then he said he wanted the same freedom as those in the book obtained, so we set a time for ministry. He was very eager for help, so it didn't take long to discover he was being troubled by an evil spirit. However, it took three sessions of nearly three hours each before he revealed the fact that he had engaged in just one homosexual experience (Romans 1:26, 27) during his time in the military. **Just one time.** When he confessed that act and asked God to forgive him, the spirit soon surrendered and left when commanded in the name of Jesus to begone. A couple years later, Lu and I accidentally (sure) met him and his family in Kona, Hawaii, and he was still rejoicing in his freedom.

Q & A (questions and answers)

1. Do you **see** any of the three definitions of **faith** as pointed out in Rx 14? Explain your answer.

2. Read or review Rx 22.

3. Read, consider, and discuss (if possible): Matthew 6:9-13, Mark 16:17, I John 1:9.

Rx27

Rx
SEEK AND
YOU SHALL
FIND

Have you ever been ready to go someplace, but when you went to get your keys or glasses you couldn't locate them? Frustrating, isn't it? It has happened to all of us. Finally you give up. Next you go to the mirror to check your hair or some other aspect of your personal appearance, and guess what? To your amazement you discover your glasses resting comfortably upon your forehead. Laughable, isn't it? This is the point: There are areas of our person that our eyes are unable to inspect by themselves. Sometimes we need a little outside help. The word of God is no different. We all need the assistance of the Holy Spirit to reveal what's been there all along.

Nonetheless, we know that the person of the Holy Spirit can reveal things to our hearts long before we discover them in God's word. However, as we continue to inspect God's word, eventually His Spirit will confirm by that very word what He had previously revealed to our hearts.

GOD'S WORD REVEALED BY HIS SPIRIT

For who among men knows the thoughts of a man except the spirit of the man, which is in him? Even so the thoughts of God no one knows except the Spirit of God. Now we have received, not the spirit of the world, but the Spirit who is from

*God, that we might know the things freely given to us by God, which things we also speak, not in words taught by human wisdom, **but in those taught by the Spirit, combining spiritual thoughts with spiritual words.***
1 Corinthians 2:11-13

Now that this is fresh in our minds, let's ask another question: have you ever sensed in your spirit that God really wants His people to be healthy, or that God really wants to heal all of His children? I'm sure there was a time in my Christian experience that I wasn't sure about the above, but as long as I can remember, I have believed God wants me healthy.

Of course, I've had many a well-meaning brother or sister try to convince me that it isn't a universal given. They have tried to tell me that it is not always God's will to heal all of His kids from sickness. Their reasoning is interesting, but I've discovered that as I earnestly inspected God's word, He has affirmed the truth: He wants all of us healthy. Long ago, God had revealed this truth to my heart by His Spirit, and eventually, His Spirit revealed this same truth in His word.

The following is just one of the ways God's Spirit used God's word to confirm that revelation. Let's start by looking at the Old Testament.

THE OLD TESTAMENT

*Then I heard the voice of the Lord, saying, "Whom shall I send, and who will go for Us?" Then I said, "Here am I. Send me!" He said, "Go, and tell this people: 'Keep on listening, but do not perceive; keep on looking, but do not understand.' Render the hearts of this people insensitive, their ears dull, and their eyes dim, otherwise they might **see** with their eyes, **hear** with their ears, **understand** with their hearts, and **return** and **be healed.***"
Isaiah 6:8-10

Here God is speaking to Isaiah and telling him to go to the people and tell them how to be healed. But wait, does the word *healed* here mean physical healing or national healing or maybe both?

At first, we might say national healing. It would seem logical. However, the Hebrew word translated *healed* overwhelming refers to physical healing.[1] So, if national healing is the meaning here, it would seem difficult to separate national healing from physical healing. Remember, in the *exodus*, the people were *nationally* set free from the bondage of Egypt, however they all left *physically* restored as well. Even though they were in the process of leaving Egypt, they were already free of physical problems, but their full salvation was still in progress. When they arrived at the Red Sea, just one look over their shoulders revealed the mightiest army on the face of the earth was heading straight for them. Not a pretty picture.

SALVATION CERTAINLY MORE THAN JUST HEALING

> *Then they said to Moses, "Is it because there are no graves in Egypt that you have taken us away to die in the wilderness? Why have you dealt with us in this way, bringing us out of Egypt (v. 11)?" But Moses said to the people, "Do not fear! Stand by and **see the salvation of the Lord** which He will accomplish for you today; for the Egyptians whom you have seen today, you will never see them again forever (v. 13)."*
> *Exodus 14:11, 13*

It would appear that salvation is a process in which healing is only one aspect.

The disciples of Jesus asked Him why He spoke to the multitudes in parables? His answer was very interesting.

JESUS QUOTES ISAIAH

---

[1] James Strong, Strong's Exhaustive Concordance of the Bible, (Grand Rapids, World Publishing, 1986), p. 624.

*"Therefore I speak to them in parables; because while seeing they do not see, and while hearing they do not hear, nor do they understand. And in this case the prophecy of Isaiah is being fulfilled, which says, 'You will keep on hearing, but will not understand; and you will keep on seeing, but will not perceive; for the heart of this people has become dull, and with their ears they scarcely hear, and they have closed their eyes lest they should **see** with their eyes, and **hear** with their ears, and **understand** with their heart and **return**, and **I should heal them.**'"*
Matthew 13:13-15

In this instance, the true author of the Bible, God, in the person of Jesus, chooses to repeat what He had said earlier through the mouth of Isaiah. And the Greek word He chose to use and that was translated *heal* means to cure, to heal, to make whole.[2] It is the exact word used *to heal* the brokenhearted (Luke 4:18), and the power of the Lord was present *to heal* them (Luke 5:17 KJV), and when He sent out His disciples to *heal* the sick (Luke 9:2), and when a royal official asked Jesus *to heal* his son, (John 4:47). It may not be obvious, but Luke, a physician, was the vessel God choose to record three of these four instances.

We have seen that God has spoken the same message twice: once in the Old Testament and once in the New Testament. Does this mean these verses are *especially* important?

With that question fresh in our minds, I would like to quote a Hall of Fame catcher, Yogi Berra, who was also known for his unintentional sense of humor. One day Yogi was asked a question about his team's unexpected lack of performance. Yogi's reply was, "It ain't over till it's over."[3] Well, (reader), It ain't over.

---

[2] Ibid., p. 264.
[3] Lawrence Berra, The Yogi Book, (New York, Workman Publishing, 1998), p. 157.

JOHN'S GOSPEL ALSO REPEATS ISAIAH

> *But though He had performed so many signs before them, yet they were not believing in Him (v. 37); for this cause they could not believe, for Isaiah said again, "He has blinded their eyes, and He hardened their hearts; least they* **see with their eyes, and perceive with their heart, and be converted, and I heal them** *(vv. 39, 40)."*
> *John 12:37, 39, 40*

Again God draws our attention to what factors either prevent or lead up to healing. And, yes, the same exact word is used for *heal* here as in the other above instances. We can see by looking at John 12:37 that Jesus is not referring to just national healing but to individual healing as well. Here, it is individuals who are refusing to believe in the signs Jesus is performing before their very eyes, which included physical healing.

Take a deep breath, it's almost over. Three times God has stated the same message, or truth. We heard it from Isaiah, and we heard it from Jesus as recorded in both Matthew's and John's account of the gospel. Would you believe, God repeats it yet another time. This time Paul, the apostle, reiterates this same message. Paul is a prisoner in Rome, and it is there that he calls for the leading men of the Jewish faith to come and hear his message.

PAUL QUOTES ISAIAH AS WELL AS JESUS

> *And when they did not agree with one another, they began leaving after Paul had spoken one parting word, "The Holy Spirit rightly spoke through Isaiah the prophet to your fathers, saying, 'Go to this people and say, "You will keep on hearing, but you will not understand; and you will keep on seeing, but you will not perceive; for the heart of this people has become dull, and with their ears they scarcely hear, and they have closed their eyes; lest they should* **see** *with their eyes,*

*and **hear** with their ears, and **understand** with their heart
and **return**, and **I should heal them**." "Let it be known to
you therefore, that **this salvation of God** has been sent to the
Gentiles; they will also listen."*
Acts 28:25-28

In this instance, Paul's emphasis is clearly upon a national
revival of the Jewish people, which would and will occur upon receiving Jesus of Nazareth as their Messiah. Fortunately, Paul does a nice
job of linking healing directly to salvation, and it has already been
demonstrated from the first three usages of this passage that physical
healing is included in the meaning. Certainly Paul wasn't speaking of
national salvation at the exclusion of personal salvation and physical
healing when he mentioned the Gentiles.

No doubt some of you are now able to quote these words, but
that is not the point of showing how frequently God repeats this
truth. The point is to emphasize **God's overwhelming desire** for
us to know and accept what He has for us and how to obtain it.
The process of SEEING God's word, HEARING God's word, and
ALLOWING the Holy Spirit to use God's word to create faith in our
hearts is the central point. God wants us to renew our trust in Him
and to believe His word more than what others say about His word.

The apostle Paul informs us that when we do the above that
we have salvation, which we understand to be a continuing experience. An experience that includes physical healing, which is just a
mere moment within a greater moment-to-moment experience that
is called salvation.

Therefore, let us allow this truth to germinate in our hearts' and
someday we will discover that if a need for healing occurs we will
not have to even ask for it. Does this seem like an incredible thing to
say? Surely to some, but it is completely biblical. A perfect example
is recorded in each of the synoptic gospels, Matthew 9:20-22, Mark
5:25-34, and Luke 8:43-48. Let's first look at Matthew's account.

300

BELIEVING IS SEEING

> *And behold, a woman who had been suffering from a hemorrhage for twelve years, came up behind Him and **touched** the fringe of His cloak; for she was saying to herself, "If I only **touch** His garment, I shall get well." But Jesus turning and seeing her said, "Daughter, take courage; **your faith has made you well.**" And at once the woman was made well.*
> *Matthew 9:20-22*

This woman didn't even ask Jesus to heal her, and certainly Jesus never said He would heal her. So the question could easily be asked, "Her faith in what?" What occurred to bring about such faith? Jairus had already asked, and Jesus had already answered. So let's look at what happened before she was healed.

SHE KNEW JESUS MADE A PROMISE TO JAIRUS

> *And one of the synagogue officials named Jairus came up and upon seeing Him (Jesus), fell at His feet, and entreated Him earnestly, saying, "My little daughter is at the point of death; **please come and lay Your hands on her, that she may get well and live. And He (Jesus) went off with him.**"*
> *Mark 5:22-24*

When Jesus left with Jairus He had agreed that **He would lay His hands** on his (Jairus') daughter and that she would live.

Why did that make such an impression on the woman?

JESUS' HANDS (TOUCH) COULD DO WHAT OTHER'S HANDS (TOUCH) COULDN'T DO

> *And a woman who had a hemorrhage for twelve years, and had endured much at **the hands** of many physicians, and had spent all that she had and was not helped at all, but*

*rather had grown worse, after **hearing** about Jesus, came up in the crowd behind Him, **and touched** His cloak.*
Mark 5:25-27

The woman believed Jesus was going to heal Jairus' daughter by simply touching her. It was **that belief** that **led** her **to act out in faith** by going and **touching** His cloak.

Did she **hear,** did she **see**, and did she **understand** what Jesus was going to do? Yes!.

THE LORD IS YOUR HEALER

*And He said, "If you will give earnest heed to the voice of the Lord, your God, and do what is right in His sight, and give ear to His commandments, and keep all His statutes, I will put none of these diseases on you which I have put on the Egyptians; for **I, the Lord, am your healer.**"*
Exodus 15:26

We can see as far back as the second book of the Old Testament that God declares He is our healer, and in the New Testament we can see that He will heal anyone.

JESUS WILL HEAL ANYONE

*I most certainly understand now that **God is not one to show partiality,** but in every nation the man who fears Him and does what is right, is welcome to Him.*
Acts 10:34, 35

Obviously somethings are worth repeating. If we are capable of reading or hearing God's word and if we allow the person of the Holy Spirt to soften our hearts, then we will understand and believe. We will experience all that is *in* Jesus. We will experience salvation to its fullness. We will experience healing. Both are *in* Jesus. Have you received Jesus? Then expect healing. You already have healing *in* Jesus. Insist upon it! Do not allow your adversary, the devil, to deceive you and keep you from experiencing what is rightfully yours. Is healing included *in* Jesus? Is healing included *in* salvation? What other answer can there be, but YES?

THIS PRESCRIPTION PROVIDES
THE FOLLOWING BENEFIT

1. Confidence that you have discovered healing is included in Jesus

CASE STUDIES

NO.11

WILL GOD RESTORE THE LOST?

The 1970s were coming to a close when a lump was noticed in my wife's thyroid. Tests were run, and it was decided surgery was the best option. The left lobe was removed by a highly respected South Bay surgeon at Little Company of Mary Hospital in Torrance, California.

Dr. E. Chester Ridgway, former president of the American Thyroid Association, stated in World Watch & Health News that thyroid tissue does not regenerate. Consequently, Lu was then placed on a thyroid medication to keep her hormone level in balance. This is a form of prophylactic treatment that would be employed for the balance of her life. Occasionally her thyroid level would be monitored to ensure the proper level was being maintained.

Subsequently we relocated to Vista, California, and eventually to Cathedral City, California. Twenty years had come and gone since her surgery, and maintenance was becoming an issue. So Lu desired that God meet her need. She wanted God to heal her thyroid. Lu didn't want to take medication any longer. However, she only had a *little faith*, meaning she didn't stop taking her medication *cold turkey*. She needed God's reassurance. I would have liked that also. So, she asked God to heal her thyroid, and continued to take her medication until such time there were signs she didn't need it any longer.

Several months went by, then Lu started experiencing symptoms of an over active thyroid, which are irritability, sweats, nervousness, etc. She went to her physician Dr. Janet Kerrigan in Palm Desert. Dr. Kerrigan had some tests run which not only showed she was receiving too much thyroid but that the left lobe of her thyroid was present (remember, this lobe had been surgically removed). Further testing showed the thyroid gland was functioning normally and she no longer needed to take thyroid medication.

Q & A (questions and answers)

1. Do you **see** any of the three definitions of **faith** as pointed out in Rx 14? Explain your answer.

2. Review Rx 25 and read Rx 32.

3. Read, consider, and discuss (if possible): Matthew 15:30, 31 (Living Bible), John 14:14.

Rx28

INSTRUCTIONS

"And behold, I am sending forth the promise of My Father upon you; but you are to stay in the city until you are clothed with power from on high."
Luke 24:49

There was a credit card company that used as a means of promoting the benefits of their card, the following slogan: *don't leave home without it*. Very catchy. God feels the same way when it comes to advancing the gospel of His kingdom.

In the 1990s our family was attending a church where a couple we knew had a son, Logan. He had just enlisted in the army. It was following the terrorist attack on the Trade Center in 2001 that Logan was deployed to Iraq. Before he saw any action, he got to return home to see his family. It was during that time that he revealed the army hadn't issued any protective plates for his unit's body armor.

When this information reached not only his father, but also, his wife's father, corrective measures began to take place. His father-in-law worked for Keebler, the cookie company, as a supervisor in the safety and machinery division. He persuaded his employer to allow his department to produce the necessary plates for Logan's entire unit. Thankfully, before his unit was sent into harm's way, every member was provided with the necessary equipment. Remarkably, Logan was hit not once but twice by enemy fire but survived.

When we opened this second prescription file, we soon became aware that God appears to have a particular message. He has chosen to use this announcement before He enters combat against Satan's kingdom: "Repent for the kingdom of God is at hand." Obviously, this message is directed toward all mankind. It is a message that demands unconditional surrender, but it is also a message promising liberation from Satan's captivity (Colossians 1:13).

It is important to realize that man isn't the only one who hears this message. Satan isn't deaf. To him this announcement, this warning, is a battle cry announcing an invasion into a sector of his kingdom, a sector he has no intentions of surrendering, a sector he will fight to maintain. Satan will come against anyone proclaiming that message. Just how might he do that? Satan is a fast learner.

UNITY BRINGS VICTORY

> But some of them said, "He casts out demons by Beelzebul, the ruler of demons (v. 15)." But He (Jesus) knew their thoughts, and said to them, "Any kingdom divided against itself falls. And **if Satan also is divided against himself, how shall his kingdom stand** (vv. 17, 18)?"
> Luke 11:15, 17, 18

We know Satan has a kingdom, and he certainly isn't about to fight himself. However, if he can bring division within God's kingdom, among God's people, then he can slow down the progress of the kingdom of God. And where did he get that idea? Why, from Jesus, Himself. Therefore, brothers, be alert. Satan has it on good authority that if he can get a brother or sister in Christ into conflict or dispute with another brother or sister in Christ, then he will be successful in slowing down the advance of God's kingdom. The body of Christ needs to be alert, 24-7-365, against this strategy. Coupled with *doubt* and *fear,* Satan will use this as one of his primary strategies.

Now, may I return to the main point of this prescription? Jesus didn't *perform* any miracles, signs, or wonders until He was accompanied by the person of the Holy Spirit. Unless we understand God's plan, the above could be difficult to grasp. Jesus lived in a time of history when the infant death rate was off the charts. He more than likely watched His earthly father, Joseph die leaving Mary, His mother a widow. Since Jesus is God, why didn't He do something in these situations? Obviously God's plan was for Jesus to be dependent on the person of the Holy Spirit to confirm His message of the kingdom. That was God's plan for Jesus and it's God's plan for His church today. Notice, Jesus sent out *the twelve* and then *the seventy,* all equipped with the presence of the person of the Holy Spirit to enforce the authority contained in the message of the good news of God's kingdom. Finally, Jesus instructed His followers that before they begin to pursue the *great commission,* they were to wait for Him to send the promise of the Father, which is the person of the Holy Spirit who will confirm the good news of the kingdom, with signs and wonders.

It is possible your uncle might send you into battle without being properly equipped but your heavenly Father would never send you into battle without seeing you were fully prepared.

Jesus didn't take on Satan without being fully prepared by having the person of the Holy Spirit with Him. Jesus was in the role of Savior-Healer and the person of the Holy Spirit was in the role of *Enforcer,* confirming Christ's message of the kingdom. After His ascension Jesus assumed among other roles the role of Baptizer of the Holy Spirit. Today Jesus is the One who equips His believers with the same power and authority that was provided to Him. It is the same power and authority He provided to *the twelve,* to *the seventy* and all His followers after the day of Pentecost.

If Jesus, as our example, didn't begin His earthly ministry until He was accompanied by the person of the Holy Spirit then why would He tell us that we would do greater things than Him (John 14:13)[1] without sending the person of the Holy Spirit to be with us to confirm the message of His kingdom (Acts 1:5-8)?[2]

Does any Christian really think our heavenly Father would send us into *the conflict to end all conflicts* equipped with a squirt gun to face an enemy armed with a flamethrower? No. Neither do I. So **DON'T**

---

[1] Matthew Henry, Matthew Henry's Commentary, (Grand Rapids, Zondervan, 1974), p. 1590.

[2] Ibid., pp. 1636-1638.

LEAVE HOME WITHOUT IT—uh, I mean without Him. You know, the person of the Holy Spirit. Why is that again? Our Heavenly Father doesn't want us to attempt to carry out His command to spread the gospel, which includes discipleship (Matthew 28:19, 20), by confronting Satan without the power that can only be provided by the person of the Holy Spirit (Acts 1:8). Consequently, He has provided that power through the promise of the Father (Acts 1:4), that *includes the gifts of the Spirit*, that Paul mentions in 1 Corinthians 12. In Paul's context, it can easily be overlooked that the primary purpose of these gifts is to facilitate the spread of the gospel as well as being for the common good of all believers (1 Corinthians 12:7).

To make this last point easier to understand, see if you can identify from the following verses in Matthew's gospel how Jesus took advantage of seven of the nine gifts mentioned in 1 Corinthians to facilitate the spreading of the gospel: (1) Matthew 21:23–27; (2) Matthew 17:27; (3) Matthew 14:22–31; (4) Matthew 14:35–36; (5) Matthew 12:28, Mark 9:38, 39; (6) Matthew 24:1, 2; and lastly, (7) Matthew 10:21–23.

Some readers who enjoy games may find this suggestion entertaining. So here is a clue. The order of the above references correlates with the order of Paul's listing in 1 Corinthians 12. Have fun.

THIS PRESCRIPTION PROVIDES
THE FOLLOWING BENEFITS

1. Confidence that Jesus voluntarily cooperated with the Godhead (the Father, the Son, the Holy Spirit) to allow the person of the Holy Spirit to confirm His words, the words of the gospel, the good news, by performing the signs and wonders that took place in His earthly ministry
2. Confidence that God isn't going to make you sick to heal you for His glory
3. Confidence that Jesus wants to equip you with the person of the Holy Spirit to confirm His message of the gospel of the kingdom of God

CASE STUDIES

NO.12

IS THERE LIFE AFTER DEATH?

I thoroughly enjoy home Bible fellowships. The informal reading and sharing of the scriptures seasoned with the experiences of other believers is very satisfying. Some of the most memorable moments of my Christian life have come from such fellowships.

One of these moments was the result of a young lady at such a fellowship who shared that she knew of a teenage girl who was expecting and whose doctor had informed her that her baby had a condition that would prevent it from being born alive. The doctor told the girl that, among other problems, the child's lungs would not develop. Her physician suggested that the baby should be aborted.

Those of us who were present that night were all moved and we discussed the situation and prayed for her. The family of the girl heard about our meeting and were informed that some of us would like to come over and pray with them. It wasn't many days later that our daughter, myself and Christina, the person who brought the girl's situation to our attention were invited to the girl's home.

To make a long story short, we had an opportunity to share the gospel of the kingdom including repentance, forgiveness, being born again, and entering God's kingdom where all things are possible. The girl accepted God's grace and then we asked her what she would like God to do for her. She answered, "I want my baby to be born alive." We laid hands on her belly and agreed with her in prayer and gave the situation to God. However, her doctor never gave her any hope the balance of her pregnancy.

Then one evening about six o'clock our daughter called to tell us the young lady was about to give birth. A half an hour later, she called again to inform my wife and me that the girl's baby was born dead. My heart dropped, and I asked our heavenly Father how He could expect me to proclaim the good news of the gospel of the kingdom if the Holy Spirit wasn't going to confirm our Lord's message. Then I ducked. Just kidding.

I sounded just like Mary and Martha, the sisters of Lazarus. I was both shocked and disappointed.

Another half hour went by before our daughter called again to inform us the young girl's baby was now alive. The baby was crying **without lungs**, which is impossible and performing other bodily functions of a typical newborn. What wasn't typical was baby Isabella had four teeth showing. This was something her grandfather was looking forward to seeing as the child grew older. Baby Isabella lived another four hours before our Lord took her home, once and for all.

Do you know what we call someone who has been deceased for a half hour? We call them a corpse. Do you know what you call someone who can hold their breath for four hours? You call them **a miracle**. That would be impossible except for the intervention of a loving God who keeps His word when others lose hope.

The resurrection has been a major part of the gospel ever since Jesus rose from the grave. He promised that one day all who believe in Him would be resurrected. That evening at Loma Linda Hospital, nearly forty family members and friends were able to have a foretaste of the truth of the resurrection. That was something they never would have experienced if Isabella had not been carried to term. Bitter but sweet.

Q & A (questions and answers)

1. Do you **see** any of the three definitions of **faith** as pointed out in Rx 14? Explain your answer.

2. Review Rx 23 and read Rx 32.

3. Read, consider, and discuss (if possible): John 11.

This concludes Section Two. What did we learn and benefit from these prescriptions? First, we learned that we all suffer from the same thing and that everyone's treatment begins the same way (Rx 15). In addition, we learned we can avoid, as well as overcome sickness, (Rx 16). We also learned that there is a way to promote our health status (Rx 17). One of the easiest ways to do that is to cleanse oneself daily from sin (Rx 18) and that, by following the orders of our Great Physician, we can avoid all types of problems (Rx 19). However, if any problems do arise, we need to be sure and discuss them with Him (Rx 20) and not to be alarmed if our recovery takes longer than anticipated (Rx 21), not losing sight of the fact that we are taking the proper course of treatment (Rx 22). There is no doubt about it. We are availing ourselves to the best treatment available (Rx 23). In addition, we have the best care staff imaginable (Rx 24). We can ask for and expect the very best (Rx 25). And we will find it in Jesus (Rx 26). Of course, once we find it, all we need to do is ask for it (Rx 27). It is so comforting to know that He is always by our side with all that we need (Rx 28).

Now let's move on to Section Three, *Restoration*, and discover what awaits us after being healed.

SECTION THREE

 RESTORATION

Restoration means to return something to its original state. Originally God created man in His own image (Genesis 1:26). Unfortunately that didn't last very long due to man's failure to believe his God, His maker (Genesis 3:6).

Ever since man's fall, which was a Humpty Dumpty event on steroids, God's intention has been to restore the human race to the image of God. But what is the image of God? What does God look like?

God tells us that Jesus is the image of the invisible God (Colossians 1:15). When we look at the life of Christ we see God's character, His love, His forgiveness, His mercy, His grace, His commitment, His obedience, His power, His authority and His intimate relationship with the other members of the Godhead. All of these things God wants to share with each of us including His power and authority.

This third and final section will hopefully help us understand how God is bringing about restoration. Surprisingly, He has chosen redeemed men and women to be His forerunners and instruments for bringing restoration to those who are still outside His kingdom.

PRESCRIPTIONS 29-42

Prescription File No. 3

(Table of Contents)

Rx29

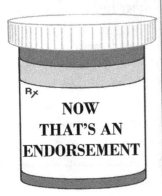

Rx

NOW
THAT'S AN
ENDORSEMENT

. . . and behold, a voice out of the heavens saying, "This is my beloved Son, in whom I am well pleased."
Matthew 3:17

One day I was cleaning out one of our closets when I came across a table board game that I had conceived in my senior year of high school. I smiled with fond memories and then I wondered, "Could I develop this into something that was marketable?" So I conducted a search to see if there was anything else like it already in the marketplace. Well to make a long story short, I fully developed the game, obtained a patent, produced a prototype and then turned my attention to obtaining capital and maybe even an endorsement.

It so happened that in the community where we were living there was an individual who at one time had been very prominent in the industry associated with my endeavor. So I asked him if he thought there might be any significant individual currently in his former profession who would possibly endorse my product. He said that would be very unlikely. Actually he said, "No!" So I sent out five letters of inquiry anyway. I figured I could only improve on "No!" Maybe, in the process, I would see how the Lord felt about what I was attempting. My acquaintance was eighty percent correct which meant he was twenty percent incorrect. One individual responded to my letter. How do you think I felt? One of the foremost individuals of his profession had just got back to me and said he was willing to discuss the possibility. Not only did he decide to endorse my endeavor but he was the catalyst for two other highly respected individuals to do so as well.

To make a long story more interesting, may I mention these individuals could demand seven figures for their endorsements? So what did I end up having to pay each of them up front? Would you believe zero? Remember I'm a nobody. Does that prove the age of miracles is still with us? John the Baptist was sort of a nobody also. He hadn't gone to an Ivy League school, he wasn't a scribe or a pharisee, his diet left something to be desired and his wardrobe was far from being Armani. John would have had a hard time trying to get a loan. If anyone needed an endorsement more than I did, it might have been John. However he wasn't going to let that stop him.

JOHN'S MESSAGE

"Repent for the kingdom of heaven is at hand."
Matthew 3:2

(Okay, maybe his approach was better than mine. Maybe!)

John's message was directed toward sinners, so his market was limitless. His message wasn't "I lost forty pounds on _____ (*fill in the blank*). However, it did require a change in lifestyle.

YOU NEED TO CHANGE YOUR WAYS

"Therefore bear fruit in keeping with repentance.
The axe is already laid at the root of the trees; therefore every tree that does not bear good fruit is cut down and thrown into the fire."
Matthew 3:9, 10

John was different and direct but that didn't stop him from attracting crowds to the Jordan river. Some even accepted his message and were baptized for the repentance of their sins.

JOHN HAD REASONABLE SUCCESS

> *Then Jerusalem was going out to him, and all Judea and all the district around the Jordan, and **they were being baptized by him in the Jordan river, as they confessed their sins.***
> *Matthew 3:5, 6*

But wait a moment! Who is this coming to John?

JESUS DOES SOMETHING UNEXPECTED

> *Then Jesus arrived from Galilee at the Jordon to be baptized by him.*
> *Matthew 3:13*

Seriously! How do you think that made John feel? Jesus didn't need to change His lifestyle.

JESUS HAD NO REASON TO BE BAPTIZED

> *But John tried to prevent Him saying, "I have need to be baptized by You, and do You come to me?"*
> *Matthew 3:14*

JESUS ENDORSES JOHN'S MESSAGE

> *But Jesus answering said to him. "Permit it at this time; for in this way it is fitting for us to fulfill all righteousness."*
> *Then he permitted Him.*
> *Matthew 3:15*

But John wasn't the only one God was endorsing.

GOD ENDORSES JESUS

> *And after being baptized, Jesus went up immediately from the water; and behold, the heavens were opened, and **he (John) saw the Spirit of God descending as a dove, and coming upon Him (Jesus), and behold, a voice out of the heavens saying, "This is My beloved Son, in whom I am well-pleased."***
> *Matthew 3:16, 17*

NOW THAT'S AN ENDORSEMENT! Back-to-back, and over-the-top, endorsements. Obviously, that meant what John had been saying was good with God. So what else had John been saying?

JOHN SPOKE OF FUTURE ENDORSEMENTS

> *As for me, I (John) baptize you with water for repentance but He (Jesus) who is coming after me is mightier than I, and I am not fit to remove His sandals; **He will baptize you with the Holy Spirit and fire.***
> *Matthew 3:11*

That means that someday Jesus would endorse what we would be saying.

Although Jesus is God, the one we refer to as the second person of the Trinity, He did not require the third person of the Trinity, the one called the Holy Spirit, in order to perform the miracles and wonders that accompanied His ministry. However Jesus voluntarily allowed His hands *to be tied behind His back* and relied on the person of the Holy Spirit to confirm His message with signs and wonders. That was God's plan because all other believers, past, present and future would and do require the person of the Holy Spirit to endorse the message of the gospel of the kingdom. Thus Jesus allowed Himself to be an example to all believers of their need, their requirement, to have and rely on the invisible-to-one's eye, presence of the person of the Holy Spirit to confirm the amazing things that the gospel of the kingdom, the gospel of Jesus Christ, proclaims. For instance, if an individual needs to be healed of whatever illness, the message in the gospel informs them that God wants them to be healthy. That's part of the message believers are to proclaim and the role of the person of the Holy Spirit is to endorse that good news by healing those who respond to the message.

THE MESSAGE OF THE GOSPEL IS TO BE CONFIRMED

> *So then, when the Lord Jesus had spoken to them, He was received up into heaven, and sat down at the right hand of God.* ***And they*** *(His disciples)* ***went out and preached everywhere, while the Lord*** *(by the invisible presence of the person of the Holy Spirit)* ***worked with them, and confirmed the word*** *(regarding the good news of the kingdom, the gospel of Christ) by signs that followed.*
> *Mark 16:19, 20*

Jesus' role in God's plan (among other things) was to proclaim the gospel of the kingdom, including the fact, that He came to be the acceptable sacrifice to God and to die for our sins and our sickness. On the other hand it is the role of the invisible person of the Holy Spirit to confirm the good news regarding the gospel of Jesus Christ and the kingdom of God. So what is our role as believers? Our role today is to proclaim Christ's message and to know the invisible presence of the person of the Holy Spirit is with us to endorse and enforce the good news of the kingdom of God. Of course, that requires the knowledge of what is contained in that good news. It is equally important to be confident that the person of the Holy Spirit is present with you to confirm that message.

THE GOSPEL IS MORE THAN JOHN 3:16

> *Jesus summoned His twelve disciples and gave them authority* (by having the presence of the person of the Holy Spirit) *over unclean spirits, to cast them out, and to heal every kind of sickness.*
> Matthew 10:1

Do you think His disciples would have been worried if Jesus would have told them something like the following: "Listen guys. The next time we talk to someone about the gospel of the kingdom, you not Me, will tell them that their heavenly Father wants them to be healthy and that He has power and authority over all sickness and disease. Rejoice when someone asks if God will heal them, because someone will ask. That's exactly what we want to happen. Just minister to them and trust Me. I will be right there with you. I've got your back." I don't think His disciples would have been worried at all. Do you?

Jesus' plan was to prepare His followers for an even more exciting moment. Today believers can't see Jesus in bodily form but His directions haven't changed. Jesus knew that this was going to be our situation. So His plan was to take believers one step at a time until all believers in all ages would know that when they followed His instructions, He would have their back, meaning the person of the Holy Spirit would be present to confirm their message of God's kingdom.

Jesus' plan was to first mature into a full grown man. A man who lived in a culture that had a a very high infant death rate. He would watch children die regularly without doing anything to keep that from happening. As I said, He likely watched His own earthly father, Joseph, die leaving His mother, Mary, a widow. He being God in the flesh could have intervened in all of the above situations however that wasn't His plan.

Jesus' second step was to endorse John's message and allow John to know something very important happened when he baptized Jesus. God, the Father, endorsed His Son and sent the person of the

Holy Spirit to be present with Him. If you are able to receive it, the person of the Holy Spirit was present with Jesus to confirm the gospel of the kingdom which Jesus preached and taught.

The next step in God's plan for equipping all believers to do the work of the ministry was to show them that the same invisible presence of the Holy Spirit that accompanied Jesus can and will accompany them. So while He was still here visibly on earth, Jesus sent out His twelve disciples with power and authority (meaning with the invisible presence of the person of the Holy Spirit) overall sickness and disease as they preached the gospel of the kingdom of God.

When it came time to expand His ministry team, Jesus increased it by seventy additional unnamed followers, disciples like you and me. He sent them out just like He had sent out the more well known twelve. He sent them out with the same message and the same power and authority, which is the invisible presence of the person of the Holy Spirit.

GUESS WHAT HAPPENED?

> *The seventy returned with joy, saying, "Lord even the demons are subject to us in your name."*
> *Luke 10:17*

I am a nobody nonetheless, I've experienced that joy. If you haven't already, you can and someday you will also experience that joy.

Jesus' plan was to school His believers for the day and time when He would no longer be visibly present with them and that day did surely arrive.

Jesus was arrested, crucified and buried. For three days His followers knew what it felt like to be without God. As strange as this might sound, it is very beneficial to know what it would be like to be without God.

Then came Christ's resurrection and His disciples would soon learn that God's plan is to equip and provide all His believers with the person of the Holy Spirit. That occurred on the day of Pentecost.

It was on that day, fifty days after Jesus was crucified and ten days after His ascension, that His disciples received the promise of the Father, the presence of the person of the Holy Spirit. It even occurred in a similar manner as when Jesus was baptized by John. It was a *sight and sound event* and it left no doubt this moment was the moment they received the promise of the Father (Acts 1:4), the baptism of the Holy Spirit.

THE PROMISE ARRIVES

> *And when the day of Pentecost had come, they were all together in one place. And suddenly **there came from heaven a noise like a violent, rushing wind,** and it filled the whole house were they were sitting. **And there appeared to them tongues as of fire distributing themselves, and they rested on each one of them. And they we all filled with the Holy Spirit** and began to speak with other tongues, as the Spirit was giving them utterance.*
> *Acts 2:1-4*

The person of the Holy Spirit was present with all of them and Peter stood up and shared the good news of Jesus with all who could hear him and then he concluded with the following.

PETER FINISHES HIS FIRST SERMON

> *Now when they (those who were listening) heard this, they were pierced to the heart, and said to Peter and the rest of the apostles, "Brethren, what shall we do?" And Peter said to them, "Repent, and let each of you be baptized in the name of Jesus Christ for the forgiveness of your sins; and **you shall receive the gift of the Holy Spirit. For the promise is for you and your children, and for all who are far off, as many as the Lord our God shall call to Himself."***
> *Acts 2:37-39*

You may not be very outgoing or assertive. You may not be surrounded by friends, in fact, you may be by yourself most of the time. However the truth is you are never alone. God promises you that He is with you in the person of the Holy Spirit and that fact alone always makes you a threat to Satan's kingdom.

THE POWER OF ONE PLUS ONE

John (His disciple) said to Him (Jesus) "Teacher, **we saw someone casting out demons in Your name,** *and we tried to prevent him because he was not following us." But Jesus said, "Do not hinder him for there is no one who will perform a miracle in My name, and be able soon afterward to speak evil of Me.*
Mark 9:38, 39

Someone means one, not two or more. It means you, just you, and with your invisible helper, the person of the Holy Spirit, you are a force Satan's kingdom can not overcome. Now that's a *feel good* endorsement.

I don't want to miss this opportunity to point out a couple of very important pieces of information these two verses contain. The first is Jesus isn't concerned about who is ministering the good news about the kingdom of God. He doesn't care if they are part of a Methodist fellowship, Baptist fellowship, a Charismatic fellowship or any other group of born again believers. It's not where you worship, it's who you worship and serve. Also Jesus' kingdom, the kingdom of God, isn't divided against itself. Jesus isn't going to shut down anyone who is following His instructions. Remember: who is the one actually performing signs and wonders? That would be the person of the Holy Spirit. He is the one who endorses the truth. No truth, no Holy Spirit, no helper, no signs and wonders.

This concludes Rx29. After the conclusion of Rx29 and through Rx42, there will appear a brief review section offering three choices.

One of those choices will be a benefit of God's health plan as mentioned in this book.

When you finish reading Rx42, you might want to return to the conclusion of this Rx and refresh your memory by going over the reviews that begin here.

THESE THREE PRESCRIPTION FILES PROVIDE
CONFIDENCE IN THE FOLLOWING BENEFIT

1. The Old Testament contains the word of God
2. Faith can come from reading the word of God
3. The New Testament contains the word of God

Select the best-response from the above three choices. (the *best-response* list is found after the Epilogue)

Rx30

THE ROAD TO RESTORATION

My most fun-filled summer may have been 1994. My wife, Lu, and I took a trip to the east coast. Our itinerary included seeing the California Angels play the Boston Red Sox at Fenway Park. We drove into Boston from Philadelphia, and we arrived a couple of hours before game time. So, we checked into our hotel, and then we consulted a map to learn the location of that storied old ballpark. We noticed a turnpike ran right by the field. That seemed very convenient however, we soon discovered there wasn't an off ramp for Fenway. The stadium was less than a minute from the highway, but there wasn't any access from the turnpike. What a surprise! We stopped at a toll station and asked one of the highway workers if they could direct us to the ballpark. Another surprise. The worker was unable to offer any help. So we drove off the turnpike and headed about a mile back into the city. There we inquired of a pedestrian the same question. Surely, the pedestrian would be able to direct us. Wrong! He was of no help either. Lu and I looked at each other in utter amazement. We couldn't have been more than two or three miles from Fenway, and yet two locals were unable to provide the necessary directions. Unbelievable but true! There we were. We could see the field from the turnpike. We had tickets in our hands that allowed us to see the game, and yet it was escaping us.

It was this incident in Boston that reminded me of the condition of today's church in America. By church, I mean those of us who have placed our faith in Jesus of Nazareth as our personal Savior. No one in Boston tried to convince us that Fenway Park no longer existed. After all, we could see it, and no one cast any doubts on our right to be at the game. Obviously, we had tickets. On the other hand, consider the church of the twentieth-first century. Have your ever heard a believer say, "Healing isn't for today," or "Miracles ceased with the close of the apostolic age" or maybe, "It isn't God's will to heal everyone?" Is it possible that you and I have even had those same thoughts?

Do we refer to Jesus as the Great Physician? Of course, we do, but why? Well, just read the gospels. It is very apparent that is exactly who He is. What would you call someone who heals the sick, casts out demons, and even raises the dead? *The not-so-great physician?* Not hardly! Now has Jesus changed?

NEVER HAS, NEVER WILL

> ***Jesus Christ is the same*** *yesterday and* ***today****, yes and forever.*
> *Hebrews 13:8*

God says no! Jesus never will change. He will always be the Great Physician.

However, the miracles of the New Testament seem far removed, even inaccessible, to those of us who live today, but is Jesus inaccessible to us? No! What Christian would make such a statement? Then why do we encounter so few people who have actually been touched by the Great Physician? Could it be that we hear more about the *road to heaven* than we hear about THE ROAD TO RESTORATION?

The problem my wife and I had in Boston was that we hadn't encountered anyone who knew how to get to Fenway Park. We simply hadn't asked directions from someone who had actually been there. The situation in the church today is very similar; too few understand THE ROAD TO RESTORATION and even fewer people are actually on it.

Does such a *road* exist? If Jesus hasn't changed, then it sure does! Others have helped me discover it. I've been down it, and I've helped others take it as well. Praise God! It leads directly to the Great Physician, Himself.

JESUS IS THE WAY

> Jesus said to him, "**I am the way** and the truth and the life, no one comes to the Father but through Me."
> John 14:6

You may be thinking, "I'm a Christian. I know Jesus. I know the way." Sure you are, and yes, you do, but remember I was in Boston, however I wasn't at Fenway Park. Boston is more than just Fenway Park, and Jesus is more than just our Savior. He is our healer.

JESUS: THE ONE WHO RESTORES

> And the Pharisees and their scribes began grumbling at His disciples; saying, "Why do you eat and drink with tax-gathers and sinners?" And Jesus answered and said to them, "**It is not those who are well who need a physician, but those who are sick. I have not come to call the righteous but sinners to repentance.**"
> Luke 5:30-32

It is interesting to notice that the Pharisees and the scribes addressed the above question to His disciples and not to Jesus. However, Jesus doesn't hesitate to interrupt and without an apology. His interjection ties together two of His ministries, savior-redeemer and physician-healer.

JESUS: SAVIOR-REDEEMER

> *For as in Adam all die, so also **in Christ all shall be made alive.***
> 1 Corinthians 15:22

JESUS: PHYSICIAN-HEALER

> *Surely **He has borne our sickness** and carried away our sorrows; yet we regarded Him as a stricken one, smitten of God, and afflicted. **But He was pierced for our transgression; He was bruised for our iniquities;** the punishment which procured our peace fell upon Him, **and with His stripes we are healed.***
> Isaiah 53:4, 5 (Berkeley)

Notice He tied these two ministries together with just one cord, repentance. (Luke 5:32). Jesus came to take care of Adam's original sin. This He did when He gave His life on the cross. In addition, He also took care of our personal sins, and the resulting diseases, with the stripes from His beating.

Now that we see these two ministries of Christ, we can look at six basic steps to restoration. THE ROAD TO RESTORATION can be a brief miraculous moment in time, or it can occur over a period of time. However, either way, the road always begins with a genuine, sincere, and true desire for help. Openness and honesty characterize this desire.

ONE: OPENNESS AND HONESTY

> ***Search me, O God, and know my heart;*** *try me and know my anxious thoughts; and see if there be any hurtful way in me, and lead me in the everlasting way.*
> Psalm 139:23, 24

The verses we read in Luke made it very clear that the tax-gathers and sinners were not trying to hide their life styles.

HONESTY IN ACTION

I acknowledged my sin unto Thee, and my iniquity I did not hide; I said, "I will confess my transgressions unto the Lord;" and Thou didst forgive the guilt of my sin.
Psalm 32:5

Honesty reveals the areas of our personal life that require the forgiving touch of our Lord. Honesty also reveals our personal sin that can give the enemy an opportunity to attack our minds and bodies. Such an attack can establish a beachhead for future destruction.

The next portion of THE ROAD TO RESTORATION is humility.

TWO: HUMILITY

"God is opposed to the proud, but gives grace to the humble." Submit therefore to God. Resist the devil and he will flee from you.
James 4:6, 7

Pride says, "I don't have a problem," or "I don't need anyone's help." Pride is in opposition to any outside help, including God's. On the other hand, humility recognizes one's personal need, and it is willing to resist the devil's attack on one's life by accepting help in whatever way God provides it. For instance, have you ever gone to see a doctor? Did you have to complete a questionnaire that asked you about your family health history? Did you hesitate to fill it out? Of course not. You wanted the best care money could buy. Well, God has always been aware of such preliminaries. He established them in His church, so His people can recover. Yes, God wants you to look, feel, and be better! And money isn't even required. God has a prepaid health plan, and Jesus paid the price in full

THREE: CONFESSION OF PERSONAL FAILURE

> *Therefore, confess your sins to one another, so that you may be healed. The effective prayer of a righteous man can accomplish much (v. 16). Is anyone among you sick? Let him call for the elders of the church, and let them pray over him, anointing him with oil in the name of the Lord; and the prayer offered in faith will restore the one who is sick, and the Lord will raise him up, and if he has committed sins, they will be forgiven him (vv. 14, 15).*
> James 5:16, 14, 15

This brings us to a stretch of the road called repentance. Remember, the word repentance was included in the opening statements in the beginning of the public ministries of John the Baptist (Matthew 3:1, 2), the disciples of Christ (Mark 5:7-12), Peter on the day of Pentecost (Acts 2:38), the apostle Paul (Acts 26:19, 20), and of course, Jesus (Matthew 4:17). Jesus said repentance was necessary before healing would occur. Let's read it one more time.

FOUR: REPENTANCE IS ESSENTIAL FOR HEALING

> *And Jesus answered and said to them, "It is not those who are well who need a physician, but those who are sick. I have not come to call the righteous but the sinners to repentance."*
> Luke 5:30-32

What is *repentance*? *Repentance* realizes our way of thinking and doing things is not God's way. *Repentance* means forsaking our way and deciding to do things God's way.

Repentance naturally takes us to the next portion of the highway. It is a section that can be very bumpy. However, when one completes it; it is very rewarding.

FIVE: THE FRUIT OF REPENTANCE (GOD'S LIFE STYLE)

> *But when he (John the Baptist) saw many of the Pharisees and Sadduces coming for baptism, he said to them, "You brood of vipers, who warned you to flee from the wrath to come?* ***Therefore bring forth fruit in keeping with repentance.***"
> *Matthew 3:7, 8*

I said this portion of the road could get very bumpy. Why? Although a Christian's spirit is in agreement with God's will, his flesh continues to be in complete disagreement. In fact, it is in total opposition to the will of God. Therefore there will be bumps.

BUMPS

> ***For the flesh sets its desire against the Spirit, and the Spirit against the flesh;*** *for these are in opposition to one another, so that you may not do the things that you please.*
> *Galatians 5:17, 18*

When one repents and decides to do things God's way, then he or she immediately enters this section of the road. And you can be sure somewhere down the road the flesh is going to say, "Forget it. I'm not going this way any longer." So what do we do when this occurs? This is when by an act of our will we must decide who is in charge. Remember, God never overpowers our will, and thank God, all the demons in Satan's realm are unable to overpower it either.

5000 TO 1: NO PROBLEM

> *And seeing Jesus from a distance,* **he ran up and bowed down before Him** *(v. 6); And He (Jesus) was asking him, "What is your name?" and he said to Him, "My name is Legion; for we are many (v. 9)." And the demons entreated Him, saying, "Send us into the swine so that we may enter them (v. 12)."*
> *Mark 5:6, 9, 12*

The flesh has a will of its own, but can you imagine what our flesh would be like under the influence of thousands of demons? Maybe you can and maybe you can't, but the bottom line is: our will is able to overpower our flesh. Yes, even flesh controlled by demons, so we can continue on THE ROAD TO RESTORATION.

So where are we now? Well, we are at an area most of us might like to skip. It's called forgiveness. We might even invite a detour, however, this is a section we cannot avoid.

A Christian has already experienced God's forgiveness for Adam's original sin. Now it's personal sin we need to deal with, and according to Jesus it needs to be dealt with on a daily basis (Luke 11:3, 4).

SIX: GOD'S FORGIVENESS

> *If we confess our sins,* **He is faithful** *and righteous* **to forgive** *us our sins and to cleanse us from all unrighteousness.*
> 1 John 1:9

Forgiveness from God allows Him to remove every evil influence from our lives. He can then cleanse us from the things that are affecting our minds and bodies. Obviously, we need God's forgiveness for our personal sin, but have you ever considered how a detour could turn into roadblock? If we have not forgiven others their sins against us, then we are at a roadblock? We can harbor unforgiveness toward others, and it can easily go unnoticed. When this occurs, it actually acts as a roadblock to God forgiving our personal sin.

UNFORGIVENESS: A ROAD BLOCK TO HEALING

> *And it came about that while He was praying in a certain place, after He had finished, one of His disciples said to Him, "Lord, teach us to pray just as John also taught his disciples." And He said to them, "When you pray, say: 'Father, hallowed be Thy name. Thy kingdom come. Give us each day our **daily** bread. And **forgive us (daily) our sins, for we ourselves also forgive everyone who is indebted to us.** And lead us not into temptation."*
> *Luke 11:1-4*

Notice, Jesus considers it a forgone conclusion that Christians daily forgive everyone who sins against them. Do we? Notice again, it is the basis for our appeal to God for His forgiveness of our personal sin. Remember, 1 John 1:9? If we block God's forgiveness of our personal sin by holding unforgiveness toward others, how can God cleanse us of the evil influences that personal sin has allowed to trouble our minds and bodies?

Okay, now we are at the most popular section of the road, *prayer*. We've all traveled this section many times, but how many of those times did we try to enter THE ROAD TO RESTORATION at the prayer *on-ramp* only to discover it didn't take us where we wanted to be? If we have not traveled the previous portions of THE ROAD TO RESTORATION then we shouldn't be surprised to find that prayer may not be a shortcut. The easy *on-ramp* was back a ways and labeled *honesty*! If we follow the right directions, then a toll pike can be turned in to a freeway.

Prayer is when we talk to God, and in our context it specifically means, when we ask God to provide the help that only He can provide.

SEVEN: PRAYER

> *"And it will come about that **whoever calls on the name of the Lord will be delivered.**"*
> *Joel 2:32*

> *"If you ask Me anything in My name, **I will do it.**"*
> *John 14:14*

Let's quickly review these six basic sections of THE ROAD TO RESTORATION. They are *honesty, humility, confession, repentance, forgiveness,* and *prayer.* When we have traveled through these portions of our journey, then God is able to restore us to health. It's not unusual for the person of the Holy Spirit to guide us through these steps without us even realizing each step is taking place. The above is mainly for teaching purposes and is not intended to do the Holy Spirit's job. On the other hand, to Satan, the enemy of our souls, minds, and bodies, this process means war.

WAR

> *For our struggle is not against flesh and blood, but against the rulers, against the powers, against the forces of this darkness, **against the spiritual forces of wickedness in heavenly places.***
> *Ephesians 6:12*

THESE THREE PRESCRIPTION FILES PROVIDE CONFIDENCE IN THE FOLLOWING BENEFIT

1. Jesus was crucified but did not die
2. Death could not hold Jesus
3. Someone stole Jesus' body from the tomb

Select the best-response from the above three choices. (the *best-response* list is found after the Epilogue)

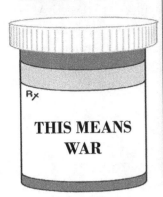

Rx31

THIS MEANS
WAR

INSTRUCTIONS

Immediately the boy's father cried out and began saying, "I do believe; help my unbelief." Mark 9:24

I once enjoyed putting together 72nd scale models of WWII aircraft. I discovered very early to make sure all the parts were present. The next thing I learned was putting all the parts together wasn't always easy. Frequently one or more parts would have an extra piece of plastic that had to be carefully removed. Sometimes a part would be warped, and occasionally, a part would even be incorrectly molded. When any of the above situations occurred, I knew I was in for a struggle. Once in a while, the struggle escalated into a battle, or even worse a war, or so it seemed.

When we decided to take THE ROAD TO RESTORATION and we went through the section called prayer then we knew all the pieces were present, and our healing could come together. However, that doesn't guarantee our restoration will be a simple process. On the other hand, it doesn't mean our restoration will be a long-drawn-out process either.

If you were in need of healing when you began reading this work, it would come as no surprise to me to learn you have already experienced your restoration. Personally, I have experienced healing that seemingly occurred in an instance. Unfortunately, I have also seen my healing appear to take days and on occasion even weeks. In addition, I have ministered to others and seen healing occur in seconds, and yes, I've seen it appear to take hours, days, and even months. When the longer scenarios are taking place, THIS MEANS WAR!

Let's take a brief moment and review. We know God has promised our healing and restoration through the finished work of His Son and our Lord, Jesus Christ.

JESUS PROVIDES COMPLETE HEALING

> *Surely He has borne our sickness and carried away or sorrows; yet we regard Him as a stricken one, smitten of God, and afflicted. But He was pierced for our transgressions; He was bruised for our iniquities; the punishment which procured our peace fell upon Him, and **with His stripes we are healed**.*
> *Isaiah 53:4, 5 (Berkeley)*

In addition, we know Jesus equipped His twelve apostles to see the same things He did, occur in their lives.

JESUS EQUIPPED THE TWELVE

> ***And He** called the twelve together, and **gave them power and authority over all demons, and to heal diseases**.*
> *Luke 9:1*

We also know Jesus didn't stop there. He continued to equip additional disciples to do the same.

JESUS EQUIPPED OTHER DISCIPLES

> *Now after this **the Lord appointed seventy others**, and sent them two and two ahead of Him to every city and place where He Himself was to come. **And He was saying to them** (vv. 1, 2). "And whatever city you enter, and they*

*receive you, eat what is set before you; and **heal those in it who are sick**, and say to them. 'The kingdom of God has come near to you (vv. 8, 9).'"*
Luke 10:1, 2, 8, 9

Jesus' plan was to continue even after His death, resurrection and ascension. He continued to equip His followers.

JESUS CONTINUED TO EQUIP HIS BELIEVERS

*And gathering them together, He commanded them not to leave Jerusalem, but to **wait for what the Father had promised**, "Which," He said, "you heard from Me; for John baptized with water, but you shall be baptized with the Holy Spirit not many days from now (vv. 4, 5). **but you shall receive power when the Holy Spirit has come upon you;** and you shall b*e My witnesses both in Jerusalem, and in all Judea and Samaria, and even to the remotest part of the earth (v. 8)."*
Acts 1:4, 5, 8

We know that on the day of Pentecost, Peter and the others received this promise, and it was at that time we learned the promise is for believers today.

JESUS EQUIPS BELIEVERS TODAY

*And Peter said to them, "Repent, and let each of you be baptized in the name of Jesus Christ for the forgiveness of your sins; and you shall receive the gift of the Holy Spirit. **For the promise is for you and your children, and for all who are far off, as many as, the Lord our God shall call to Himself.**"*
Acts 2:38, 39

The above means that Jesus has promised to equip you and me, all believers, exactly the same way He equipped Peter and Paul.

JESUS' WILL IS TO EQUIP EVERY BELIEVER

> *"And these signs will accompany those who have believed: in My name they will cast out demons, they will speak with new tongues; they will pick up serpents, and if they drink any deadly poison, it shall not hurt them; they will lay hands on the sick and they will recover."*
> *Mark 16:17, 18*

A believer doesn't have to be considered special in the eyes of the world for God to use that believer in a mighty way. A believer doesn't need a great personality or to be attractive or intelligent or wealthy or have any other asset or quality the world deems desirable. A believer only needs to be willing to accept the gift God has promised to give him or her. Then the believer is responsible to show the love of God as that believer shares the message of God's kingdom with this power and authority which is provided by the person of the Holy Spirit.

JESUS ENDORSES THE GOSPEL

> *"And now, Lord, take note of their threats, and grant that Thy bond-servants may speak Thy word with all con-fidence, **while Thou dost extend Thy hand to heal, and signs and wonders take place through the name of Thy holy servant Jesus.**" And when they had prayed, the place where they had gathered together was shaken, **and they were all filled with the Holy Spirit,** and began to speak the word of God with boldness.*
> *Acts 4:29-31*

To sum up this review, let it be simply stated that God has promised to equip every believer with the person of the Holy Spirit so the message of the gospel of Jesus Christ, which includes salvation and healing, is confirmed by the presence and manifestation of God's power. God uses the ordinary in an extraordinary way.

JESUS EQUIPS THE ORDINARY TO BE EXTRAORDINARY

*And when I came to you brethren, I did not come with superiority of speech or of wisdom, proclaiming to you the testimony of God. For I determined to know nothing among you except Jesus Christ, and Him crucified. And I was with you in weakness and in fear and in much trembling. **And my message and preaching were** not in persuasive words of wisdom, but **in demonstration of the Spirit and of power, that your faith should not rest on the wisdom of men, but on the power of God.***
1 Corinthians 2:1-5

For our gospel did not come to you in word only, but also in power and in the Holy Spirit *and with full conviction; just as you know what kind of men we proved to be among you for your sake.*
1 Thessalonians 1:5

Now that we have this fresh in mind, we can look forward and prepare ourselves for the type of war Satan will conduct.

SATAN: LIKE A ROARING LION

*Be of sober spirit, be on the alert. **Your adversary, the devil, prowls about like a roaring lion**, seeking someone to devour.*
1 Peter 5:8

Satan, like a lion, needs to be kept under lock and key. A cage is the ideal place for a lion, especially if you've put him on a diet. We know a starving lion can't hurt us as long as it is in a cage.

Consequently, Satan will do everything he can to trick us to let him out of his cage. Remember, Satan is the master of deception, so we can expect him to assume a role other than a lion in his effort to escape his bondage. The church can keep him in bondage, or unfortunately, we can let him loose.

THE CHURCH: THE KEEPER OF THE CAGE

> *"And I also say to you that you are Peter, and upon this rock I will build My church; and the gates of Hades shall not overpower it. I will give you the keys to the kingdom of heaven; and **whatever you shall bind on earth shall be bound in heaven, and whatever you shall loose on earth shall be loosen in heaven."***
> *Matthew 16:18, 19*

So what other role might Satan assume? The Bible tells us his most successful role is that of the serpent.

SATAN: THE SERPENT

> *Now **the serpent was** more **crafty** than any beast of the field.*
> *Genesis 3:1*

> *And the dragon was thrown down, **the serpent of old who is call the devil and Satan, who deceives the whole world**; he was thrown down to the earth, and his angels were thrown down with him.*
> *Revelations 12:9*

You will recall, in the garden of Eden, Satan did not overpower Adam and Eve. He had no authority to do so; they were sinless. However, he was allowed to deceive them, and Eve was deceived. It will do us well to review his deceptive attack.

SATAN ATTACKS OUR KNOWLEDGE OF GOD'S WORD

> *And he (Satan) said to the woman, **"Indeed, has God
> said**, 'You shall not eat from any tree in the garden?'"*
> Genesis 3:1

Eve's reply added to what God had said, and God's word doesn't
need any help.

EVE'S REPLY TO THE SERPENT

> *And the woman said to the serpent, "From the fruit of
> the trees of the garden we may eat; but the fruit from the tree
> which is in the middle of the garden, God has said, 'You shall
> not eat from it, **or touch it**, lest you die.'"*
> Genesis 3:3

So Eve wasn't correct. What's the big deal? Satan detected Eve's
uncertainty of what God had said. So now, he attacks her faith.

SATAN ATTACKS OUR FAITH

> *And the serpent said to the woman, **"You surely shall
> not die!"***
> Genesis 3:4

Remember, faith comes from knowing God's word. Eve demonstrated she didn't understand the importance of knowing God's word.
Satan could almost sense his release. He was so close to changing his
role from serpent to lion; he could almost taste it. The only thing
preventing him was Eve's will to act on God's word, but Eve wasn't
certain and certainly not confident regarding what God had said
about her situation. So would Eve exercise her will in favor of what
she had now been told to doubt? Remember, *doubt* is "checkmate" as

far as Satan is concerned. Eve had to decide who she would believe, and then act on it.

SATAN ATTACKS OUR WILL

*"For God knows that in the day you eat from it your eyes will be opened, and you will be like God, knowing good and evil." When the woman saw that the tree was good for food, and that it was a delight to the eyes, and that the tree was desirable to make one wise, **she took** from its fruit and ate; and **she gave** also to her husband with her, and **he ate**. Genesis 3:5, 6*

Eve decided to act on what Satan had said, rather than what God had said. Satan, with that deceptive victory, not only robbed the human race of spiritual life but condemned all of us to living in bodies that are at war with God's will (Galatians 5:17). However, once we take THE ROAD TO RESTORATION Satan can no longer overpower us like a mighty lion. He has now been caged so expect his deceptive tactics once more.

SATAN DECEIVED CHRIST'S DISCIPLES

*And when they came back to the disciples, they saw a large crowd around them, and some scribes arguing with them. And immediately, when the entire crowd saw Him, they were amazed and began running up to greet Him. And He asked them, "What are you discussing with them?" And one of the crowd answered Him, "Teacher, I brought You my son, possessed with a spirit which makes him mute; and whenever it siezes him, it dashes him to the ground and he foams at the mouth, and grinds his teeth, and stiffens out. **And I told Your disciples to cast it out, and they could not do it**." And He answered them and said, "**O unbeliev-***

ing generation, how long shall I be with you? How long shall I put up with you?"
Mark 9:14-19

Here we see Satan's demon created doubt in the minds of Christ's disciples as well as the boy's father. The demon deceived His disciples by not leaving as quickly as they had anticipated. Doubt began to creep in. **Never forget this! Deception is designed to cause us to fall away from a position of faith; to stop believing what God has said.** How does it work? It works when we focus our attention on things that seemingly contradict God's word, such as persistent or lingering symptoms. For instance, when did God take back the power and authority he had given His disciples over all demons and disease (Luke 9:1)? He never did take it back! His disciples were involved in a kingdom vs kingdom battle and Jesus was physically somewhere else. Thus the demon resisted and that gave an opportunity for His disciples to doubt.

CANCER: SATAN IS STILL DECEIVING CHRIST'S DISCIPLES

The April 2, 1996, edition of the Los Angeles Times reported that researchers at U.C.L.A. had discovered a certain form of brain cancer produces a substance called TGF-B. TGF-B cloaks the cancer cells so the human immune system is not aware of their presence. This substance deceives the immune system, and consequently, our bodies which God created to fight cancer, take no action. However, the researchers also stated that when cells from the tumor are taken from the body and modified so they no longer secrete TGF-B and then are placed back into the individual with the tumor, the individual's immune system fights off the cancer.

What have we just learned? First, God created a body that shows it is not God's will for people to have or die from cancer. Second, we see that Satan's real power is in deception but when deception is uncovered, Satan is powerless.

Warfare only takes place where faith already exists. Deception is used to create a reason for unbelief. It is designed to erode faith that had previously existed. If this process goes unchecked and is not reversed, then we will discover we have a starving lion loose in our backyard. Now, what would you do if you walked into your backyard and found your son or daughter was about to be attacked by a lion? Would you stop and pray? Or would you take a gun and shoot it? This is not meant to be a funny or ridiculous question. It is meant to illustrate there is a time for prayer and there is a time for action, war, if you will. In a war the stronger army wins. Man cannot defeat Satan or his demons. However, with the power and authority of the person of the Holy Spirt, victory is assured.

The apostle Paul in his letter to the church at Ephesus informs us how we need to be equipped to defeat a deceptive foe. He refers to this equipment as the armor of God, and if you look closely, you'll notice each piece is designed to withstand the strategy of a deceptive enemy. Let's look at three particular pieces of this armor.

ARMOR FOR VICTORY

*In addition to all, taking up the **shield of faith** with which you will be able to extinguish all the flaming missiles of the evil one. And take the **helmet of salvation**, and **the sword of the Spirit**, which is the word of God.*
Ephesians 6:16, 17

What is Paul saying? He is telling us to protect our minds. We must know God's word; we must know we are the children of God. The helmet of salvation must be in place. Paul is also saying we must know what God has said He will do in and through us regarding our particular situation. If healing is our need, then we must know what God has promised about healing. When we act on that knowledge, we are acting in faith, and faith shields us from the enemy's deceptive actions, such as fear and doubt. Finally Paul is saying when we use the word of God that applies to our situation then the person of the

Holy Spirit turns it into His own spiritual sword to cut the enemy down.

In conclusion, when we pray we are addressing our heavenly Father regarding our personal needs and reminding Him what He has promised us about our situation. On the other hand, in warfare, we are speaking to Satan and his demons what God has promised in the name of Jesus, which then is enforced by the person of the Holy Spirit.

Jesus is our example. He spoke with authority to demons and the conditions they brought about. He did so, not simply because He is the Son of God but because He, as our example, had received the promise of the Father, which is the person of the Holy Spirit.

A SPECIAL PROMISE

"Truly, truly, I say to you, he who believes in Me, the works that I do shall he do also; and greater works than these shall he do; because I go to the Father."
John 14:12

THESE THREE PRESCRIPTION FILES PROVIDE CONFIDENCE IN THE FOLLOWING BENEFIT

1. People die because Eve believed Satan
2. People die because they sin
3. People die because Adam ate from the forbidden tree.

Select the best-response from the above three choices. (the *best-response* list is found after the Epilogue)

Rx32

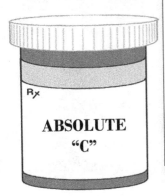

Rx

ABSOLUTE "C"

For I am confident of this very thing, that He who began a good work in you will perfect it until the day of Christ Jesus Philippians 1:6

Have you decided to take THE ROAD TO RESTORATION? Do you find yourself on a battlefield? Wars are fought over property. Who controls what? God has purchased our bodies with the precious blood of His Son, Jesus. Do you think Satan wants to give up control? The greatest battlefield any of us will ever be on is the battlefield we call our mind. Who is going to win this war? Our answer to this last question is pivotal to the outcome.

THE BATTLE OF FAITH VERSUS DOUBT

> *But let him ask in faith without doubting,* for the
> one who doubts is like the surf of the sea driven and tossed by
> the wind. For let not that man expect he will receive anything
> from the Lord.
> James 1:6, 7

Anyone, even the disciples of Jesus, can find themselves in a battle that has turned bad. A situation turns bad when an individual takes his or her focus off the word of God and redirects it upon the circumstances that led them to THE ROAD TO RESTORATION. Please allow me to illustrate.

PETER'S FAITH SINKS

> *And Peter answered Him and said, "Lord if it is You,*
> *command me to come to You on the water." And He said,*
> *"Come!" And Peter got out of the boat, and walked on the*
> *water and came toward Jesus.* ***But seeing the wind, he***
> ***became afraid****, and beginning to sink, he cried out saying,*
> *"Lord, save me!" And immediately Jesus stretched out His*
> *hand and took hold of him, and said to him, "**O you of little***
> ***faith, why did you doubt?****"*
> *Matthew 14:28-31*

When Peter followed Jesus' words, he demonstrated faith and he was able to walk on the water. However, when he reconsidered his situation, he became fearful (check) and then doubted (checkmate), and those two things sank Peter and his faith. Now listen closely to what Jesus said about this incident. "O you of little faith." Did Jesus say Peter had faith? Yes! What else did Jesus say? "Why did you doubt?" Could Jesus have added, "You still believed I would save you, and I did". Was Peter's problem lack of faith or the presence of doubt?

DOUBT WILL CANCEL OUT FAITH

> *And Jesus answered and said to them, "Truly I say to*
> *you, if you have faith,* ***and do not doubt****, you shall not only*
> *do what was done to the fig tree, but even if you say to this*
> *mountain, 'Be taken up and cast into the sea,' it shall happen."*
> *Matthew 21:21*

Jesus isn't saying lack of faith is the problem. Here Jesus is saying the presence of doubt is the determining factor for unanswered prayer. What could be clearer? If we want to see God's promises take place in our lives, then we must believe God's word, act on God's word and not allow doubt any room. Everything and everyone might say, "It can't happen," but God says, "Oh yes it will." We can't believe

God and consider other possibilities at the same time. That is doubt. In physics, two objects can't occupy the same space at the same time. In the dynamics of spiritual truth, the key to the door of God's promises is either faith to open the door or doubt to lock it shut. Both keys cannot operate at the same time.

What can we do to proceed toward ABSOLUTE "C", absolute confidence in God's word? Let me share with you what works best for me. I believe the most important aspects of obtaining absolute confidence in the word of God are faith and the absence of doubt. Let's consider faith first. How does a believer increase in faith? Below you will find biblical answers:

HEAR AND KNOW GOD'S WORD

> **So faith comes from hearing,** and hearing by the word of Christ.
> Romans 10:17

We already know this, but let's take God at His word. Try reading the Bible out loud. Does this seem absurd? Let me assure you it correlates with a later truth, which deals with overcoming doubt.

FASTING AND PRAYER

> Then came the disciples of Jesus apart, and said, "Why could not we cast him out?" And Jesus said unto them, "Because of your unbelief. . . How be it this kind goeth not out by **prayer and fasting.**"
> Matthew 17:19-21 (KJV)

Can faith that is sinking into unbelief be buoyed by fasting and prayer? (Rx14).

PRAYING IN THE HOLY SPIRIT

> *But you beloved,* **building yourselves up on your**
> **most holy faith; praying in the Holy Spirit.**
> *Jude 20*

The apostle Paul tells us this type of prayer goes hand in hand with the word of God and guarding your mind (Ephesians 6:17, 18). We need to know what it means to pray in the Holy Spirit (1 Corinthians 14:14, 15).

I encourage you to become familiar with and understand each of these sources, and then exercise them routinely.

Now let's consider doubt. Hopefully, what I share here will make a significant change in your life. It certainly has in mine. How do we overcome doubt? Here are three truths I believe will be helpful.

I believe I can use THE ROAD TO RESTORATION for any need in my life. Of course, I understand that once I begin on that road Satan will be on the defensive. He will no longer go unchallenged. Instead, the Lord and I will be on the offensive. The longer I remain on that course the sooner Satan will have to retreat to his stronghold. Now, that isn't a bad thing. In fact, that is a good thing. A stronghold is a place of final defense. A fortress or a castle would be a good example. I understand the Greek word for stronghold was used to describe such a place of defense. I also understand that the same Greek word was used in a legal sense to refer to a lawyer's argument. These two facts lead me to conclude that Satan's strongholds are his final defense, and guess what? They are just arguments to continue his actions against us. For instance, a medical diagnosis of cancer is a powerful argument. It could be a very doubt producing circumstance. It's important to realize nobody wins a war in a castle. However, lawyers make their living by using strong arguments to win their cases. Satan comes to rob, to kill and to destroy, and he is confident he can do it with just an argument.

What are we going to do about it? As Christians, we need to be prepared with the weapons provided in God's word. They are mighty enough to put doubt in its place!

PUT DOUBT IN ITS PLACE

(for the weapons of our warfare are not carnal, but mighty through God to the pulling down of strongholds;) casting down imaginations and every high thing that exalted itself against the knowledge of God, and bringing into captivity every thought to the obedience of Christ.
2 Corinthians 10:4, 5 (KJV)

All of us have experienced doubt at one time or anther. It's Satan's modus operandi. Just review chapter 3 of Genesis. Satan wants us to doubt God's word above all else. Never underestimate him. He is a liar and the father of all lies (John 8:44). The things that cause us to doubt God's word are very well conceived, and they are very convincing arguments. But in reality they are twisted imaginations and thoughts based on some element of truth. Nevertheless, they are designed to lead us to a conclusion that is not absolute truth. So, in this regard, they are just lies. In other words, a doubt is a lying thought. It cannot take authority over your faith unless you allow it. On the contrary, it is our option to allow our faith in God's word, which is the weapon of the Holy Spirit, to take action against any and all doubts. You can decide to doubt God's word, or you can choose to doubt your doubts. God's word can render every doubt ineffective and place them in captivity. Think about it. The individual with a weapon (God's word) is not at the mercy of the one (Satan) who has just an argument. But a word of caution. We must not pretend doubt cannot exist. If doubt does exist, then we must expose it and confess it. The following is the first step in removing doubt.

DOUBT NEEDS TO BE CONFESSED

*And one of the crowd answered Him, "Teacher, I brought
You my son, possessed with a spirit which makes him mute;
and whenever it seizes him, it dashes him to the ground and he
foams at the mouth, and grinds his teeth, and stiffens out. And
I told Your disciples to cast it out, and they could not do it."
And He answered them and said, "O unbelieving generation,
how long shall I be with you? How long shall I put up with
you? Bring him to Me!" And they brought the boy to Him. And
when he saw Him, immediately the spirit threw him into a
convulsion, and falling to the ground, he began rolling about
and foaming at the mouth. And He asked his father, "How
long has this been happening to him?" And he said, "From
childhood. And it has often thrown him both into the fire and
into the water to destroy him. But if You can do anything, take
pity on us and help us!" And Jesus said to him, "'If You can!'
All things are possible to him who believes." Immediately the
boy's father cried out and began saying, **"I do believe; help
my unbelief."** And when Jesus saw that a crowd was rapidly
gathering, He rebuked the unclean spirit, saying to it, "You
deaf and dumb spirit, I command you come out of him and do
not enter him again." And after crying out and throwing him
into terrible convulsions, it came out; and the boy became so
much like a corpse that most of them said, "He is dead!" But
Jesus took him by the hand and raised him; and he got up.
Mark 9:17-27*

We looked at this portion of scripture to a lesser extent in the
previous prescription. Now, let's look at a greater portion of this incident. So much is laid out before us in this more complete account.
We can see the boy's need, we can see the father's request or prayer,
we can see the father's faith, we can see the disciples unbelief, we
can even see doubt challenging Jesus, we can see Christ's reaction to
doubt, we can see the father confess his doubt and finally we can see

the boy's healing. Let me say it again. Where faith and doubt coexist, doubt will always win out. We must confess our doubts, because doubt, which is acted upon, becomes sin: sin in the sense of not believing God's word.

DOUBT IN ACTION IS SIN

> *But he who **doubts** is condemned if he eats, because his eating is not from faith; and whatever is not from faith **is sin**. Romans 14:23*

Paul in this portion of his letter to the church at Rome is explaining that there is a spiritual reason to allow one to eat meat offered to idols as well as a reason not to eat such food. But Paul's point is simply one's action to eat or not to eat must not be accompanied by doubt. In such an instance, doubt would be sin. But sin can be forgiven. Remember forgiven sin is forgotten sin. It no longer exists in the mind of our heavenly Father. It never happened. Consequently faith remains alone. Doubt no longer exists, and when this occurs, even a little faith will release the promises of God.

We obviously don't want to act in doubt, but what does faith in action look like? The answer may be easy to say, but it may be more difficult to do. Certainly Satan will try to stop us. After all, who wants their castle torn down? Too bad! Spoiler alert! Here's the answer. We need to speak God's promises out loud. We need to direct God's promises verbally and with confidence toward our need. This act allows the person of the Holy Spirit to use His weapon, the word of God, to bring down all strongholds. In so doing our faith is being strengthened at the same time.

THE WEAPON TO TEAR DOWN STRONGHOLDS

> *And take the helmet of salvation, **and the sword of the Spirit, which is the word of God**. Galatians 6:17*

You can have absolute confidence the person of the Holy Spirit will use the spoken word of God to accomplish its purpose. This is the only way the early church knew how to function.

LET THE HOLY SPIRIT USE HIS WEAPON

> *"And now, Lord, take note of their threats, and **grant that Thy bond-servants may speak Thy word with all confidence**, while Thou dost extend Thy hand to heal, and signs and wonders take place through the name of Thy holy servant Jesus." And when they had prayed, the place where they had gathered together was shaken, and **they were filled with the Holy Spirit, and began to speak the word of God with boldness** (vv. 29, 30). And with great power the apostles were giving witness to the resurrection of the Lord Jesus, and abundant grace was upon them all (v. 33).*
> *Acts 4:29, 30, 33*

Threats and persecution are strong arguments. However, the Holy Spirit uses God's people as an extension of His own hand, especially when they speak His word with bold confidence.

To recognize and confess doubt is a big step forward. The next step is to allow the Holy Spirit to put doubt in its place by speaking the word of promise. Now, let me share with you what really helps my faith.

There are occasions, mainly of my own making, when I feel I have no faith at all. I certainly don't feel I have enough faith to move a mountain. Do you ever feel that way? At times, I'm not sure I have enough faith to take my next involuntary breath. Do you get my drift? It's in moments like these that I feel I need a prayer partner. It's normal. Many of us seek out others to join us in prayer especially when we have a big need. We covet the prayers of those who we perceive to have greater faith than ourselves. How would you like to know Billy Graham had personally prayed for your need? Oh sure, there are others who might be up there on your list. To some, it might be the Pope. Wouldn't it be great if Paul the apostle was here today, and you knew he was praying for you? Well, if you can relate to what I'm saying, then allow me to let you in on my secret. There are three very special individuals who pray for me constantly.

GOD, THE HOLY SPIRIT, IS PRAYING FOR MY NEEDS

> *And in the same way the Spirit also helps our weakness; for we do not know how to pray as we should, but **the Spirit Himself intercedes for us** with groanings too deep for words, and He who searches the hearts knows what the mind of the Spirit is, because He intercedes for the saints according to the will of God.*
> *Romans 8:26, 27*

Wow! The Holy Spirit is praying for me, and obviously according to the will of God. But there is another one who is praying for me.

JESUS, THE SON OF GOD, IS PRAYING FOR MY FAITH

> *"Ron, Ron behold Satan has demanded permission to sift you like wheat; but **I have prayed for you, that your faith may not fail;** and you, when once you have turned again, strengthen your brothers."*
> *Luke 22:31, 32*

Okay, Okay! I know the Bible says Peter instead of Ron, but it was the same Peter who gave me permission to put my name in place of his. Listen to Peter.

GOD DOESN'T HAVE ANY FAVORITES

> *And opening his moth, **Peter said:** "I most certainly understand now that **God is not one to show partiality.***
> *Acts 10:34*

If Jesus prayed for Peter's faith, then He is praying for you and me as well. Jesus wants us to have absolute confidence in His word. He wants us to defeat every doubt. But someone else is also praying for you and me. You might be thinking, "Who needs anyone else?" The answer to that question is unquestionably, "No one!" But what could it hurt?

GOD, THE FATHER IS PRAYING FOR ME

> *Jesus therefore answered and was saying to them, "Truly, truly, I say to you, the Son can do nothing of Himself, unless it is something He sees the Father doing; for **whatever the Father does, these things the Son also does in like manner.***
> *John 5:19*

The reason Jesus prayed for Peter and the reason He is praying for you and me is because He first saw the Father doing the same. In fact, the entire process began with God the Father. Someone might be thinking, "Who does God the Father need to pray to?" "No one," might be your first response, and it would certainly be correct. But I would like you to consider this. The entire Godhead, the Trinity, is praying concerning your life and mine. They jointly discuss our individual situations. That discussion I consider prayer. Each of them is talking to God. In addition, they want us to partner with them, the Holy Trinity. We're looking for that special prayer partner, and all the time God is looking for you and me to be His prayer partner.

WE CAN LIVE IN ABSOLUTE "C"

> *And this is the confidence which we have before Him, that if we ask anything according to His will, He hears us. And if we know He hears us in whatever we ask, **we know that we have the requests which we have asked from Him.***
> *1 John 5:14, 15*

Are we going to win this war for faith? There's no *doubt* about it. No pun intended. Well, maybe a little.

THESE THREE PRESCRIPTION FILES PROVIDE THE FOLLOWING BENEFIT

1. Sin can lead to sickness
2. Sin won't lead to sickness
3. Sin and sickness have nothing to do with each other

Select the best-response from the above three choices. (the *best-response* list is found after the Epilogue)

Rx33

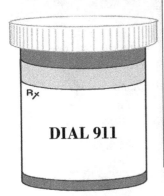

DIAL 911

Now before I proceed any further, I should mention that this prescription is slanted toward pastors. Although it will be interesting and illuminating to all believers.

The mid 1960s witnessed a revolution in American music amusingly referred to as the British Invasion. The influence of English rock music, spearheaded by groups such as the Beatles, left a long-term effect on the American music scene.

Nonetheless, there were American artists who maintained their own unique style among those were the Beach Boys and a singer named Johnny Rivers. The later recorded a song called Outside Help, and one of the lines in that song says, "Give me some outside help. I can't make it by myself."

Outside help is something that is familiar to most of us. We commonly refer to it as DIAL 911. This is the emergency telephone number. When someone needs immediate outside assistance in the areas of fire, police or medical attention, they dial 911, and the operator promptly dispatches the required help.

A believer who is experiencing sickness has a similar line available. Only it calls for inside help.

CHRISTIAN INSIDE HELP

> *Is anyone among you sick? Let him call for the elders of the church,* and let them pray over him anointing him with oil in the name of the Lord; and the prayer offered in faith will restore the one who is sick, and the Lord will raise him up, and if he has committed sins they will be forgiven him.
> James 5:14, 15

In the spiritual realm, the elders of the church take the place of the 911 operator. They are the first responders. But who or what is an elder? The word elder itself suggests a comparison, and indeed, a New Testament elder would be considered a believer who is more mature in his or her knowledge and experience in the Lord. The Bible gives us a divine set of qualifications to allow us to know who is eligible to be an elder.

WHO IS AN ELDER?

> *To Titus, my true child in a common faith: Grace and peace from God the Father and Christ Jesus our Savior. For this reason I left you in Crete, that you might set in order what remains, and* **appoint elders** *in every city as I directed you, namely,* **if any man be above reproach, the husband of one wife, having children who believe, not accused of dissipation or rebellion.** *For the overseer must be above reproach as God's steward,* **not self-willed, not quick-tempered, not addicted to wine, not pugnacious, not fond of sordid gain, but hospitable, loving what is good, sensible, just, devout, self-controlled, holding fast the faithful word which is in accordance with the teaching, that he may be able both to exhort in sound doctrine and to refute those who contradict.**
> Titus 1:4-9

Here Paul gives a rather lengthly list of qualifications for an elder. However I would like to ask what will appear to be a laughable question. Why doesn't Paul include that it is essential for an elder to be a Christian? Isn't that important? Of course it is. I'm sure it is. However, thank our Lord that it just so happens that Paul not only gave such a list to Titus, but he also gave a similar list to Timothy.

WHO IS AN ELDER? PART TWO

> *He must be one who manages his own household well, keeping his children under control with all dignity (but if a man does not know how to manage his household, how will he take care of the church of God?);* ***and not a new convert,*** *lest he become conceited and fall into the condemnation incurred by the devil.*
> *1 Timothy 3:4-7*

In the book of Titus, Paul informs us that the children of an elder must be believers and in Timothy he tells us that an elder shouldn't be a new believer but he doesn't actually say that an elder must be a believer. Obviously, that is a given.

When a brother or sister in Christ is troubled about their well-being, meaning they are sick to the point of concern; they are to call for the elders of the church to pray for them.

But wait! Before we go any further are there any other qualifications that Paul didn't mention concerning elders? Thank God, Paul loved lists. In his first letter to the church at Corinth he needed to instruct them on the proper usage of spiritual gifts, gifts provided by the person of the Holy Spirit to individual members of Christ's body. It wouldn't hurt to remind ourselves of two important facts that we could easily take for granted.

JESUS IS THE HEAD OF THE CHURCH

> *For the husband is the head of the wife, as* ***Christ also is the head of the church***, *He Himself being Savior of the body.*
> *Epheisans 5:23*

THE CHURCH IS THE BODY OF CHRIST

> ***Now you (believers) are Christ's body*** *and individually members of it.*
> *1 Corinthians 12:27*

These two verses inform our minds that there is a collective spiritual body consisting of Jesus as the head and all other believers as forming the remainder of His body. We understand that the body doesn't tell the head what to do nor how to do it. Rather, it is the head that informs the body what and how to do what it wishes.

Consequently, it should come as no surprise to learn that Jesus in His earthly ministry was instructing His body of the different ways ministry can be approached because of the presence of the person of the Holy Spirit and the gifts He provides. This is an excellent time to look at another of Paul's list. Paul mentions in his first letter to the believers at Corinth a list he calls the gifts of the Spirit.

SPIRITUAL GIFTS AVAILABLE FROM THE HOLY SPIRIT

1. The word of wisdom (1 Corinthians 12:8)
2. The word of knowledge (1 Corinthians 12:8)
3. The gift of faith (1 Corinthians 12:9)
4. Gifts of healing (1 Corinthians 12:9)
5. The effecting of miracles (1 Corinthians 12:10)
6. The gift of prophecy (1 Corinthians 12:10)
7. The distinguishing of spirits (1 Corinthians 12:10)
8. Various kinds of tongues (1 Corinthians 12:10)
9. The interpretations of tongues (1 Corinthians 12:10)

Remember, in His first coming Jesus came in the role of Savior-Healer. Now, lets ask ourselves, did Jesus demonstrate in His role as Savior the use of any of the above spiritual gifts while ministering to or leading an individual into salvation?

JESUS-SAVIOR: THE SAMARITAN WOMAN
AND THE WORD OF KNOWLEDGE

> *He (Jesus) said to her (the Samaritan woman) "Go, call your husband, and come here." The woman answered and said, "I have no husband." Jesus said to her,* **"You have well said, 'I have no husband', for you have had five husbands, and the one whom you have is not your husband; this you have said truly."** *The woman said to Him, "Sir I perceive that You are a prophet (vv. 16-19)." "Come, see a man who told me all the things that I have done; this is not the Christ, is it (v. 29)?"*
> *John 4:16-19, 29*

It isn't difficult to recognize that Jesus demonstrated the use of *the word of knowledge* in this situation.

Now, let's see if Jesus as Healer, not Savior, ever demonstrated using any of the gifts provided by the person of the Holy Spirit to restore an individual's health. I don't think it will be necessary to scour the four gospels to find our answer. I believe we will find it in chapters eight and nine of Matthew's gospel.

JESUS: HEALING THE SICK AND THE WORD OF WISDOM

> *And getting into a boat, he crossed over, and came to His own city. And behold, they were bringing to Him a paralytic, lying on a bed; and* **Jesus seeing their faith said to the paralytic, "Take courage, My son, your sins are forgiven** *(vv. 1, 2)." And he rose, and went home. (v. 7).*
> *Matthew 9:1, 2, 7*

Here Jesus recognizes the faith of those who are bringing the paralytic, and no doubt, that of the paralytic as well. However, it is the gift of *the word of wisdom* that allows the paralytic to be freed from the crippling influence of unforgiven sin. Should one think this deduction is a *stretch* then please look at James 5:15 one more time.

JESUS: HEALING THE SICK AND THE WORD OF KNOWLEDGE

> *And behold, a woman who had been suffering from a hemorrhage for twelve years, came up behind Him and touched the fringe of His cloak; for she was saying to herself, "If I only touch His garment, I shall get well." **But Jesus turning and seeing her said, "Daughter, take courage; your faith has made you well."***
> *Matthew 9:20-22*

In this incident Jesus was gifted by *the word of knowledge* to know who had touched Him. Mark 5:31 and Luke 8:45 make it very clear that many people had touched Him, but the person of the Holy Spirit provided Jesus with the exact knowledge of who the woman was who was seeking healing. When Jesus informed her He knew it was she, and He knew of her faith, she was healed immediately.

JESUS: HEALING THE SICK AND THE GIFT OF FAITH

> *And Jesus came into the official's house, and saw the flute-players and the crowd in noisy disorder, He began to say, **"Depart; for the girl has not died, but is asleep."** And they began laughing at Him. But when the crowd had been put out, **He entered and took her by the hand; and the girl arose.***
> *Matthew 9:23-25*

If we had any questions about the girl being dead, then Luke's gospel should put them to rest, because it tells us her spirit returned to her (Luke 8:55). So we see that it was by *a gift of faith* that Jesus said she is asleep. It certainly wasn't the girl's faith, nor her parents' who had summoned Jesus to heal her and not to raise her.

JESUS: HEALING THE SICK AND GIFTS OF HEALING

> *And when Jesus had come to Peter's home He saw his mother-in-law lying sick in bed with a fever. And **He touched her hand, and the fever left her; and she arose,** and waited on Him.*
> *Matthew 8:14, 15*

Certainly the disciples had as much faith as those who brought the paralytic. Just as it was in the former situation, so it is here. The question is not the faith of the others; instead it is the giver who is really the center of focus. Earlier Jesus exercised the gift of the word of wisdom to the paralytic but here He simply gives Peter's mother-in-law *a gift of healing*, a healing she did not request, but obviously one she did receive. Remember that one does not ask for a gift or it no longer is a gift. A gift comes from the giver.

JESUS: HEALING THE SICK AND THE EFFECTING OF MIRACLES

> *And as they were going out, behold, a dumb man demon possessed, was brought to Him. **And after the demon was cast out, the dumb man spoke**; and the multitudes marveled, saying, "Nothing like this was ever seen in Israel."*
> *Matthew 9:32, 33*

It would be difficult for me not to consider everything mentioned above as miraculous, but Jesus, Himself, defined this form of healing specifically as being *a miracle*.

CASTING OUT OF DEMONS: THE EFFECTING OF MIRACLES

*John said to Him, "Teacher, we saw **someone casting out demons in Your name,** and we tried to hinder him because he was not following us." But Jesus said, "Do not hinder him, for there is **no one who shall perform a miracle in My name,** and be able soon afterward to speak evil of Me."*
Mark 9:38, 39

JESUS: HEALING THE SICK AND THE GIFT OF PROPHECY

*And when He had come down from the mountain, great multitudes followed Him. And behold a leper, came to Him, and bowed down to Him, saying, "Lord, **if you are willing,** You can make me clean." And He stretched out His hand and touched him, saying, "**I am willing;** be cleansed." And immediately his leprosy was cleansed.*
Matthew 8:1-3

The *gift of prophecy* is speaking forth the word and will of God. Here the leper did not know the will of God concerning his healing. He certainly did not doubt God could heal him, but only if God wanted to heal him. Here Jesus exercises the *gift of prophecy* to inform the leper that it is God's desire and will for him to recover from his leprosy.

JESUS: HEALING THE SICK AND THE DISTINGUISHING OF SPIRITS

*And when evening had come, **they brought to Him many who were demon possessed; and He cast out the spirits with a word,** and healed all who were ill in order that what was spoken through Isaiah the prophet might be fulfilled, saying, "He Himself took our infirmities, and carried away our diseases."*
Matthew 8:16, 17

In these very brief two verses we see Jesus was able to *distinguish spirits,* in those who needed to be set free from demons, and to also inform us that the Lord desires to heal all of us.

Jesus is God and He didn't need the person of the Holy Spirit to be present in order to provide Him with any of the above gifts in order to carry out His ministry. However, that is what the Trinity, decided to do because His body, the church, would need these gifts to perform at the level desired by God the Father that would be at the same level of His Son.

So that begs the question, "Then why in neither of Paul's list of qualifications for an elder does he mention any of the gifts of the Spirit? It was James who tells us that the sick are to call for the elders to pray for them (James 5:14-16). Wouldn't it be beneficial for those elders to be gifted in the areas of the *gifts of healing, the effecting of miracles* and the *distinguishing of spirits*? Why would Paul neglect to include these on his list of qualifications? Could the answer be as simple as why Paul didn't instruct Titus that an elder needs to be a Christian? Could it be that being spiritually gifted was also a given?

This should not go left unmentioned. I believe that it is very easy to overlook the obvious. You know *you can't see the forest for the trees* sort of thing. This is what I mean. If the believers at Corinth had not been misusing the gifts provided for them by the person of the Holy Spirit, then Paul would not have addressed them about proper usage. If Paul would not have addressed them about proper usage, then we would not have a list of nine spiritual gifts provided by the Holy Spirit. Thus it logically follows that we would not be aware of how helpful, dare I say essential, they are for leading others to Jesus, as well as restoring health. Is it possible that we take this listing for granted or do we realize how easily it could have been excluded from the New Testament.

I will not attempt to mention *the gift of tongues* nor *the interpretation of tongues* in regards to ministering or leading individuals to Christ in this Rx because it would be unnecessarily controversial.

THERE IS NO SUCH THING AS COINCIDENCE

> *As we know that God causes **all things to work together for good to those who love God**, to those who are called according to His purpose.*
> *Romans 8:28*

If one were to observe the body of Christ in the twenty-first century and also reflect upon the church of the first-century one might conclude that the gifts of the Spirit were far more prevalent in the first century than today. Such a comparison could raise many questions but hopefully it would also remind us that man is the one who gives *titles* and God is the one who gives *gifts*. We should never loose sight of that fact.

However is it possible the early church accepted the fact that the person of the Holy Spirit wanted to equip them for service more than the church of today recognizes its need?

THESE THREE PRESCRIPTION FILES PROVIDE THE FOLLOWING BENEFIT

1. God hears all your prayers
2. God hears most of your prayers
3. You can keep God from hearing your prayers

Select the best-response from the above three choices. (the *best-response* follows the Epilogue)

Rx34

Rx

AN OUNCE OF
PREVENTION

The last half of the twentieth-century saw the medical profession, and people in general, realize that the old saying, "An ounce of prevention is worth a pound of cure," is an excellent guideline.

Today the medical profession stresses regular check ups including very thorough physicals. These check ups serve as early detection systems. On the other hand, people in general are paying more attention to proper diet, exercise and rest.

We could conclude that both the medical profession and the populace have experienced a needed awakening, but where does spiritual awareness fit into these preventive programs? In most cases it is virtually ignored. However I am convinced it is more important than either of the other two areas, and that is not failing to recognize their importance. Now, why would I make such a statement? Simple! God promised each of us good health if we will simply obey His word. Let's read His promise for ourselves.

GOD'S PROMISE OF GOOD HEALTH

*"Therefore, you shall keep the commandments and statutes and the judgments which I am commanding you today, to do them. **Then it shall come about, because you listen to these judgments and keep and do them,** that the Lord your*

*God will keep with you His covenant and His loving kindness which He swore to your forefathers (vv. 11, 12). And **the Lord will remove from you all sickness; and He will not put on you any of the harmful diseases of Egypt** which you have known, but He will lay them on all who hate you (v. 15)."*
Deuteronomy 7:11, 12, 15

Now that's preventive medicine dear brother and sister! But in all honesty, we have a problem.

ALL HAVE BEEN EXPOSED TO SICKNESS

*For **all** have sinned and fall short of the glory of God.*
Romans 3:23

This certainly accounts for sickness before one becomes a Christian and receives God's forgiveness through Christ, but what about afterward? Unfortunately, when most of us received Jesus as our Savior no one informed us of the physical benefits we received simultaneously.

GOD REMOVES SIN AND SICKNESS

Bless the Lord**, oh my soul, and forget none of His benefits; **who pardons all your iniquities, who heals all your diseases.
Psalm 103:2, 3

Now that's what I call a real fresh start, but let's return to our basic problem. We still commit sin.

THE BASIC PROBLEM

***If we say that we have no sin we are deceiving ourselves**, and the truth is not in us.*
1 John 1:8

Okay! So where do we go from here? How do we get back to spiritual preventive medicine?

GOD'S PREVENTION PROGRAM: AN OUNCE OF PREVENTION

We have already seen that God endorses a life style, that He guarantees will keep us free of sickness. Sadly, we have also seen that all of us are going along a course that exposes ourselves to sickness. However, the apostle John informs us we have a way out of our dilemma.

THE WAY OUT: A NEW FRESH START

> *If we confess our sins,* He is faithful and righteous to forgive us our sins and to cleanse us from all unrighteousness. 1 John 1:9

This verse is the New Testament counterpart of Psalms 103:2, 3. Forgiveness is the first aspect of God's prevention plan, but if God did not provide cleansing as well, the plan could not be effective. That makes perfect sense to me. What if I had voluntarily violated a quarantine sign, and I exposed myself to the Ebola virus? Forgiveness for my act would be kind, but by itself it would offer little hope of saving my life. Therefore, I will ask for God's forgiveness, and I will accept His forgiveness, and I will also confidently receive His cleansing. Thank You, Lord.

But how does one practice good spiritual preventive medicine? This is a very important question, but it is one I don't believe is very difficult to answer. We might ask ourselves how are the other forms of preventative medicine and fitness practiced? When it comes to routine physical checkups, appointments must be scheduled and kept. Good, now that wasn't so hard, but what about proper fitness? Obviously, proper diet, exercise and rest are to be practiced on a daily basis if they are to be of any benefit. Surely, eating like a pig, being a couch potato and staying up all night is not the best program. And we haven't even mentioned abusing one's body with alcohol, tobacco or drugs. Obviously, living in sin is a no-no!

BAD PROGRAM

> *What shall we say then? Are we to continue in sin that grace might increase?* **May it never be!** *How shall we who died to sin still live in it?*
> *Romans 6:1, 2*

THE CORRECT PROGRAM

> *And He said to them, "When you pray, say:* **'Father,** *hallowed be Thy name. Thy kingdom come. Give us* **each day** *our daily bread. And* **forgive us our sins,** *for we ourselves also forgive everyone who is indebted to us. And lead us not into temptation.'"*
> *Luke 11:2-4*

The best program includes examining one's life on a daily basis and asking God for His forgiveness daily. The only improvement on this basic program would be to ask for His forgiveness as soon as possible after committing a sin. That would certainly slam the door of opportunity in Satan's face.

GOD'S PROGRAM ALSO INCLUDES: A POUND OF CURE

Now that we have dealt with AN OUNCE OF PREVENTION we can move on to a more serious situation: *a pound of cure.* This is a more serious situation because we are now dealing with sickness. However, the cure involves the same subject as prevention: and that is forgiveness.

FORGIVENESS: KEY FOR A CURE

*And He said to them. "When you pray, say: '**Father,** hallowed be Thy name. Thy kingdom come. Give us **each day** our daily bread. And forgive us our sins, for **we ourselves also forgive everyone who is indebted to us.** And lead us not into temptation.'"*
Luke 11:2-4

When we examine the Lord's Prayer a little closer we notice God will forgive us because we have forgiven others. We all must be very honest here. Have we forgiven everyone who is indebted to us or who has sinned against us? If we have not, we may still have God's forgiveness, but it's unlikely we will have experienced His cleansing from all unrighteousness. That cleansing includes the removal of the influence of all evil from our lives, or spiritual decontamination. You may not think unforgiveness could keep you from receiving all the benefits of forgiveness from God, but just listen to Jesus as He responds to Peter's question regarding forgiveness of others.

FORGIVING OTHERS: THE KEY TO A CURE

*Then Peter came and said to Him, "Lord, how often shall my brother sin against me and I forgive him? Up to seven times?" Jesus said to him, "I do not say to you, up to seven times, but up to seventy times seven. For this reason the kingdom of heaven may be compared to a certain king who wished to settle accounts with his slaves. And when he had begun to settle them, there was brought to him one who owed him ten thousand talents. But since he did not have the means to repay, his lord commanded him to be sold, along with his wife and children and all that he had, and repayment to be made. The slave therefore falling down, prostrated himself before him, saying, 'Have patience with me, and I will repay you everything.' **And the lord of that slave felt compassion***

and released him and forgave him the debt. But that slave went out and found one of his fellow slaves who owed him a hundred denarii, and he seized him and began to choke him, saying, 'Pay back what you owe.' So his fellow slave fell down and began to entreat him, saying, 'Have patience with me and I will repay you.' He was unwilling however, but went and threw him in prison until he should pay back what was owed. So when his fellow slaves saw what had happened, they were deeply grieved and came and reported to their lord all that had happened. Then summoning him, his lord said, to him, 'You wicked slave. **I forgave you all that debt because you entreated me.** Should you not also have had mercy on your fellow slave, even as I had mercy on you?' **And his lord, moved with anger, handed him over to the torturers until he should repay all that was owed him.** So shall My heavenly Father also do to you, if each of you does not forgive his brother from your heart."
Matthew 18: 21-35

May all of us have ears to hear this! The lord of the slave in the above illustration forgave that slave his entire debt. The slave had total forgiveness. His debt was canceled out completely. But that slave in turn did not forgive his fellow slave. In fact, he had his fellow slave put into prison until he should pay back his debt. Now, how can a man pay off his debt from prison? Nobody was writing books in prison back then. So here is where our problems begin. When the slave's lord was informed of his actions and unforgiveness, he turned that slave over to *the torturers* until he should repay all that was owed. Listen up! Who are the torturers? Do torturers make you feel better or worse? Would you like to be handed over to torturers?

Could torturers produce sicknesses? How is this slave to be free from his torturers if he has to repay a debt that has been canceled? If the torturers are the cause of our sicknesses, then this is a dilemma that must be answered. What is the answer? The only debt that is still owed, the only debt that can still be repaid is the debt that is owed to the unforgiving slave, the slave who has been handed over to the torturers. What must that slave do in order to be released from his captors? He must forgive the slave who is in debt to him. As soon as he forgives his fellow slave, his lord's anger will disappear and his lord will see that he is set free from his torturers, his sicknesses, etc. Forgiveness will then be united with being cleansed from all unrighteousness. We are to imitate our Lord. We are to forgive others completely from our heart.

Remember, God promised us health, if we will only keep His commandments.

THE GUIDELINE FOR A HEALTHY LIFE

> *And He said to him, "You shall love the Lord your God with all your heart, and with all your soul, and with all your mind.' This is the great and foremost commandment. The second is like it, 'You shall love your neighbor as yourself.'* **On these two commandments depends the whole Law and the Prophets."**
> *Matthew 22:37-40*

THESE THREE PRESCRIPTION FILES PROVIDE CONFIDENCE IN THE FOLLOWING BENEFIT

1. God mentions His desire to heal in the Old Testament
2. God mentions His desire to heal in all parts of the Bible
3. God mentions His desire to heal in the New Testament only

Select the best-response from the above three choices. (the *best-response* list is found after the Epilogue)

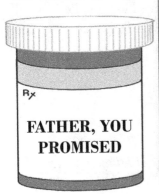

Rx35

The Spirit of the Lord God is upon me, because the Lord has anointed me . . .
Isaiah 61:1

FATHER, YOU PROMISED

Felicity is the name of our first grandchild. When she was three years old she would want to help her grandfather mow the lawn. Of course, it was out of the question for her to actually push the gas-powered mower by herself. So I would allow her to stand beside me and place her hands on the mower's handlebar, and the two of us would walk behind the mower as I mowed the lawn. It made her feel like a big helper, and it made me feel good to see her enjoy helping her grandfather do his work.

We were all children at one time, and some of us have children of our own. Certainly we can relate to the above situation. Children like to feel they can do the same things that their mom and dad do. It's not unusual to find a child grow up and want to do what his mom and dad does. My father was a pharmacist, and I decided to become a pharmacist. However, as children, it is frequently impossible for a child to do the same things as their parents, unless their parents of course, help them.

I understand that when I received Jesus as my personal Savior that I became a child of God. I became one of God's kids.

WE ARE GOD'S CHILDREN

> **But as many as received Him, to them He gave the right to become children of God**, even to those who believe in His name.
> 1 John 1:12

It shouldn't come as a surprise, that since I am a child of God I want to do the same things I see my Heavenly Father do. Isn't that exactly the same way His own unique Son, Jesus of Nazareth, the Christ, felt and did?

LIKE FATHER, LIKE SON

*Jesus therefore answered and was saying to them, "Truly, truly, I say to you, the Son can do nothing of Himself, unless it is something He sees the Father doing; for **whatever the Father does, these things the Son also does in like manner.** John 5:19*

Unfortunately, I have a problem. My problem is I don't see my heavenly Father doing much these days. Why is this the case? Why don't I see demons being cast out, the sick being healed, and on occasion, the dead being raised? Could the reason simply be we don't hear that being taught today? How can I, or you for that matter, believe what we don't hear? If few are proclaiming this portion of the gospel, then certainly few will have the faith to believe these truths and consequently, the opportunity to act accordingly.

NO MESSAGE, NO MIRACLES

So faith comes from hearing, and hearing by the word of Christ.
Romans 10:17

How did Luke, the author of the book of Acts, begin that book?

JESUS STARTED WHAT WE ARE TO FINISH

*The first account I composed, Theophilus, about **all that Jesus began to do and teach.** Acts 1:1*

Nowhere does Luke indicate that Jesus' ministry of doing and teaching is to stop. On the contrary, the book of Acts would indicate the opposite. The church, comprised of those who believe on the Lord Jesus Christ, is to continue His ministry.

I see the Lord healing the sick, casting out demons, and raising the dead in the gospels. I also see those who believed in Him doing the same things in the book of Acts, but what do I see today? Not much! In fact, I hear many who believe in Him making learned explanations why these things should not be expected to happen today. Do the reasons they give really agree with God's word? Do they satisfy you? They don't satisfy me, and I don't see they agree with God's word.

WHO CHANGED, GOD OR MAN?

> ***Jesus Christ is the same*** *yesterday, and **today**, yes and forever.*
> *Hebrews 13:8*

So I have a problem, you have a problem, and to a great extent the remainder of the body of Christ has a problem. What should we do?

We all agree that Jesus left His church with what we refer to as *the great commission.*

THE GREAT COMMISSION

> *And Jesus came up and spoke to them, saying, "All authority has been given to Me in heaven and on earth. Go therefore and **make disciples of all the nations**, baptizing them in the name of the Father and the Son and the Holy Spirit, **teaching them to observe ALL that I have commanded you**; and lo I am with you always, even to the end of the age."*
> *Matthew 28:18-20*

If you have been a Christian for any time at all, and if you have taken the opportunity to regularly attend a local fellowship, then more than likely you have become familiar with the above portion of God's word. Nonetheless, you and I are nearly two thousand years removed from the time it was initially given. In two thousand years a lot can occur, including how the church perceives this commission, and how it is to be carried out. But let's ask ourselves one question: could we go wrong if we examined the life of Jesus and then followed in His footsteps? After all, we are to imitate Him. Do you remember, the words of the apostle Paul?

JESUS IS OUR EXAMPLE

Be imitators *of me, just as I also am* **of Christ**.
1 Corinthians 11:1

Is Paul saying we are to imitate Jesus in all things except healing the sick, casting out demons, and raising the dead? Did Paul heal the sick? Yes (Acts 14:8-10)! Did Paul cast out demons? Yes (Acts 16:16-18)! And did Paul raise the dead? Yes (Acts 20:9-10)!

If we are expected to follow after Christ in water baptism, shouldn't we be expected to follow Him in the Holy Spirit baptism as well? Why not? Should we expect to follow in His footsteps when it comes to ministry? Of course! Is this an overwhelming thought? Can you imagine yourself doing the same miracles Jesus performed? Who said you can't? Certainly, Jesus never made that statement but He did tell us how that would happen.

Jesus was and is all God. He could and can do anything. Yes, He could have, but He realized there was no way for us to carry out the great commission in our own strength and wisdom. Therefore, the Trinity decided that Jesus would carry out this commission in the exact same manner that His followers would be expected to continue it. That decision by the Trinity meant that Jesus would **wait** for the outside assistance of the third person of the Trinity, the Holy Spirit. Jesus would **wait** for the promise of the Father before He began to carry out the great commission. So Jesus **waited** until the person of the Holy Spirit came along side Him to confirm His words with signs and wonders.

ENTER THE HOLY SPIRIT

> *Now it came about when all the people were baptized, that Jesus also was baptized, and while **He was praying** heaven was opened, **and the Holy Spirit descended upon Him** in bodily form like a dove, and a voice came out of heaven, "Thou art My beloved Son, in Thee I am well pleased."*
> Luke 3:21, 22

Jesus knew what His Father had promised through Isaiah 61:1. Jesus knew it was time to begin His public ministry, and it wouldn't surprise me at all to someday learn while Jesus was praying He was reminding His Father of the promise He (God) made through the prophet. In very human terms, I can visualize Jesus saying to His Father, "Dad, you promised." **God had promised Jesus that the Holy Spirit would come upon Him in order that His mission and ministry would be successful.** Jesus would be ministering to individuals who were spiritually dead but who were very alive to the power of Satan and his demonic influences. Jesus knew His believers would need outside help in order to be successful against this type of power. Therefore, Jesus pioneered God's plan for conducting the great commission.

THE FATHER'S PROMISE TO HIS SON

> ***The Spirit of the Lord God is upon me, because the Lord has anointed me to bring good news to the afflicted.*** *He has sent me to bind up the broken hearted, to proclaim liberty to captives, and freedom to prisoners; to proclaim the favorable year of the Lord.*
> Isaiah 61:1

This promise was made hundreds of years before Christ was born, and we see that Jesus specifically tells us it was made regarding Him.

JESUS RECEIVED HIS FATHER'S PROMISE

> And the book of the prophet Isaiah was handed to Him. And He opened the book, and found the place where it is written, **"The Spirit of the Lord is upon Me, because He anointed Me to preach the gospel** to the poor, He has sent Me to proclaim release to the captives, and recovery of sight to the blind, to set free those who are downtrodden, to proclaim the favorable year of the Lord."
> Luke 4:17-19

Now, are you ready for a sobering thought? If the Holy Spirit had not come upon Jesus would Christ's message have been any different? I don't think so. Do you? His message would have sounded very similar to the message of His church today, but would His ministry have been any different? I'm afraid so! Oh, His work on the cross would have been exactly the same, His resurrection would have been exactly the same but the casting out of demons, healing the sick and raising the dead along with all the other miracles that followed His message would have been missing. Does this sound like heresy or for the first time in your life has this truth hit home? God had decided to impose upon His Son the same limitations that every believer would find in their own life, the same limitations His church would experience. God decided His Son would need to rely on the assistance of the Holy Spirit to confirm His message. Consequently, Jesus waited for the moment the Holy Spirit would come upon Him before He consummated God's great plan of salvation as well as commencing God's great commission.

The most remarkable difference between the life of Jesus and the life of His church is the difference between His ministry and the ministry of His church in general. God does not want us to ignore it, or explain it; He simply wants us to explore it and then correct it. God has made every provision for this correction. Jesus **waited** for the promise of His Father and accepted it. He is our example, and His instructions are clear and simple.

JESUS SAID, "WAIT"

> *And gathering them together, He commanded them not to leave Jerusalem, but to* **wait for what the Father had promised,** *"Which" He said, "You heard from Me; for John baptized with water, but* **you shall be baptized with the Holy Spirit** *not many days from now."*
> *Acts 1:4, 5*

These instructions are an essential part of our Lord's last few recorded words. Jesus was giving His disciples His final earthly instructions, and this portion is so important that **He states them as commands**. Jesus knows what it takes to have a powerful and successful ministry. He also knows the plan God predetermined to ensure such ministry. It is the ministry God wants His believers, His church, to experience. God desires signs and wonders because His kingdom is far superior to Satan's kingdom, and He has no reservations demonstrating that truth.

POWERFUL BELIEVERS MAKE A POWERFUL CHURCH

> *And He said to them, "Go into all the world and preach the gospel to all creation. He who has believed and has been baptized shall be saved; but he who has disbelieved shall be condemned. And these signs will accompany those who have believed; in* **My name they will cast out demons,** *they will speak with new tongues; they will pick up serpents, and if they drink any deadly poison, it shall not hurt them;* **they will lay hands on the sick and they will recover."**
> *Mark 16:15-18*

God the Father, promised God the Son, this ministry, which was to be confirmed by God the Holy Spirit. Here, Jesus, the Son is making the same promise to His believers. I hope this truth encourages and excites you the same way it does me because there is no way we will be able to carry out the great commission the way God intended without our complete reliance upon the person of the Holy Spirit. My granddaughter was unable to accomplish my work without my help, and the same truth can be applied to God's work. We must have His help.

I see some very desirable qualities in the church today, things like dedication, determination, and degrees. These are all very admirable traits and accomplishments. However, the first-century church, which we consider enormously successful, realized that honesty, humility, and holy voices lifted up to God acknowledging it's need and dependence upon the work of the person of the Holy Spirit is indispensable.

WILLING BUT WANTING

*And when they heard this, they lifted their voices to God with one accord and said, "O Lord, it is Thou who didst make the heaven and the earth and the sea, and all that is in them, who by the Holy Spirit through the mouth of our father David, Thy servant, didst say, 'Why did the Gentiles rage, and the people devise futile things? The kings of the earth took their stand, and the rulers were gathered together against the Lord, and against His Christ.' "For truly in this city there gathered together against thy holy servant Jesus, whom Thou didst anoint, both Herod and Pontius Pilate, along with the Gentiles and the people of Israel, to do whatever Thy hand and Thy purpose predestined to occur. And now, Lord, take note of their threats, and grant that Thy bond-servants may speak Thy word with all confidence, **while Thou dost extend Thy hand to heal, and signs and wonders take place through the name of Thy holy servant Jesus." And when they***

*had prayed, the place where they had gathered together was shaken, **and they were all filled with the Holy Spirit,** and began to speak the word of God with boldness.*
Acts 4:24-31

The first-century church certainly wasn't lacking in dedication or determination. Maybe it was lacking in degrees, at least compared to today's church, but that was offset by its willingness to sacrifice. However, the thought that the person of the Holy Spirit might not be present to confirm the message was all but unbearable to the first-century church. I hope this thought is becoming increasingly unbearable to each of us, but what can we do? Certainly, we can begin just as our Lord began, when He was baptized by John. Let each of us find the time and the place to say, "**Father, You promised.** I desire your promise, the person of the Holy Spirit and His powerful confirming presence."

KEEP THIS IN MIND

Jesus received the Holy Spirit while He was praying (Luke 3:21, 21). His disciples also received the Holy Spirit on the day of Pentecost while they were praying.[1] (Acts 2:1-4). And once again His disciples were *filled* while praying later in the book of Acts. (Acts 4:24-31).

GOD DOESN'T BREAK A PROMISE

*For as many as may be the promises of God, in Him **they are yes;** wherefore also by Him is our Amen **to the glory of God through us.***
2 Corinthians 1:20

---

[1]   Finis Dake, The Dake's Annotated Reference Bible, The New Testament, (Dake Publishing, Inc., Lawrenceville, Georgia, 2014), p. 215* i.

DR. RON GIRARDIN

THESE THREE PRESCRIPTION FILES PROVIDE CONFIDENCE IN THE FOLLOWING BENEFIT

1. Satan is able to stop you from praying
2. Satan totally controls sinners
3. Satan cannot control your will

Select the best-response from the above three choices. (The *best-response* list is found after the Epilogue)

Rx36

INSTRUCTIONS

"... You shall receive power when the Holy Spirit has come upon you; and you shall be my witnesses both in Jerusalem, and in all Judea and Samaria and even to the remotest part of the earth."
Acts 1:8

ARMED AND DANGEROUS

Most of us live unspectacular lives at least in our own eyes. True, a few of us do escape this norm at least in the eyes of others, but the operative word here is *few*. The first thirty years of Christ's life were very similar to the first thirty years of almost anyone's life at least in the eyes of others. That may be why so little has remained in writing regarding His earlier years. True, we know there was one extremely notable exception that being He was sinless. But Jesus came for a specific purpose. He had a job to do. Unquestionably, He came to show us exactly what God is like and how God feels about each of us.

JESUS SHOWS US WHAT GOD IS LIKE

> *Philip said to Him, "Lord, show us the Father, and it is enough for us." Jesus said to him, "Have I been so long with you, and yet you have not come to know Me, Philip?* **He who has seen Me has seen the Father;** *how do you say, 'Show us the Father'?"*
> *John 14:9-10*

Christ's entire life demonstrated this truth and so should the lives of those who believe in Him. In addition, and of paramount importance, Jesus came to provide a way back into God's grace and favor.

JESUS IS THE WAY TO GOD

> *Jesus said to him, "I am the way, the truth, and the life;* **no man comes to the Father but through Me."**
> *John 14:6*

Jesus gave His sinless life's blood to make this possible.

JESUS BLOOD CLEANSES US FROM SIN

> *If, however, we walk about in the light, as He Himself is in the light, then we enjoy mutual fellowship, and **the blood of His Son Jesus cleanses us from all sin.***
> *1 John 1:7 (Berkeley)*

But that is not all He came to accomplish. He also came to take our sickness and our diseases upon Himself.

JESUS BORE OUR SICKNESS

> *Surely **He has borne our sickness** and carried away our sorrows; yet we regarded Him as a stricken one, smitten of God, and afflicted. But He was pierced for our transgression; and He was bruised for iniquities; the punishment which procured our peace fell upon Him, **and with His stripes we are healed.***
> *Isaiah 53:4-5 (Berkeley)*

A healthy mind and body are just two of the things Jesus provides so that we can have a better quality of life.

JESUS CAME TO PROVIDE A BETTER LIFE

> *"The thief comes only to steal and kill, and destroy;* **I came that they might have life, and might have it abundantly.**"
> *John 10:10*

He made these things possible when He experienced all the physical abuse surrounding His crucifixion. He came for these expressed purposes: to show us the Father, to make it possible to be reunited with our God, to have a healthy body and mind, and to have a better quality of life.

Now, let's ask ourselves a couple of questions. Did the Holy Spirit die for us? No! Is the Holy Spirit our Savior? Of course not! Nevertheless, the Holy Spirit also has a very specific *job profile*. We need to concentrate on one aspect of that profile. Remember, I said that Jesus' life was rather ordinary until the time He began His public ministry. What made the difference? Clearly, the answer is revealed by the fact that the person of the Holy Spirit had come upon Him. This occurred while He was being baptized by John. Now the two of them were walking as one.

THE HOLY SPIRIT COMES UPON JESUS

> *Now it came about when all the people were baptized, that Jesus also was baptized, and while He was praying, heaven opened, and the* **Holy Spirit descended upon Him** *in bodily form like a dove, and a voice came out of heaven, "Thou art My beloved Son, in Thee I am well-pleased."*
> *Luke 3:21, 22*

This was the time God's purpose for Jesus' life became His sole motivation. Everything He did was centered around the kingdom of God and the great commission.

A FOCUSED LIFE

*And Jesus, **full of the Holy Spirit**, returned from the Jordan and was led about by the Spirit in the wilderness. Luke 4:1*

We have no idea what kind of a nuisance Satan was to Jesus before He was baptized by John, but we know for certain that Satan was hot on His trail as soon as the Holy Spirit came upon Him. Why? Because Jesus was now ARMED AND DANGEROUS. If anyone understands the awesome disarming power of sin, it is Satan. He knows how effective sin can be when it comes to disarming anyone who has invited the Holy Spirit to come upon their lives. No doubt you have heard of at least one notable individual of God who was toppled by sin. Jesus resisted Satan's efforts, and consequently He began His powerful ministry.

THE HOLY SPIRIT PROVIDES THE POWER

*And when the devil had finished every temptation, he departed from Him until an opportune time. **And Jesus returned to Galilee in the power of the Holy Spirit**; and news about Him spread through all the surrounding district. Luke 4:13, 14*

Jesus shows us how to have a powerful ministry. It isn't because of who we are rather it is because of what Jesus did and what the person of the Holy Spirit is here to do. Jesus wants His believers to minister in the exact same way as He ministered.

HIS MINISTRY IS OUR MINISTRY

*Jesus therefore said to them again, "Peace be with you; **as the Father has sent Me, I also send you.**" And when*

He had said this, He breathed on them, and said to them,
"Receive the Holy Spirit."
John 20:21, 22

When and how did the Father send Jesus? Not until the Holy Spirit was upon His ministry. His ministry is our ministry. This means we are to tell and show others how God the Father feels about them. We are to help others have a better quality of life through the ministry of the person of the Holy Spirit. We are to offer others salvation and a way back into God's grace and favor. We are to inform them God wants them to be healthy, which is something His Son has made possible. Jesus makes our ministry perfectly clear, and He makes it equally clear that it can not be accomplished without our dependence upon the person of the Holy Spirit. Jesus commands us to allow the Spirit to accomplish God's work through us.

It's staggering to think that God wants to do miracles through you and me. However, this conclusion is unavoidable. We can see God revealing this desire when Jesus sent His twelve disciples, two by two.

GOD SHARES HIS POWER WITH HIS OWN

*And He called the twelve together, and **gave them power and authority over all the demons, and to heal diseases**. And He sent them out to proclaim the kingdom of God, **and to perform healing**.*
Luke 9:1, 2

God doesn't expect us to proclaim the kingdom of God without the power and the authority to cast out demons and heal diseases. However, when we go out today to proclaim the kingdom of God, do we go with this understanding? Do we go expecting the Holy Spirit to confirm our message? Is our message complete?

The gospels have preserved the names of the twelve disciples, those who Jesus personally selected. We have just seen how the Lord equipped them with power and authority provided by the person of the Holy Spirit. It would be easy to think of them as being very special people. However, Jesus sent out an additional seventy who have remained nameless. Not so special? Were they any less equipped? Were they not equals when it came to effectiveness?

GOD WANTS TO SHARE HIS POWER

> *Now after the Lord appointed seventy others,* and *sent them two and two ahead of Him to every city and place where He Himself was going to come. And He was saying to them* . . . (vv. 1, 2). *"And whatever city you enter, and they receive you, eat what is set before you; and **heal those in it who are sick**, and say to them, 'The kingdom of God has come near to you (vv. 8, 9).'"*
> Luke 10:1, 2, 8, 9

Here again we see that God does not expect those who carry out the great commission to do so without the power and authority to cast out demons and heal the sick. This time we see that Jesus sent out not twelve but seventy ordinary people. We have no idea of who they were, but who they were isn't the point. The point is: Did Jesus equip them, and how effective were they?

THEY WERE ARMED AND DANGEROUS

> *And the seventy returned with joy, saying, **"Lord, even the demons are subject to us in your name."***
> Luke 10:17

It may still be difficult to imagine that God wants to share His power and authority with you. But consider this: have you ever thought of denying Jesus or betraying Him? Judas not only thought about it he did it. Jesus knew Judas would betray Him, but even with that foreknowledge Jesus still shared His power and authority with Judas. Now, do you still think He won't share it with you?

Do you want to be ARMED AND DANGEROUS? Me too! But what are we going to do, or what is going to happen to make us so threatening to Satan's domain? Well, what does God's word say? First, Jesus promises that He will send the promise of His Father upon us.

JESUS MAKES A PROMISE TO EACH OF US

> *And He opened their minds to understand the Scriptures, and He said to them, "Thus it is written, that the Christ should suffer and rise again the third day; and that repentance for forgiveness of sins should be proclaimed in His name to all the nations, beginning from Jerusalem. You are witnesses of these things. And behold,* **I am sending forth the promise of My Father upon you; but you are to stay in the city until you are clothed with power from on high."**
> *Luke 24:45-49*

Okay, Jesus has promised that we will also have the promise of the Father. Why? So we can continue the great commission and continue it the exact same way He conducted it. But how does this all come about?

HOLY SPIRIT BAPTISM ESSENTIAL

> *And gathering them together,* **He commanded them** *not to leave Jerusalem, but* **to wait** *for what the Father had promised, "Which," He said, "You heard from Me; for John baptized with water, but* **you shall be baptized with the Holy Spirit** *not many days from now."*
> *Acts 1:4-5*

We know John baptized Jesus with water, but who baptizes with the Holy Spirit?

JESUS BAPTIZES WITH THE HOLY SPIRIT

> *As for me, I (John) baptize you with water for repentance, but He who is coming after me is mightier than I, and I am not fit to remove His sandals,* **He (Jesus) will baptize you with the Holy Spirit** *and fire.*
> *Matthew 3:11*

We know Jesus is the baptizer, but whom will He baptize? It is generally accepted that Jesus baptized His disciples on the day of Pentecost. They certainly ceased to *wait* after that moment, but will He baptize you and me in this time of history?

THE PROMISE IS FOR ALL BELIEVERS

> *This Jesus God raised up again, to which we are all witnesses. Therefore having been exalted to the right hand of God, and having received from the Father, the promise of the Holy Spirit, He has poured forth this, which you both see and hear (vv. 32, 33). And Peter said to them, "Repent, and let each of you be baptized in the name of Jesus Christ for the forgiveness of your sins; and you shall receive the gift of the Holy Spirit.* **For the promise is for** *you and your children, and for all who are far off,* **as many as the Lord our God shall call to Himself** *(vv. 38, 39)."*
> *Acts 2:32, 33, 38, 39*

The gift of the Holy Spirit is another one of those gifts or benefits included in Jesus. So the promise is to as many as the Lord our God shall call to Himself. That's you and that's me!

If Jesus is the one who is going to baptize us with the Holy Spirit, then do you think anything bad could come from it?

GOD GIVES ONLY GOOD THINGS

If you then, being evil, know how to give good gifts to your children, **How much more shall your heavenly Father give the Holy Spirit to those who ask Him?**
Luke 11:13

What is there to fear? It is Satan who should be afraid. So, what are we waiting for? Let's become ARMED AND DANGEROUS. Dear Jesus, my prayer is for you to baptize me with the Holy Spirit, and fill me as necessary. Amen!

THESE THREE PRESCRIPTION FILES PROVIDE CONFIDENCE IN THE FOLLOWING BENEFIT

1. John the baptizer's message on repentance was for the first century only
2. John's message is to continue until Christ's return
3. John's message is ineffective today

Select the best-response from the above three choices. (the *best-response* list is found after the Epilogue)

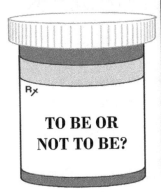

Rx37

TO BE OR NOT TO BE?

William Shakespeare is probably the most well-known author in English literature, and his famous line from Hamlet, "To be or not to be?" may be the most recognized words he ever penned. However, the question "To be or not to be?" is a question every Christian who has considered the promise of the Father, or who has desired that promise or who has received that promise should ask themselves. In fact, that is why this chapter carries its title, TO BE OR NOT TO BE?

The United States Army has used a recruiting slogan for some time that goes something like this: "Be all that you can be join the Army." A Christian is already a member of God's army and a Christian solider. In addition, if you have received the promise of the Father, you are also a member of God's special forces. A member of God's special forces is obligated to special training just as if he or she was a member of the special forces in any branch of the military. Please allow me to explain.

I'm sure you are aware Christians experience temptation every-day of their lives. And because we experience daily temptations, Jesus instructed us to ask our heavenly Father, not to lead us into temptation.

GOD'S DESIRE IS FOR US TO AVOID DAILY TEMPTATIONS

> *And He said to them, "When you pray say: 'Father, hallowed be Thy name. Thy kingdom come. (on earth as it is in heaven) Give us our daily bread. And forgive us our sins, for we ourselves also forgive everyone who is indebted to us. **And lead us not into temptation.**"'*
> Luke 11:2-4

God is willing to help us avoid the temptations, which as we all know can be very attractive to our flesh.

THE FLESH HAS ITS OWN DIRECTION IN MIND

> *But each one is tempted **when he is carried away** and enticed **by his own lust**.*
> James 1:14

The lust of our flesh is certainly the principle factor in temptation, but there is another factor to consider.

The scriptures indicate that Jesus faced temptations daily. These temptations were very similar to the temptations you and I experience on a daily basis.

JESUS WAS TEMPTED JUST LIKE YOU AND ME

> *For we do not have a high priest who cannot sympathize with your weaknesses, but **one who has been tempted in all things as we are**, yet without sin.*
> Hebrews 4:15

This one scripture covers Christ's entire life, but it spares us the details. Yet it informs us that Jesus experienced numerous temptations before His baptism in the Jordan. It was then and there that He received the promise of the Father.

JESUS RECEIVES THE HOLY SPIRIT FOR MINISTRY

> *And after being baptized, Jesus went up immediately from the water; and behold, the heavens opened and he saw **the Spirit of God descending as a dove and coming upon Him.***
> Matthew 3:16

What happened next is what should command our attention.

LISTEN TO THIS: JESUS HAD SPECIAL TRAINING

> ***Then Jesus was led up by the Spirit** into the wilderness **to be tempted by the devil.***
> Matthew 4:1

Didn't we just learn that God wants us to ask Him not to lead us into temptation? Yes we did! Therefore what is about to happen to Jesus is unusual and obviously very important. Up to this point we have been spared the details of any temptations Jesus may have experienced. Now God is going into great detail. Why? Jesus had just received the promise of the Father, so why didn't He immediately begin His powerful public ministry? These are serious questions, however, we must never forget.

JESUS IS OUR EXAMPLE

> ***Be imitators** of me, just as I also am **of Christ.***
> 1 Corinthians 11:1

I believe the reason the Holy Spirit led Jesus into the wilderness to be tempted was to provide us with information that we must have for our own special training: training we must successfully complete before our ministry begins.

We know that if we ask God, He will help direct us away from daily temptations and those we do encounter we can overcome.

WITH GOD WE CAN DO ALL THINGS

> *I can do all things through Him* who strengthens me.
> *Philippians 4:13*

But special training is just that: **special**. It isn't an everyday thing. I said earlier there is another factor in temptation besides our flesh. That factor is Satan himself, the tempter. God wants you and me to know that if we have received the promise of the Father, Satan isn't about to sit back and allow you and me plus the person of the Holy Spirit to cut through his kingdom's plans like a hot knife through butter. Satan knew that God's intentions for Jesus were not only for Him to be the redeemer of every human being (what's that to Satan?), but Christ was also to restore mankind's power and authority over the devil, which includes all demons and diseases.

GOD'S INTENTIONS FOR JESUS

> *The Son of God appeared for this purpose, that **He**
> *might destroy the works of the devil.***
> 1 John 3:8

If anyone hesitates to believe this purpose was not to be extended to His believers, then we need to refresh our memories.

JESUS' INTENTIONS FOR THOSE WHO BELIEVE IN HIM

> *And **He** called the twelve together, and **gave them power**
> **and authority over all demons, and to heal diseases.***
> *Luke 9:1*

And if we believe those were His intentions for only the twelve, then we need to continue to refresh our memories.

JESUS' INTENTIONS OBVIOUSLY EXTENDED

> *Now after this **the Lord appointed seventy others,** and sent them two by two ahead of Him to every city and place where He Himself was going to come* (v. 1). *And the seventy returned with joy saying,* **"Lord even the demons are subject to us in Your name."** (v.17).
> Luke 10:1, 17

And if there are still lingering doubts that Christ's intentions include each of us, then we need one more time to refresh our memories.

JESUS' INTENTIONS FOR YOU AND ME

> **"And these signs will accompany those who have believed**: in My name they will cast out demons, they will lay hands on the sick, and they will recover."
> Mark 16:17, 18

However, God's intentions do not eliminate the need for special training. It is very easy to get caught up in different aspects of *the promise of the Father* and to overlook the very special training and temptations that will shortly follow the reception of that promise. To become ARMED AND DANGEROUS is one thing, but to remain a serious threat to Satan and his kingdom's objectives is something else. The devil has a program of temptations to keep any and all such believers from becoming all that they can be for God. And that is precisely why God took great care to preserve the record of Christ's special training.

I would like to illustrate the importance of this record for each of us. When I graduated from high school, I had my own agenda. It was to complete my pre-pharmacy training at a nearby community college and then transfer to the University of Southern California's School of Pharmacy. There I would complete my education just as my dad had done before me. I completed my studies at El Camino Community College, and I was accepted at U.S.C. However, my freshman year was a real eye opener. I had a very difficult time making good grades. I had several friends in my class, and I didn't find them remarkably different than myself, but they seemed to be doing better academically. So what was my problem? It wasn't until my sophomore year that I discovered the answer. It was in that year that I was asked to pledge one of the pharmacy fraternities. I considered it, but since I didn't live on or near campus, I decided not to join. That's when I noticed that some of my friends who had also been struggling academically began to improve greatly. They were catching on, and I wasn't. At least that is what I thought. How depressing. Then one of my friends who had recently joined a fraternity asked me if I would like to study with him for an up coming exam. So I said, "Sure, why not?" Maybe he could show me where I was going wrong. Grades in pharmacy courses were usually scored on the curve. You could score eighty percent and be last in the class. Or stated another way: you could be a well-informed failure. Anyway, when I arrived at my friend's room at the dorm, I discovered several other of his fraternity brothers were present and also studying. That's when my problem became clear.

I had been studying the wrong materials. I had been studying my notes from class, and I took great notes. I also had been studying the materials in the textbooks. Both amounted to an overwhelming amount of material. Anyway, how could I have been so wrong? My friend and his fraternity brothers were studying the questions that had been given on similar exams over the past five years along with the appropriate answers. Now I ask you isn't that what everyone should study? I learned that anytime an exam was given, a fraternity brother was designated to smuggle out an extra exam and enter it into the fraternity's exam file.

So what have we learned? We have a brother in Jesus who took the exam and left a copy for our inspection. He knows all the questions, and He has all the right answers.

My professors rarely made any significant changes on any of their exams. And guess what? Neither does Satan. So let's look at the file.

THE FIRST ADAM AND THE FIRST EXAM

Problem No. 1 - Is the tree good for food?
        (the lust of the flesh)
Problem No. 2 - Is the tree a delight to the eyes?
        (the lust of the eyes)
Problem No. 3 - Is the tree desirable to make one wise?
        (the boastful pride of life)
Genesis 3:6

God had already given Adam the answer to each problem: don't eat from that tree no matter how great the temptation (Genesis 2:17). Notice, Adam failed, even though he knew the correct response, and failure meant immediate spiritual death, which included the loss of power and authority over the devil. Oh yeah! It also meant eventual physical death as well. Adam picked a bad test to fail. However, there would be another Adam, and another test.

THE LAST ADAM

So also it is written, "The first man, Adam, became a living soul." The last Adam became a life-giving spirit.
1 Corinthians 15:45

And with Christ, who is the last Adam, came the next exam.

CHRIST AND THE NEXT EXAM

Problem No. 1 - "*If you are the Son of God,*
command that these stones become bread"
(the lust of the flesh)
Matthew 4:3

Problem No. 2 - "*If you are the Son of God, throw yourself down*
for it is written, 'He will give His angels
charge concerning You'; and 'On their hands
they will bear You up, lest You strike Your
foot against a stone.'"
(the boastful pride of life)
Matthew 4:5, 6

Problem No. 3 - Again, the devil took Him to a very high moun-
tain, and showed Him all the kingdoms of the
world, and their glory; and said to Him,
"*All these things will I give You if*
You fall down and worship me."
(the lust of the eyes)
Matthew 4:8, 9

We have seen the exam Satan gave Adam, as well as the one he gave Christ. What do we observe? The test hasn't changed. That's the same conclusion John the apostle made.

JOHN'S CONCLUSION

Do not love the world, nor the things in the world. If anyone loves the world, the love of the Father is not in him. **For all that is in the world, the lust of the flesh, and the lust of the eyes, and the boastful pride of life,** *is not from the Father, but is from the world.*
1 John 2:15, 16

We see the exam contains three basic areas of testing. Adam and Eve failed, but Jesus passed. So let's look at how Christ successfully completed His training.

I cannot over emphasize the fact that Jesus is our example. He first tells us the correct response, and then He shows us how to apply it.

JESUS KNEW THE ANSWERS AND
JESUS SPOKE THE ANSWERS

Answer No. 1   *But He (Jesus) answered and said,* **"It is written** *(**Jesus knew the answer**), 'Man shall not live on bread alone, but on every word that proceeds out of the mouth of God (**Jesus spoke the answer**).'"*
Matthew 4:4

Answer No. 2   *Jesus said to him, "On the other hand,* **it is writ-** **ten** *(**Jesus knew the answer**), 'You shall not put the Lord your God to the test (**Jesus spoke the answer**).'"*
Matthew 4:7

Answer No. 3   *Then Jesus said to him, "Begone, Satan! For* **it is written** *(**Jesus knew the answer**), 'You shall worship the Lord your God and serve Him only (**Jesus spoke the answer**).'"*
Matthew 4:10

Jesus shows us the correct answer is the word of God, which applies to our situation. However, to know the correct answer is only one half of the solution. Let me explain what I mean. I had to successfully pass a state board examination before I would be empowered or licensed to practice pharmacy. What good would it have done me to know the correct answer to every question if I didn't write down or speak out the appropriate responses? If I hadn't demonstrated the fact I knew the answers I would have failed.

If we would allow ourselves to objectively look at the church today, the body of Christ, we might conclude that not many have successfully passed the exam and kept going. And in one respect, we would be right. However, God wants all of His children not only to take that exam but also to pass it. He has provided the file, He has provided a study buddy in the person of the Holy Spirit, and He has provided the knowledge of the right answers and how to use them. He has made all the necessary provisions for us to successfully complete our training. God in the person of the Holy Spirit didn't lead Jesus into the wilderness to fail, and He is not about to provide you with the promise of the Father just to fail.

THE HOLY SPIRIT IS PRESENT TO SEE YOU PASS

> *No temptation has overtaken you but such is common to man, and **God is faithful, who will not allow you to be tempted beyond what you are able**, but with the temptation will provide the way to escape (His written word) also, that you may be able to endure it.*
> *1 Corinthians 10:13*

I guess that only leaves one question to be asked and answered: TO BE OR NOT TO BE? The choice is ours. TO BE means personal revival and a renewed ministry of power and authority. It means local, national, and international revival. Believers are praying for revival from God and God is waiting for believers to complete His special training which begins with being baptized in the person of the Holy Spirit.

DECIDE: TO BE

> *And when the devil had finished every temptation, he departed from Him until and opportune time. **And Jesus returned to Galilee in the power of the Spirit**; and news about Him spread through all the surrounding district.*
> *Luke 4:13, 14*

THESE THREE PRESCRIPTION FILES PROVIDE
CONFIDENCE IN THE FOLLOWING BENEFIT

1. Nothing follows death
2. God's judgement follows death
3. Some will escape judgement

Select the best-response from the above three choices. (the *best-response* list is found after the Epilogue)

Rx38

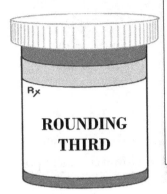

ROUNDING THIRD

I was introduced to the great American pastime, that is, the game of baseball when I was in the third grade. And believe me, it didn't take very long before I found myself in a lifelong love affair that millions had entered before me and countless others will encounter in the future. I must admit, *I love baseball!*

I grew up in Los Angeles, California during the 1940s and 50s. Major league baseball hadn't moved to the West Coast yet, but the area had two minor league teams: the Hollywood Stars and the Los Angeles Angels. The Stars and the Angels provided all the excitement a young boy needed.

The Hollywood Stars once had a manager whose name was Fred Haney. Fred had done it all. He had been a major league player, a manager, a radio announcer, and one day he would become the first general manager of a new major league franchise, the Los Angeles Angels. When Fred was still an announcer, he would close out each of his broadcasts with his well-known sign off: "This is Fred Haney, ROUNDING THIRD and heading for home."

Rounding third and heading for home is a baseball expression, that indicates a player or a team has an immediate opportunity to score. Jesus knows all about scoring, and when He returned to Galilee from His wilderness testing, we all know plenty of scoring occurred.

SCORE! SCORE! SCORE!

And Jesus returned to Galilee in the power of the Spirit; and news about Him spread through all the **surrounding districts.**
Luke 4:14

Jesus scored in real life, not in baseball, and He scored not with a bat but with a powerful, life-changing ministry. However, His opponent was and still is anything but a quitter. Satan will take advantage of any opportunity to *block the plate* and prevent powerful ministry.

SATAN NEVER QUITS

And when the devil had finished every temptation, **he departed from Him until an opportune time.**
Luke 4:13

Obviously, Jesus never quits either, and we know He never sinned as well. Unfortunately, we are very capable of sinning, and Satan generally doesn't have to wait very long for another opportunity to test us. God wants us to understand our situation and its consequences. In addition, there is one particular satanic opportunity that God wants us to fully recognize. It's an opportunity Jesus did not provide to Satan, but it's one that I'm sure each of us has already provided him. Jesus never had to ask forgiveness from anyone, but what about you and me? When Satan finds either you or me in need of asking for someone's forgiveness, then he is able to trap us in a *spiritual run down* between third and home very similar to the game of baseball. When this occurs, our chances of scoring have become extremely compromised, or more correctly stated, our success in ministry has been drastically diminished. Let's listen to how Jesus describes this particular situation and its solution.

MINISTRY ON HOLD

"You have heard that the ancients were told, 'You shall not commit murder and whoever commits murder shall be liable to the court.' But I say to you that everyone who is angry with his brother shall be guilty before the court; and whoever shall say to his brother, 'Raca,' shall be guilty before the supreme court; and whoever shall say, 'You fool,' shall be guilty enough to go into the fiery hell. **If therefore you are presenting your offering at the altar, and there remember that your brother has something against you, leave your offering there before the altar, and go your way; first be reconciled to your brother, and then come and present your offering."**
Matthew 5:21-24

Jesus is simply saying, when we offer our life as a living sacrifice to our Lord, He would like to be able to use it to its fullest extent. In order for God to use our lives to the maximum we have the responsibility of removing any obstacles that still may be in place because of our need to ask forgiveness from others. Yes, we know we have been instructed to forgive others and our Christian brothers and sisters have been instructed to forgive us but here we are being instructed to ask for forgiveness, and the failure to do so can be extremely costly to our ministry.

The goal of the promise of the Father is to equip us for powerful, life-changing ministry, and the goal of our personal testing is to allow God to endorse that ministry. Now, the goal of this current instruction is to keep Satan from frustrating the first two goals. Why be stuck in a run-down or held at third?

STUCK ON THIRD

"Make friends quickly with your opponent at law while you are with him on the way, **in order that your opponent**

may not deliver you to the judge and the judge to the officer, and you be thrown into prison.
Matthew 5:25

Our failure to attempt reconciliation with those we have offended can put us into a spiritual prison, and our ministry will suffer. Offenses will occur. We must not allow them to remain unresolved. Satan will do everything in his power to turn offenses into hurt, hurt into bitterness, bitterness into anger and anger into unforgiveness, which equates to a spiritual prison. Stuck on third indefinitely!

Jesus says, don't wait. Resolve the situation quickly.

HOW TO SCORE

"Truly I say to you, you shall not come out of there until you have paid up the last cent."
Matthew 5:26

It is imperative that each of us examines our lives with the assistance of the person of the Holy Spirit and recall anyone we may have offended. This sounds like a big job for me, and that is why I say we must ask for the Holy Spirit's help. He will prioritize as well as give us no more than we can bear. Whenever possible, we need to make contact with any and all we have offended and request their forgiveness. In some cases, restitution may even be required. Again I remind us to trust the person of the Holy Spirit.

When we forgive others and when we receive forgiveness from others, then the last cent has been paid, and all of us can *score*.

ROUNDING THIRD AND HEADING FOR HOME

And so, as those who have been chosen of God, holy and beloved, put on a heart of compassion, kindness, humility, gentleness and patience; bearing one another and forgiving

each other, whoever has a complaint against anyone; **just as the Lord forgave you, so also should you.**
Colossians 3:12, 13

THESE THREE PRESCRIPTION FILES PROVIDE CONFIDENCE IN THE FOLLOWING BENEFIT

1. Doubt might cancel out faith
2. Doubt and faith are merely descriptions
3. Doubt cancels out faith

Select the best-response from the above three choices. (the *best-response* list is found after the Epilogue)

Rx39

Rx

THE DREAM

INSTRUCTIONS

"And it will come about after this that I will pour out My Spirit on all mankind; and your sons and daughters will prophesy, your old men will dream dreams, your young men will see visions."
Joel 2:28

You may recall I mentioned in the introduction that God revealed three biblical truths to me in a dream. I would like to present all three truths together in this prescription so they escape no one.

The first truth is:

CREATION REVEALS GOD WANTS US HEALTHY

> *For since the creation of the world His invisible attri-butes,* ***His eternal power and divine nature, have been clearly seen, being understood through what has been made,*** *so they are without excuse.*
> *Romans 1:20*

The apostle Paul is telling us we can know, as well as understand, God's will by simply examining what He has made. Of course, that would include our bodies. And when we examine our bodies, we learn that when we bleed, our blood clots; when we become infected, our body fights the infection; when we break a bone, the body repairs the bone; and as we learned in Rx 11, READ MY LIPS, when our body suffers a heart attack, the major organ systems in the body come to the aid of our heart. This last process is referred to as homeostasis. Again, we learned in Rx 31, THIS MEANS WAR, when our body recognizes the presence of (at least one type of) cancer, it attacks that cancer. All these things help us understand that God's will is for us to be and remain healthy. That's been God's will from the beginning.

The second biblical truth is recorded in all three synoptic gospels (Matthew 12:22-31; Mark 3:22-29; Luke 11:14-23).

GOD NEVER MAKES ANYONE SICK

> *And the scribes who came down from Jerusalem were saying "He is possessed by Beelzebub," and "He casts out demons by the ruler of demons." And He called them to Himself and began speaking to them in parables,* **"How can Satan cast out Satan? And if a kingdom is divided against itself, that kingdom cannot stand.** *And if a house is divided against itself, that house will not be able to stand. And if Satan has risen up against himself and is divided, he cannot stand, but he is finished. But no one can enter the strong man's house and plunder his property unless he first binds the strong man, and then he will plunder his house. Truly I say to you, all sins shall be forgiven the sons of men, and whatever blasphemies they utter; but whoever blasphemies against the Holy Spirit never has forgiveness but is guilty of an eternal sin."*
> *Mark 3:22-29*

God isn't schizophrenic nor is He bipolar nor does He have a split personality. God isn't double-minded. He doesn't need to make people ill to show He can heal. In addition, these eight verses are a source of some other valuable information. Consider the following:

ANYONE CAN BECOME A CHILD OF GOD

> *"For God so loved the world, that He gave His only begotten Son, that* **whoever believes in Him shall not perish**, *but have eternal life.*
> *John 3:16*

> *But as many as received Him to them He gave the*
> *right to become children of God, even to those who believe*
> *in His name.*
> *John 1:12*

Now that brings us to the third truth, a truth that should uplift every Christian. So pay attention! There are two special benefits that are only available to God's kids. I refer to these two benefits as His supplemental health benefits. As I mentioned, they are for family members only.

FOR FAMILY MEMBERS ONLY

> *We have fixed our hope on the living God, who is the*
> *savior of all men, **especially believers**.*
> *1 Timothy 4:10*

Our heavenly Father has made it possible for everyone to become a part of His family. However, His special health benefits are only available to His children. There are two specific benefits.

BENEFIT NO. 1: NEW OWNERSHIP

> *Or do you not know **that your body is a temple of the***
> ***Holy Spirit who is in you**, whom you have from God, and*
> ***that you are not your own**? For you have been bought with*
> *a price: therefore glorify God in your body.*
> *1 Corinthians 6:19, 20*

A healthy body glorifies God. If God owns your body, then disease, be it mental or physical, is a trespasser. Notify God at the first sign of any trespasser. Ask Him in the name of Jesus to take immediate action. Then cooperate with His authority to remove the trespasser and its influence.

BENEFIT NO. 2: AN ON SITE CAREGIVER

> *But if the Spirit of Him who raised Jesus from the dead dwells in you,* **He who raised Christ Jesus from the dead will also give life to your mortal bodies through His Spirit who indwells you.**
> *Romans 8:11*

God doesn't want anyone to remain in an unhealthy state. If you're still not sure of this truth, then please review His basic health plan. This plan is available to all. When you become a child of God, He obtains the title deed to your life, your soul, and your body. You belong to Him, and He became your on-site caregiver. Naturally, God doesn't desire His property to contribute to a neighborhood of neglect. Just the contrary, God wants us to glorify Him with our physical bodies as well as with our intellect, emotions and will. To do that, we don't have to be a Mr. or Miss Universe. We don't have to be an Einstein or Mr. or Miss Perfectly Well-Adjusted or someone whose will cannot be changed. You can glorify God in your body by simply experiencing health.

These last two benefits combine to form the third biblical truth God revealed to me. However you should understand you don't have to take advantage of this supplemental benefit. It's free to His kids, but you can cancel or suspend this benefit at anytime. Just allow the influence of unconfessed, unrepented and unforgiven sin to remain in your life. So please be advised of your rights.

THESE ARE YOUR RIGHTS

> **If we confess our sins,** *He is faithful and righteous to forgive us our sins and to cleanse us from all unrighteousness.*
> *1 John 1:9, 10*

You do have the right to remain silent, but I do not recommend it.

Near the conclusion of Rx 5, YOUR VERDICT PLEASE, it was suggested some readers may not have made a decision yet. Hopefully, everyone has made that decision by this time. But if this is the moment you would like to make that decision, I suggest you review Rx 18, WATSON, THE GAME IS AFOOT. This is going to be the best decision you'll ever make.

The next two prescriptions are going to be far more helpful if you are a member of the family of God. So why not become a member today?

THESE THREE PRESCRIPTION FILES PROVIDE
CONFIDENCE IN THE FOLLOWING BENEFIT

1. Satan uses sin as a permission slip to make people sick
2. Sometimes you just have to accept sickness
3. It is impossible to be blameless in God's eyes

Select the best-response from the above three choices. (the *best-response* list is found after the Epilogue)

Rx40

YOU REMIND ME OF YOUR FATHER

"Rock a bye baby in the tree top, when the wind blows the cradle will rock. When the bow breaks, the cradle will fall, and down will come baby, cradle and all." For centuries, those words could bring a smile to the face of the hardest soul. Those words could easily rekindle fond memories of one's childhood.

Nursery rhymes have existed for hundreds of years. Soon they may be relegated to a disc or a chip and stored away in some unexplored corner of a public library, or they may be simply lost in a home computer, or *in the cloud*.

Maybe you are familiar with these words? "Humpty Dumpty sat on a wall. Humpty Dumpty had a great fall. All the king's horses and all the king's men couldn't put Humpty Dumpty together again."

Christians have no trouble relating to a great fall. They just have to remember their earliest ancestors, Adam and Eve. Talk about a great fall! Man has attempted to restore himself ever since Eden but with no more success than all of the king's men. God even gave us a measuring stick to check our progress. Christians and Jews as well, recognized that measuring stick as the Ten Commandments. However:

MAN CAN NOT RESTORE HIMSELF

> *"Cursed is everyone who does not abide by all things written in the book of the law, to perform them."*
> Galatians 3:10

Does man have a problem he can't solve? We sure do! Is there a solution? Yes there is! God gave us the Law to point us to the only solution.

THE LAW POINTS US TO GOD'S SOLUTION

> *Therefore the Law has become our tutor to lead us to Christ, that we may be justified by faith.*
> Galatians 3:24

When we realize no effort of our own can ever restore us in God's sight, we are able to come to Jesus and allow His work to begin God's restoration process.

JESUS PROVIDES TRUE RESTORATION

> *Christ redeemed us from the curse of the Law,* having become a curse for us - for it is written, *"Cursed is everyone who hangs on a tree."*
> Galatians 3:13

The restoration process begins when an individual realizes and accepts the fact that Jesus suffered the curse each of us deserves to suffer.

RESTORATION BEGINS WHEN WE BECOME A CHILD OF GOD

> *But as many as received Him,* **to them He gave the** **right to become children of God,** *even to those who believe in His name.*
> *John 1:12*

The moment an individual receives Jesus as their personal Savior they not only become a child of God, but they also become holy.

FROM UNHOLY TO HOLY

> *And although you were formerly alienated and hostile in mind, engaged in evil deeds, yet* **He has now reconciled** **you** *in His fleshly body through death,* **in order to present** **you before Him, holy** *and blameless and beyond reproach.*
> *Colossians 1:21, 22*

That is good news. But if we are already holy, why does the apostle Peter tell us to be holy?

CHRISTIANS ARE TO REVEAL THEIR HOLINESS

> *But like the Holy One who called you,* **be holy your-** **selves also in all your behavior,** *because it is written, "You shall be holy for I am Holy."*
> *1 Peter 1:15, 16*

Peter tells us to demonstrate outwardly what we already are inwardly. Maybe the following illustration will help clear up any confusion. Let me begin by asking a question. How many of us actually installed the electricity in our dwellings? Not many of us, correct? The point is: none of us are capable of becoming a child of God without the work of Jesus Christ. He is the only one capable of installing holiness into our being and into our lives. He connects us to God. Now, consider this. What good is it for a residence to be wired with electricity if no one ever turns it on? Here is another illustration. The United States of America has had a two-party political system for many years. There are the Republicans and the Democrats. Most registered voters belong to one party or the other. When an election approaches, each party encourages its members to go to the poll and vote for its party's candidates. That opportunity will present itself only a few times a year at the most. Now, do you think acting like a child of God a few times during the year is the type of Christian Peter is telling us to be? Do you think that's what God expects when He says:

BE HOLY

> For I am the Lord your God. **Consecrate yourselves therefore, and be holy;**
> for I am holy.
> Leviticus 11:44

Do you believe God is only saying, "Go to church on Sunday because you are a Christian"? Or do you think He means something more than church attendance?

This is how Jesus expressed it.

DON'T HIDE THE TRUTH

> "**No one, after lighting a lamp, puts it away in a cellar, nor under a peck measure, but on the lampstand, in order that those who enter may see the light** (v. 33). If therefore your whole body is full of light, with no dark part in it, it shall be wholly illuminated, as when the lamp illuminates you with rays (v. 36)."
> Luke 11:33, 36

God turns His light on inside everyone who believes in His Son, Jesus. In addition, He has told us not to hide what has happened to us. In fact, just the opposite. We are to reveal His light to everyone around us. We are not to keep it a secret or cover it up because of fear, nor are we to diminish it by sin. Our behavior is to reveal the holiness that God has personally placed within us. Our job is not to ignore what God has installed within but rather to turn on the switch. God's holiness and power are present, but it's our responsibility to reveal them.

Now that we have touched upon holiness and God's desire for us to express it, let's turn our attention to a complimentary aspect of restoration. Do you remember Humpty Dumpty? If we were going to attempt to restore this Mother Goose character, we would need to know how he originally appeared. That's a given. Doesn't it follow that we need to know what our original image was in order to proceed toward our own restoration?

MAN WAS CREATED IN GOD'S IMAGE

> *Then God said, "Let us make man in Our own image according to Our likeness; and let them rule over the fish of the sea and over the birds of the sky and over the cattle and over all the earth."* **And God created man in His own image**, *in the image of God He created him, male and female He created them.*
> Genesis 1:26, 27

Man isn't Humpty Dumpty, but his fall in the Garden of Eden shattered his image. Today we are distorted beyond our own repair.

Ever since the fall of Adam, no one has been able to look at another person and get an accurate picture or even a glimpse of the true image of God.

EVERYBODY'S IMAGE IS DISTORTED

> For **all** have sinned and **fall short of the glory of God**.
> Romans 3:23

So where does one get an idea of the true image of God? There isn't a single soul, living or dead that we can look at to see what true and complete restoration means. Or is there? Let's see. We are told Adam and Eve were created in God's image, which included authority. However, that was very short lived, and their lives' provide little insight into what that actually means. If Adam could only have maintained his original image long enough to have left an example, then we could know how the image of God was to be expressed. Just two or three years of record would have been extremely helpful. But wait. We do have at least a three-year period that has been carefully preserved, and it portrays exactly the image of God.

JESUS: THE EXACT IMAGE OF GOD

> God, *after He spoke long ago to the fathers in the prophets in many portions and in many ways, in these last days has spoken to us in His son, whom He appointed heir of all things, through whom also He made the world. And **He is the radiance of His glory and the exact representation of His nature**, and upholds all things by the word of His power.*
> Hebrews 1:1-3

> For He delivered us from the domain of darkness; and transferred us to the kingdom of His beloved Son (v. 13). And **He is the image of the invisible God**, the first born of all creation (v. 15).
> Colossians 1:13, 15

I was twenty-three years old when I received Jesus as my personal Savior. I can remember those formative Christian years very clearly.

When a situation would arise where I was required to make a crucial decision, I would ask myself, "What would Jesus do?" Unconsciously I was choosing to conform to the image of God. Later, I realized that everything that happens to me has a specific purpose in restoring my image to the image of God.

GOD WANTS TO RESTORE US TO HIS IMAGE

> *And we know that God causes all things to work together for good to those who love God, to those who are called according to His purpose.* **For whom He foreknew, He also predestined to become conformed to the image of His Son,** *that He might be the first-born among many brethren.*
> Romans 8:28, 29

The Bible repeatedly informs us that Jesus is the image of God, but that doesn't mean it is always an easy fact to recognize. At least one of His disciples struggled with this truth. However . . .

MAN CAN SEE GOD'S IMAGE

> *Philip said to Him, "Lord show us the Father, and it is enough for us." Jesus said to him, "Have I been so long with you and yet you have not come to know Me, Philip?* **He who has seen Me has seen the Father;** *how do you say, 'Show us the Father'?"*
> John 14:8, 9

Philip walked and talked with Jesus for over three years, yet it was still difficult for him to recognize the image of God. Did Philip see Jesus heal the sick or cast out demons or even raise the dead? Of course, he did. The nature of God the Father was the motivating factor in all of those miracles. Everything Jesus did was motivated by God's nature, and His nature or image can be described in a single word.

THE IMAGE OF GOD DEFINED IN A WORD

*Beloved, let us love one another, for love is from God; and everyone who loves is born of God and knows God. The one who does not love does not know God, for **God is love**.*
John 4:7, 8

Philip should have recognized God the Father by Christ's exceptional loving attitude and actions. However, God has explained the word *love* so we can better understand what He means.

LOVE MORE FULLY EXPLAINED

Love is patient, love is kind, and is not jealous; love does not brag and is not arrogant, does not act unbecomingly; does not seek its own, is not provoked, does not take into account a wrong suffered, does not rejoice in unrighteousness, but rejoices with the truth; bears all things, believes all things, hopes all things, endures all things.
1 Corinthians 13:4-7

This is the form of love that reflects God's nature, God's image. God wants to pour forth His love upon all mankind. Initially Jesus carried out that role, but now He has passed that role onto us who believe in Him. We are to carry out God's will.

TO LOVE IS TO DO GOD'S WILL

*"If you love Me, **you will keep my commandments**."*
John 14:15

This might seem like an impossible task, but God has only two requests or commandments.

NUMBER ONE: LOVE GOD

*"Teacher, which is the greatest commandment in the Law?" And He said to him, '**You shall love the Lord your God with all your heart, and with all your soul, and with all your mind**.' This is the great and foremost commandment."*
Matthew 22:36-38

NUMBER TWO: LOVE YOURSELF AND OTHERS ALSO

*"The second is like it, '**You shall love your neighbor as yourself.**' On these two commandments depend the whole Law and the Prophets."*
Matthew 22:39, 40

Love fulfills every requirement of God. When you see love, you see God.

Now we come to a section most of us would like to avoid. Unfortunately, it's unavoidable. In fact, it would be unfair to everyone if it went unmentioned. Remember, I said it is the responsibility of each believer to turn on the power or to reveal the holiness that God has so graciously placed within us. You know there is a cost involved when you turn on the power at your residence. Well, there is also a cost involved when a believer chooses to reveal the image of God to others.

THERE IS A COST INVOLVED

*I urge you therefore, brethren by the mercies of God, **to present your bodies a living and holy sacrifice**, acceptable to God, which is your spiritual service of worship.*
Romans 12:1

The apostle Paul is telling us that the cost is billed to our bodies. Our born again spirit would never consider it a cost. The cost is being a holy and living sacrifice. God wants to use our living bodies, but He wants them to be crucified to self-indulgence. Instead of Satan's kingdom ruling in our bodies, God wants to be given that opportunity.

DEAD YET ALIVE

> *"I have been crucified with Christ; and it is no longer I who live, but Christ lives in me; and the life which I now live in the flesh I live by faith in the Son of God, who loved me, and delivered Himself up for me."*
> Galatians 2:20

> **Now those who belong to Christ Jesus have crucified the flesh with its passions and desires.**
> Galatians 5:24

I constantly need to remind myself that crucifixion is not the same as a bullet through the brain. In fact it's just the opposite. It's a comparatively slow process of dying. Therefore, when you or I decide to allow the holiness of God to come forth and reveal the image of God, we shouldn't expect it to happen overnight.

When God starts to move in your life it's going to be great, even fun; but it won't always be fun and games. I'm going to offer two examples that will show a cost involved with the above choice. I love my wife very much, and she frequently asks me to rub her back. That's not always convenient, and I can never remember asking her if she would like her back rubbed. I'm sure some of you husbands recognize this as being included in *a living sacrifice*. Just kidding! However, I do hope you get the point. This is an oversimplified but accurate form of loving your neighbor.

Let's move on to the next example. The night my wife and I celebrated our seventh wedding anniversary, we received a phone call around midnight. We had just gone to bed, and sleep hadn't become foremost in our thinking. The call was from a good friend of ours,

Steve, who was the husband of a couple in the church. The couple only lived a few houses away. Steve said his wife was acting very strange. He asked if I would please come over. Surely you understand, this is one time I wanted to rub my wife's back. However, my loving wife gave me permission, and I left our anniversary bed and went over to our friends. About two hours later Steve's wife was freed of an adulterous spirit. When this spirit left, Steve's wife cried out with a loud scream. It was so loud I thought the neighbors would probably call the police.

I can remember walking home that night and thinking, *this isn't fun anymore.* And I equally remember sensing the Lord's reply, *when did I say this was going to be fun?* This is the type of living sacrifice that is logical. It makes sense. It is reasonable (Romans 12:1). Would it be reasonable to you to wake up in the middle of the night deathly sick, and call out to God, only to hear, *Take two aspirins and call Me in the morning?* God asks for us not only to love Him but to love our fellow man as well.

In the last incident, both my wife and I happened to demonstrate a sacrificial love toward God and our neighbors. Oh, if we would always choose to do so. When we choose, and it is moment-to-moment, to be a living sacrifice, we will feel the cost. I should say, "Our flesh will feel the cost." In those moments, our rule of thumb should not be sacrifice till it *hurts.* Rather, it should be sacrifice till it *feels good.* When sacrifice goes beyond hurting to feeling good, then you know the flesh has been crucified.

I mentioned earlier it was difficult for those closest to Jesus to realize they were beholding the image of God. It was even more difficult for them to accept the fact they could portray that same image, but listen to what Jesus told Philip.

IF GOD IS IN US, HIS IMAGE IS IN US

"Do you not believe that I am in the Father, and the Father in Me? The words that I say to you I do not speak on My own initiative, but the Father abiding in Me does His

works. Believe Me that I am in the Father, and the Father in Me; otherwise believe on account of the works themselves. Truly, truly, I say to you, he who believes in Me, the works that I do shall he do also; and greater works than these shall he do; because I go to the Father (vv. 10-12)." ***In that day you shall know that I am in My Father, and you in Me, and I in you*** *(v. 20)."*
John 14:10-12, 20

If I were a poetic individual I might attempt to paraphrase what Jesus said in these words: "What you get and what you see is because God is in me, and when others see you they should see God too."

God the Father, Jesus the Son, and you and I who have been born again all have the same spiritual DNA. God has made all the necessary preparations for each of His children to have a very special life.

DESIGNED FOR DESTINY

For we are His workmanship, created in Christ Jesus for good works, *which God prepared beforehand, that we should walk in them.*
Ephesians 2:10

To those who don't claim Jesus as their personal Savior, image is everything. I can remember working in Malibu, California, a very nice area. One day, one of our many high-profile clientele sent his houseboy to pick up some medicine. He entered the store all excited and invited us to come outside to see his new car. What we saw was a brand-new Mercedes convertible. We asked, "How did you manage to get this beauty?" He said his employer had some friends over one afternoon, and they happened to be coming up the driveway as he was going down. They asked their host, "Who was that leaving in the older model car; the car in apparent need of repair?" Or words to that effect. This young man's former vehicle had become an embarrassment to his employer, so his employer made sure it went, and he provided him with a brand new car.

Well, guess what! Image is a priority with God as well. Who we are reflects upon Him, so He has provided us with holiness, authority, and power so that reflection is accurate. Maybe you have heard someone say, "The closest anyone on this earth will ever get to seeing God is when they see you or me." That is not meant to be an arrogant statement, although it may be a very scary thought. The responsibility is now ours. This is a truth God has always known. It is a truth He established, and it is a truth He has made possible to achieve through His Son. Jesus came to show us the Father, both in word and in deed. We are redeemed to do the same. Dear believer, please understand, this is:

THE BOTTOM LINE

> *Now the Lord is the Spirit; and where the Spirit of the Lord is, there is liberty. But **we all**, with unveiled face beholding as in a mirror the glory of the Lord, **are being transformed into the same image from glory to glory**, just as from the Lord, the Spirit.*
> *2 Corinthians 3:17, 18*

THESE THREE PRESCRIPTION FILES PROVIDE CONFIDENCE IN THE FOLLOWING BENEFIT

1. Doctors are on God's side
2. God only cares about sin
3. Not all sickness can be overcome

Select the best-response from the above three choices. (the *best-response* list is found after the Epilogue)

Rx41

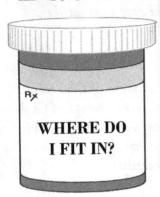

WHERE DO I FIT IN?

Hans Christian Anderson was a nineteenth-century European author. One of his most popular stories is titled "The Ugly Duckling". "The Ugly Duckling" is about a baby swan that finds himself among a group of baby ducklings. He doesn't realize he is a swan, and the ducklings don't realize he isn't a duck. Consequently, the ducklings notice how different he is from the rest of them, and they make fun of him. Naturally, that hurts his feelings; but eventually he becomes reunited with his own kind, and the story has a happy ending.

God, in the person of Jesus Christ, took on human form and became like us. One reason God became one of us was so we could see with our own eyes exactly what God is like, both in attitude and in action. God wants us to know exactly how He feels about each of us.

GOD BECOMES LIKE ONE OF US

> God, after he spoke long ago to the fathers in the prophets in many portions and in many ways, in these last days has spoken to us in His Son, whom He appointed heir to all things, through whom also He made the world. And He is the radiance of His glory and **the exact representation of His nature**, and upholds all things by the word of His power.

When He had made purification of sins, he sat down at the right hand of the Majesty on high.
Hebrews 1:1-3

Today the church is the physical representation of God to our world. Today the church is supposed to be the mirror image of God. The only two ways the world has to know how God feels about His people is by reading about His Son, Jesus, as revealed in the Bible, or by observing the church, His visible body on earth.

THE CHURCH IS THE BODY OF CHRIST

Now you are Christ's body, *and individually members of it.*
1 Corinthians 12:27

Consequently, we who have placed our faith in Christ are the visible earthly manifestation of God. That means God, used Jesus, the head of the church, to show the world what God is like. Today He uses each of us, who make up the body of Christ, to advance that same purpose. That should be a very sobering fact. We are His body today.

Jesus is in charge of assembling His body of believers. This body He refers to as His church.

JESUS IS IN CHARGE OF THE BUILDING

*And Simon Peter answered and said, "Thou art the Christ, the Son of the living God." And Jesus answered and said to him, "Blessed are you Simon Barjona, because flesh and blood did not reveal this to you, but My Father who is in Heaven. And I also say to you that you are Peter, and upon this rock **I will build my church**; and the gates of Hades shall not overpower it."*
Matthew 16:18

Jesus assembles His body with a specific purpose in mind. That purpose is to achieve the great commission. That purpose will not be overpowered by the motives and activities of Hades. Jesus has a way of ensuring this will not happen. He designed His body, His church, so each member fits into a specific location. Where we fit in is no accident. It's part of Christ's plan so that His ultimate goal will be accomplished. Remember that Jesus allowed Himself to be empowered and directed by the Holy Spirit. Therefore, it should come as no surprise that Jesus has put the person of the Holy Spirit in charge of placing each of us in His body exactly where He wants us to fit in.

THE HOLY SPIRIT PUTS US ALTOGETHER

> *For even as the body is one and yet has many members, and all the members of the body, though they are many are one body, so also is Christ **for by one Spirit we were all baptized into one body**, whether Jews or Greeks, whether slave or free, and we are all made to drink of one Spirit. For the body is not one member, but many.*
> *1 Corinthians 12:12, 13*

Location is the key factor in the world of real estate. Beachfront property is more desirable than mountainous terrain. In real estate, location is everything.

LOCATION BY DESIGN

> *But now God has placed the members, each one of them, in the body, **just as He desired**.*
> *1 Corinthians 12:18*

God had a good reason for designing our physical bodies the way they are designed. For instance, can you imagine what would happen if God had designed our body with our nose on our buttocks? Think about it! Every time you sat down, your eyes would water. Did you think I was going to write something else? Bad design! Thank God, He thought it through, and that wasn't His design. Could it be some of us, at sometime in our lives, have volunteered to be transplants in the body of Christ? If so, who did the transplanting, and what were the results? Are we fitted into place according to God's design for His body?

In the previous prescriptions we discussed the importance of having the person of the Holy Spirit present with us to confirm the truth of Jesus the Christ and His message to the world. The greatest concern of the early church was not persecution but rather that God would confirm His message delivered by them through the presence and power of the person of the Holy Spirit.

THE PRAYER OF THE EARLY CHURCH

> "And now, Lord, take note of their threats, and grant that Thy bondservants may speak Thy word with all confidence. **While Thou dost extend thy hand to heal, and signs and wonders take place through the name of Thy holy servant Jesus.**" And when they had prayed, the place where they had gathered together was shaken, and they were all filled with the Holy Spirit, and began to speak the word of God with boldness.
> Acts 4:29-31

I always have chuckled at this section, because I can envision God saying, "Amen" in such a way as to explain why the place where they had gathered together was shaken. At any rate, God certainly answered that prayer, and the fear (remember, fear is *check*) of persecution didn't matter.

GOD DESIRES TO CONFIRM HIS WORD

> But Peter and the apostles answered and said, "We must obey God rather than men. The God of our fathers raised up

Jesus, whom you had put to death by hanging Him on a cross. He is the one whom God exalted to His right hand as a Prince and a Savior, to grant repentance to Israel, and forgiveness of sins. **And we are witnesses of these things; and so is the Holy Spirit, whom God has given to those who obey Him.**"
Acts 5:29-32

Now that we've reminded ourselves of the importance of having God's Spirit present with us to confirm His word, let's return to the importance of where we are to fit in or serve with the Holy Spirit's presence and power. Location is of absolute importance in real estate, but it's even more important in warfare. Obviously, the church is involved in warfare against spiritual forces.

THE CHURCH IS AT WAR

For our struggle is *not against flesh and blood, but against the rulers, against the powers, and against the world forces of this darkness,* **against spiritual forces of wickedness in heavenly places.**
Ephesians 6:12

The church is at war, and the real estate it is acquiring is spiritual property. It is the spirits and lives of all those who exist outside of God's kingdom and the saving grace that is in Jesus Christ. Therefore, where and how we use God's power is highly important. So for purposes of illustration, let's consider what the consequences could have been if during World War II, the war in the Pacific had conclude before the conflict in Europe. Germany had developed the V-2 rocket, which was capable of traversing long distances of ground. Just think about the ranges of rockets today. Those rockets could easily have been equipped with subsequent nuclear warheads. However, the United States succeeded in being the first country to develop a nuclear weapon, and coupled with the B-29 Super Fortress, it had the capability of delivering such a weapon. What would have happened if a European target had been selected instead of a target in the Pacific? What if the navigational instruments on the bomber malfunctioned? What if above the cloud cover, the bomb dropped on the wrong target, possibly a highly populated city of one of our allies? I hope the point is clear. Spiritual power must be dispatched and directed by the Holy Spirit. The body of Christ does not need any loose cannons. Spiritual victories are assured when we are where we should be. So how can we be confident that we are really where we do fit in, that is, according to the Lord's design? I would like to suggest three criteria, but first, I want to say that if we have a good relationship with our Lord, He is capable of answering that question directly from His Spirit to our spirit, then the following three points will only serve as confirmation of His voice.

The three points that should all agree are: feeling, feeding and functioning. A believer should feel good about where he or she is fellowshipping. A believer should feel that he or she is a part of the whole and not just fulfilling a religious obligation. Personal relationships should be developing and community should be resulting. What do I mean by community?

BELIEVERS SHOULD FEEL GOOD
ABOUT THEIR FELLOWSHIP

So then, those who had received his word where baptized; and there were added that day about three thousand souls. And they were continually devoting themselves to the apostle's teaching and to fellowship, to the breaking of bread and to prayer. And everyone kept feeling a sense of awe; and many wonders and signs were taking place through the apostles. ***And all those who had believed were together and had all things in common; and they began selling their property and possessions, and were sharing them with all, as anyone might have need. And day by day continuing with one mind in the temple, and breaking bread from house to***

house, they were taking their meals together with gladness and sincerity of heart, praising God, and having favor with all the people. And the Lord was adding to their number day by day, those who were being saved.
Acts 2:41-47

Next, when a believer is where he or she should be, they will be receiving spiritual food and developing in spiritual power and grace.

BELIEVERS ARE TO BE FED

*And from Miletus he (Paul) sent to Ephesus and called to him the elders of the church. And when they were come to him, he said to them (vv. 17, 18). "Take heed therefore unto yourselves, and to all the flock over which the Holy Ghost hath made you overseers, to **feed the church of God, which He hath purchased with His own blood** (v. 28).*
Acts 20:17, 18, 28 (KJV)

The last of the three points we need to recognize emphasizes that the body of Christ exists to further advance the completion of the great commission. Every member of the body of Christ must be equipped, encouraged, and allowed to function toward that end.

EVERY BELIEVER IS TO FUNCTION

And he gave some as apostles, and some as prophets, and some as evangelists, and some as pastors and teachers, for the equipping of the saints for the work of service, to the building up of the body of Christ; until we all attain the unity of the faith, and to the knowledge of the Son of God, to a mature man to the measure of the stature which belongs to the fullness of Christ.
Ephesians 4:11-13

Is your relationship with the other members of God's family what you would expect it to be in a godly home? Are you comfortable and lifted up when everyone worships together? Are you being fed well on God's word? Do you notice your faith increasing? And have you discovered how you contribute to the welfare of God's family and His great commission? If most of the answers to the above questions are yes, then I suspect you are currently where the Holy Spirit has placed you. However, if the majority of those answers are no, then I would guess you feel like you are punching a spiritual time clock on Sunday mornings. When church becomes an obligation instead of a celebration, something is obviously missing or wrong.

Well, let me assure you, it has nothing to do with your decision to accept Christ as your personal Savior. That thought would be a lying suggestion. And here's another such suggestion: things are the way they are because you are living a life of sin. Sin can mess up your life, but you can be living a life of forgiveness and still feel the same way. What you're likely experiencing is the urging of the Holy Spirit who is within you. He wants to lead you to the place God has for you. So ask for His help, then be willing to listen. Be sensitive to what's happening in your life. You will only be blessed. Know that gnawing feeling inside is only the tugging of His Spirit, saying, *Let's go*. He wants to replace that uneasy feeling with peace. God has a purpose and a place for you. God has a church home for you. Allow Him to lead you into your own promised land. Be flexible. God can choose any way He wants to lead you there.

FOLLOW GOD AND HE WILL FIT YOU IN

*And **the Lord was going before them** in a pillar of cloud by day **to lead them on the way**, and a pillar of fire by night to give them light, that they might travel **by day and by night**.*
Exodus 13:21

God is available twenty-four hours a day to lead you to where you fit in. He may lead you to a congregation of 12,000, like He has many in South Korea. Or it may be 1200 believers which is not uncommon in America. Of course, He may lead you to a smaller group of believers, possibly only 120. That would be very normal. But don't be surprised if you find yourself in an intimate fellowship whose number is closer to 12. This size group will possibly be associated with a lager body of believers. However, your opportunity to achieve your full restoration, as well as our Lord's great commission, can be just as great in this setting as it is in a larger one. You may have already discovered this truth: THE ROAD TO RESTORATION is a very fulfilling and rewarding journey.

THESE THREE PRESCRIPTION FILES PROVIDE CONFIDENCE IN THE FOLLOWING BENEFIT

1. God can heal any condition immediately
2. You don't always see God's healing immediately
3. Both 1 and 2 are accurate

Select the best-response from the above three choices. (the *best-response* list is found after the Epilogue)

Rx42

THAT'S ALL FOLKS

When I review my life, I conclude that I have been greatly blessed. Sure, I can think of several things I wish had been different. However, I am extremely grateful. As I mentioned earlier, one of my favorite recollections is the Saturday afternoon matinee at the local theater. One or more of my childhood friends, Ron Corder, Bill Field, or someone else, and I would meet at my father's pharmacy at 110th Street and Vermont in southwest Los Angeles. Then we would walk a few blocks south on Vermont to the Southside Theatre, which was located at Vermont and Imperial. There we would see not one but two feature films. But that's not all. In addition, we would see a newsreel on current events and at least one cartoon. That was a long time ago. Since then, television has become the medium for *newsreels* and cartoons.

Warner Brothers generally produced the cartoons we saw. They had a great collection of characters, and Mel Blanc gave each of them a very special voice. I remember Yosemite Sam, Daffy Duck, Tweedy Pie and Sylvester, the Road Runner and Wiley Coyote, Elmer Fudd and Bugs Bunny and who could forget Porky Pig. Each cartoon would conclude with the familiar WB filling the screen and the words *That's All Folk's* being scrolled over them. In the background you could hear Porky Pig sputtering out, "Ba-peep, ba-peep, THAT'S ALL FOLKS." And so another cartoon would conclude. But my friends and I all knew next Saturday we would see another adventure of one of those zany characters.

Some things you never forget, and this book doesn't say all that could be said. However, I trust you have read things in these pages you will never forget, truth that will influence and change your life forever. Words that will produce a positive impact and create special memories. I own a book that has done that for me. It is called *Healing The Sick*, and it was written by a worldwide evangelist named T. L. Osborn. It has had a tremendous influence on my life, and it has been the catalyst of many precious memories.

In his book, Mr. Osborn mentions many people whose stand for the truth served as a catalyst and produced a similar impact on his life. And if we could ask those individuals, I am sure we would hear the names of others who came before them and had a similar effect on their lives. And if we were able to continue backward, eventually we would find ourselves speaking to the apostles themselves, who would refer back to Jesus of Nazareth. This is how truth is passed on from generation to generation. God allows each generation to express His truth in words it can easily understand. Because of this, I understand those who read these pages will communicate the truth to others with their own vocabulary and with their own personality. And if the Lord does not return in our lifetime, someone else will bridge this period of time and communicate the same truth with either a book, an audio, a video, a disc or whatever means of preservation is common at the time. One thing is for sure, THAT'S ALL FOLKS never applies to spreading the truth of God's love for people as demonstrated in His Son, Jesus Christ.

THESE THREE PRESCRIPTION FILES PROVIDE CONFIDENCE IN THE FOLLOWING BENEFIT

1. Do you believe God can heal you?
2. Do you want God to heal you?
3. Will you ask God to heal you?

Select the best-response from the above three choices. (the *best-response* list is found after the Epilogue)

ADDENDUM

A WORD ABOUT COVID 19

Since this book was initially published in 2018 a worldwide pandemic has occurred. Sorry for the oxymoron. Since it has only been four years since this book became available, I thought this addendum should be included in the next publication.

Since the advent of the COVID 19 virus which occurred in the last months of 2019 and the first of 2020, 14 million lives were collectively lost in 2020 and 2021 alone. Just to get a grip on how tragic that is, in the six years of WWII there was somewhere between 40 and 50 million lives lost. So, if we split the difference and say approximately 45 million lives were lost then the average for a two-year period would be 15 million lives lost.

How would you describe the loss of 15 million lives? Tragic? At least! So then how would you describe the loss of 14 million innocent lives? Tearfully sad? Oh, my Lord, yes! But for additional perspective, allow me to take a brief tangent. How would **I** describe the anticipated loss of 42 million lives in 2022 alone? That is the number the World Health Organization (W.H.O.) anticipates being lost. To What? Heart disease? No. Cancer? No. The definition of murder is premeditation to take an innocent human life…except when it applies to abortion. What is in a name? "A rose by any other name…" William Shakespeare. Legal or illegal murder has eventual consequences. Just like any other sin. In this case it is probably national consequences. A permission slip is a permission slip, regardless of its' name and it allows Satan to work his will. Ah, but, as I said, "I digress."

Back to COVID 19. In 2020 the Center for Disease Control (C.D.C.) issued three strong *physical,* guidelines to follow in an effort to reduce one's likelihood of becoming infected.

They were:

FIRST: PHYSICALLY WEAR A FACE MASK
covering the nose and the mouth in the presence of others.

SECOND: PHYSICALLY PRACTICE SOCIAL DISTANCING
by being no closer than six feet from the person closest to you, and

THIRD: PHYSICALLY PRACTICE INDIVIDUAL DECON-
TAMINATION
by frequently washing one's hands for at least twenty seconds each time.

Of course, they also recommended that if and when a vaccine became available that one should become vaccinated and take advantage of any boosters that may later become available.

Our family followed the above precautions except for availing ourselves to the vaccine when it became available for reasons which I will not state in this book.

I have earlier employed comparisons to get us to this point, and I will continue to do so. It isn't likely the C.D.C. was aware that thousands of years earlier God had informed His people of comparable *spiritual* practices to employ to prevent diseases.

FIRST: SPIRITUALLY WEAR HIS WORDS
on your eyes and your heart (like a mask over your nose and mouth).

My son give attention to My words incline your ear to My sayings (the Word of God). *Do not let them depart from your sight; keep them in the midst of your heart. For they are life to those who find them and health to their whole body.*
Proverbs 4:20-22

SECOND: SPIRITUALLY PRACTICE SOCIAL DISTANCING

> *But you shall serve the Lord your God* (separate yourself from worldly ways) *and He will bless your bread, and your water; and I will remove sickness from your midst.*
> *Exodus 23:25*

OK. How is one to do that? Fair question. God was very aware of the difficulty man would have avoiding contaminating himself with sin. May I be down to earth enough to say, "Duh!"?

THIRD: SPIRITUAL CLEANSING

> *Cleanse your* (physical) *hands* (of wrongdoing), *you sinners; and purify* (spiritually) *your hearts, you double-minded people.*
> *James 4:8b*

OK. How do we (I) do that?

> *If we confess our sins* (physically), *He is faithful and righteous to forgive us our sins and to cleanse us* (spiritually) *from all unrighteousness* (the consequences of our (my) sins).
> *1 John 1:9*

How often should we do that?

> *And He* (Jesus) *said to them, "When you pray, say...* '*And forgive us* **(this day)** *our sins, For we ourselves also forgive everyone who is indebted to us,'*" (do we?).
> *Luke 11:2, 4*

Do you notice the similarities between the recommendations of the C.D.C. and God's Word?

Do you think one might be more effective than the other? You might be thinking I am biased, and you would be correct. However, is it bias when what you believe is the truth? After all, who are you going to believe?

May I share a personal testimony? My wife and I begrudgingly must admit we are now senior citizens (an endangered species according to the C.D.C.) and we both have been Christians for most of our lives.

At the beginning of 2022 we both tested positive for having COVID. Of course, we took the antibiotics our doctor prescribed, (a 10-day dose) and my wife even had an infusion. However, we also followed our Lord's direction and neither one of us displayed the typical symptoms of the virus from hell. Thank you, Jesus.

EPILOGUE

If you picked up this book because you hoped the information inside might result in your healing then you were right. However, I strongly recommend that you don't read this portion of the book until you have read everything that comes before it.

The first part of this book tells you what faith is, a gift from God, and it comes with and is included in His word. This entire book is filled with the word of God. It is a seed bed of faith, and it is presented in a way to develop your faith to the point where you are able to receive what God has for you: forgiveness, healing and restoration. These are all gifts God has for you and all you have to do is believe they are for you and receive them. These are all things God wants you to have because He loves you. He not only wants you to have eternal life with Him, but He desires you start today by having an abundant life.

If you still haven't received what God has for you, then don't worry or doubt. No problem. I believe I can help you go these next few inches until you reach the goal line. Trust me. You're right there. I can almost hear the angels in heaven cheering. Okay. Here we go. Let me ask you ten simple questions and you will discover you are there. Your life will never be the same.

	QUESTIONS	ANSWERS
1.	Do you need healing?	YES_____ NO_____
2.	Will you allow God to heal you?	YES_____ NO_____
3.	Have you repented of your sin?	YES_____ NO_____
4.	Have you asked God to forgive you?	YES_____ NO_____
5.	Do you believe God has forgiven you?	YES_____ NO_____

6. Can you honestly say, Romans 10:10? YES_____ NO_____

7. Do you understand you are now a child of God? YES_____ NO_____

8. Can you ask your heavenly Father to heal you through His Son, Jesus? YES_____ NO_____

9. Will you read Psalms 103:2-3? YES_____ NO_____

10. Do you believe your heavenly Father healed you when He forgave your sins? That's what He tells us. (1 Peter 2:24). YES_____ NO_____

If you answered "Yes" to these questions, then according to God, you are healed. That's the good news.

Now, ask yourself this question: what can I do to show God I believe Him and thank Him at the same time? Remember, faith is believing what God said and then acting like you believe it. Oh, does Satan hate that.

May I share with you how one believer answered this question? In the book *Ever Increasing Faith* by Smith Wigglesworth, he gives us this account: *"One day I was having a meeting in Bury, Lancashire, England. A young woman from a place called Ramsbottom came to be healed of a goiter. Before she came she said 'I am going to be healed of this goiter, mother.' After one meeting, she came forward and was prayed for. At the next meeting she got up and testified that she had been wonderfully healed. She said, 'I will be happy to go tell mother about my healing.'*

She went to her home and testified how wonderfully she had been healed. The next year, we were having the convention, she came again. From a human perspective, it looked as though the goiter was just as big as ever, but that young women was believing God. Soon she was on her feet giving testimony, saying, 'I was here last year, and the Lord wonderfully healed me. I want to tell you that this has been the best year of my life.' She seemed to be greatly blessed in that meeting and she went home to testify more strongly than ever that the Lord had healed her.

She believed God. The third year, she was at the meeting again, and some people who looked at her said, 'Look how big that goiter has become!' But when the time came for testimonies, she was on her feet and testified, 'Two years ago, the Lord gloriously healed me of a goiter. Oh, I had a most wonderful healing. It's grand to be healed by the power of God.'

That day someone questioned her and said, 'People will think there's something wrong with you. Why don't you look in the mirror? You will see your goiter is bigger than ever.' The young women went to the Lord about it and said, 'Lord, You so wonderfully healed me two years ago. Won't You show all the people that You healed me?' She went to sleep peacefully that night still believing God. When she came down the next day, there was not a trace or a mark of that goiter."[1]

The Christian woman in the above account neither HUNG IN THERE BABY nor did she *pray-through*. Instead she *fearlessly* demonstrated faith (Rx 14) and *praised-through*, to defeat *doubt*.

That's all well and good but how was this woman able to maintain her belief for so long in the face of such apparent evidence to the contrary? Are you able to conceive of doing that yourself?

Would you believe in the United States every year thousands, if not millions of non-believers do something similar?That's right non-believers.

May I cite an example from everyday life? If you work for a living in America, then you file an income tax form every year. Many individuals learn the government is going to send them a refund of hundreds, and some even thousands of dollars. Do you think those individuals are elated? I would be. Do you think they might share their good news with family, friends and maybe others? I would.

However, when they learned about this fact did they have the money in their hands? No. In fact it could take thirty days or longer before that occurred. Do you think they ever doubted they would receive it? If you happened to have been one of those individuals, did you ever doubt you would receive it? I never did. After all the government said I would receive it. In fact, I had a piece of paper saying I would.

[1] Smith Wigglesworth, Ever Increasing Faith, (New Kensington, Whitaker House, 2001), p. 99.

As Christians, do we realize we have a piece of paper that not only says we have forgiveness and eternal life but that God has also healed us? That paper is called the Bible.

The above modern-day parable reminds me, who do I believe more, the government or God?

Remember: Doubt and fear are the enemies of faith and God allows Satan to use both of them against us, just so Satan can't claim foul.

The healing that Jesus has purchased for us (Isaiah 53:5, 1 Peter 2:24) occurs immediately when we accept it by faith (Rx 14). However, there are occasions when what Jesus has done takes longer than immediately to become obvious (Mark 8:23-25, Luke 17:12-14). Do you remember Patrica who was mentioned in the Introduction of this book? Her healing became apparent over a period of sixty days. In all such situations, positive results are ushered in by acting on Romans 10:10: if we confess, with our mouth, what we believe in our heart then that confession is our act of faith.

A FINAL THOUGHT

Did you ever think, "I'm never going to finish this book?" Well, you did. Most of you read this book because you were hoping it might improve or resolve your health issues. Right? Some of you are extremely thankful you did read it because you have experienced the truth contained within these pages. Of course, some of you are disappointed or even depressed because you haven't seen any difference in your physical or mental state. Well, don't be. I can assure you that there is a difference.

Think about this. When you have had a headache, did you ever take a medication hoping it would remove the pain? Who hasn't? How long did it take for the pain to leave or diminish? A half an hour? Maybe an hour? Were you glad when the pain was gone? Did a doctor ever prescribe antibiotics for you when you had an infection? If so, it could have taken up to ten days for the infection to clear up. Correct? Unfortunately, if you are someone who has high blood pressure, you probably will be on medication the rest of your life. How many of you are going to stop taking pain mediation when needed or antibiotics if required or medications to prolong your life. What? No takers?

Believe me, you are different than before you read this book (you did read the book?), because by doing so you have spread the seed of healing and recovery all over your mind, your heart, your soul, and your spirit. Right now, whether you realize it or not, the truth in God's word is at work germinating in your life, sending down roots into your spirit. Once that occurs it will start to grow and fulfill its purpose, which is to produce the fruit it promises. The seed in Dispensing Truth produces health, providing of course, you believe it and act on it (Rx 14).

Eve was sinless but she still doubted God's Word and then acted on her doubt by eating the forbidden fruit. You and I are not sinless. Do you think you are not capable of doubting God's promises? Let's don't kid ourselves. We have and we do. Every day I battle doubt by reminding the enemy, Satan, of what God has said or promised by telling him, "It is written (followed by the appropriate Word of God)." For instance, I might say, "It is written, with His stripes we are healed (Isaiah 53:5)." That makes God happy because He sees His child making the right decision.

If you have doubts (and you will), then doubt your doubts, never God's Word. You can do that. Say, "It is written..." plus the appropriate Word of God. Satan won't be happy. You might be thinking, "I do that all the time." I have thought that too. Sometimes I think, sooner or later *God will have to respond.* Be careful. Faith is a process not a program. Allow the Word of God to produce the faith it promised (Romans 10:17). Then you will have your own experience of God.

It was the renown twentieth century English evangelist, Leonard Ravenhill, who said, "The man with an experience of God is never at the mercy of a man with an argument." You will be the one with the experience of God and guess who will be the one with an argument.

In closing I want to be very clear. The truth in this book is not meant to be a "fix all" formula. It isn't. It is a *spiritual process* rather than a human program.

TRUTH IS SPIRITUALLY DISCERNED

*But **the natural man receiveth not the things of the Spirit** of God: for they are foolishness unto him: neither can he know them, **because they are spiritually discerned**.*
1 Corinthians 2:14 (KJV)

IN CLOSING

The phrase, "Easy for you to say", is ringing in my ears because I suspect some readers are thinking those very words. Why am I suspecting that? Because I have been told that before; that's why. No problem. I get it. I know where you are coming from. I have been there myself on my own journey on the road going from faith to faith (Romans 1:17).

Thus, from experience the best advice and encouragement I can offer you is to remember the truth God uses to bring about faith (Romans 10:17) **doesn't result from a program** with predetermined commencement and completion times. Rather, **it is a process** that begins with becoming familiar with God's word and continues until one believes that word so much that they live their life by it. That's called faith. How did this take place in my own life pertaining to healing? Read Case Study No. 2 beginning on page 203.

Every member in my immediate and most intimate family has had a similar experience, not just me. May I elaborate? 1. Our daughter was freed from 15 years of drug and alcohol addiction by believing the truth. 2. Our son was born with ¼ of a functioning kidney, and he has led a "normal" life for nearly 50 years (without needing dialysis). 3. My wife had an entire lobe of her thyroid surgically removed and then 20 years later God replaced the lobe out of nothing. 4. Our son-in-law had a severe heart attack and the doctors at Desert Memorial Hospital in Palm Springs, CA, where he was taken, gave him no hope of survival. However, a couple of months later he was back to working full time and has resumed his normal routine. 5. Finally, I was diagnosed with an incurable condition, dupuytrens contracture disease, but God through faith in His promises that are printed in this book, released me from that condition. That was 30 years ago, and my hands are still perfectly healthy.

I know how difficult it is not to believe your eyes or what your doctors tell you about your condition, however when man's treatments fall short (Luke 9:43, 44), continue to believe God's promises won't fail. Keep repeating, it is written, "… by His stripes I've been healed." isn't that exactly how Jesus successfully dealt with Satan during His 40 days in the wildness (Matthew 4:4, 7, 10)?

I pray I have shared the truth with you that will change your life now as well as make you a powerful-life changing child of God in the future…so more lives will be touched like yours.

In other words, I am a man on a spiritual mission. Believe me, there are easier missions because spiritual things are spiritually discerned or understood and not because of a fresh or cute presentation, which I hope you enjoyed. If you received the truth in this book, it isn't because of the author. Oh no! It is because the person of the Holy Spirit has touched and enlightened your heart, your soul, and your spirit (Ephesians 6:17; Hebrews 4:12).

If you have read the entire book many of you may still have questions. You will probably share those questions with other believers to see what they have to say, that's natural. However, I believe reading these scriptures over and over coupled with prayer will bring about the answers you seek (Acts 17:11, 12).

As John the apostle said at the conclusion of his gospel and I paraphrase, If I had included all that I could have shared with you about healing, then this book might have become too heavy to pick up (John 21:25).

God bless, your friend and author.

OK, now let's have some fun!

BIBLICAL HEALTH SEED

Jesus liken the word of God to seed. (Matthew 15:18, 19). In addition, Jesus guaranteed divine seed will always germinate (Matthew 13:5-8).

The following are divine seed that are capable of producing healing and health. God also informs us how to insure the seed will be fruitful: resulting in healing and health. (see trouble shooting below).

Now correctly match the seed (references) in the left hand column with the appropriate fruit (verses) in the right hand column.

SEED	FRUIT
A. Psalm 107:20	G. And these signs will accompany those who have believed: in My name they will cast out demons; they will lay hands on the sick, and they will recover.
B. James 5:14-16	H. Bless the Lord, O my soul, and forget none of His benefits; who pardons all your iniquities; who heals all your diseases.

SEED	FRUIT

SEED   **FRUIT**

C. Isaiah 53:5

I. He Himself bore our sins in His body on the cross, that we might die to sin and live to righteousness; for by His wounds you were healed.

D. 1 Peter 2:24

J. The chastening for our well-being fell upon Him, and by His scourging we are healed.

E. Psalms 103:2, 3

K. He sent His word and healed them and delivered them from their destructions.

F. Mark 16:17, 18

L. The prayer offered in faith will restore the one who is sick, and the Lord will raise him up.

Correct matches are found on the next page beneath *benefits*.

TROUBLE SHOOTING (to insure seeds produce fruit)

PROBLEM   **SOLUTIONS**

1. Loss of seed

1. Sow more seed (Romans 10:17)

2. Seed lands on rocky ground

2. Endure persecution and affliction (Romans 8:35-37)

3. Seed is sown among thorns

3. Ignore the cares and worries of this world (1 Peter 5:6, 7)

THESE PRESCRIPTIONS PROVIDE THE FOLLOWING BENEFIT

Rx Number	The Best Response	Source of Response
Rx 29	2	Rx 1
Rx 30	2	Rx 4
Rx 31	3	Rx 6
Rx 32	1	Rx 8
Rx 33	3	Rx 10
Rx 34	2	Rx 12
Rx 35	3	Rx 13
Rx 36	2	Rx 15
Rx 37	2	Rx 16
Rx 38	3	Rx 17
Rx 39	1	Rx 18
Rx 40	1	Rx 20
Rx 41	3	Rx 23
Rx 42	More than one number can be the best response	Ask your heart

CORRECT MATCHES (for SEED with FRUIT from pp. 465 and 466) A&K, B&L, C&J, D&I, E&H, F&G

ABOUT THE AUTHOR

Dr. Ronald Girardin is a member of two of the most trusted professions in the United States, a licensed pharmacist, and an ordained minister. He has been active as a personal evangelist for over 30 years, repeatedly seeing individual lives dramatically transformed spiritually, emotionally and physically, by the love and healing power of Jesus Christ.

Dr. Girardin and his wife, Luetta-Rae, are dedicated to discipling those who desire to see New Testament ministry as a part of their lives. They refer to this process as Another 12 Ministries.

We welcome your inquires regarding church leadership training sessions, congregational discipleship seminars, healing services and the request for individual "healing cloths" (Acts 19:11).
Inquiries can be made by contacting:

Another 12 Ministries
P.O. Box 2712
Cathedral City, CA 92235
Email: another12ministeries@aol.com
Text: 760-861-2527